THE
BRITISH

ALSO BY NORMAN GELB

The Irresistible Impulse

Enemy in the Shadows

THE
BRITISH

A PORTRAIT
OF AN
INDOMITABLE ISLAND PEOPLE

by Norman Gelb

NEW YORK   EVEREST HOUSE   PUBLISHERS

Library of Congress Cataloging in Publication Data:

Gelb, Norman.
   The British : a portrait of an indomitable
island people.

   Bibliography: p. 219
   Includes index.
   1. National characteristics, British. 2. Great
Britain—Social life and customs—1945–
I. Title.
DA118.G4   1982   941.085   81-22219
ISBN 0-89696-107-9   AACR2

FOR
Mallary & Amos

CONTENTS

PREFACE
9

ONE
The Island People
15

TWO
Tribes of Britain
38

THREE
A Woman's Place—A Man's World
70

FOUR
To Love or Not To Love
91

FIVE
London Town
104

SIX
The Other Britons
123

SEVEN
The Royal Image
149

EIGHT
Ruling the Roost
179

NINE
Foreigners and Other Peculiar Things
197

TEN
What Next?
215

BIBLIOGRAPHY
219

INDEX
221

PREFACE

TO TRY TO PIN the British down between the covers of a book is a presumptuous undertaking. In their long, eventful history, they have been exposed to countless influences which have left various residues. They are, as a result, a complex and often enigmatic people with many engaging and some curious characteristics.

As noted in the following pages, they are scrupulously fair, immensely loyal, and emotionally inhibited. They are compulsive about what's right and what's wrong, which doesn't keep them from honoring eccentrics. They display deep-rooted masochistic leanings. Each is a firm believer in being as good as the next person but virtually all of them are locked into rigid class identities which give some of them privileges others may not share. Like people elsewhere, the British are subject to ongoing changes and, from time to time, are victims of diabolical, disorienting economic blights. That further complicates the task of drawing up a reasonably authentic account of what they are, where they come from, and where they are going.

But this book is neither an academic treatise nor a sociological tract. In fashioning an image of the British, it recklessly indulges in generalizations of the kind usually scorned by scholars. The fact is, however, that despite the existence of a goodly number of individuals among the British whose mannerisms and attitudes march blithely against the prevailing grain, there are distinct British characteristics which outlive temporary upheavals in fashions and values. That, in part, is what this book is about.

No people can be understood out of context. Britain is a place of prodigious diversity. The British panorama is one of both charming and drab towns and cities, rolling countryside and industrial sprawl, great national pride and waves of bitter strikes, the pleasures of the pub and soccer madness. It is a landscape of splendid stately homes and architectural eyesores, winding country roads and high-speed highways, morning tea (before breakfast) and afternoon tea (before dinner), church rummage sales and village fairs with contests for who can grow the biggest scallions. Britain is a nation with a turbulent past and, despite recent street riots in British cities, a relatively well-ordered present. It is content with its queen and almost invariably fed up with its government. And that's what this book is also about.

It has become fashionable of late to catalog Britain's defects. They are real and some of them are very worrying. But it should be clear to anyone who knows them that the British are an imaginative, resilient people. They have good reason to be neither bowed nor cowed by their current adversity, or the attention paid to it.

Nevertheless, as this book took shape, I felt that maybe I was stepping out of line. The British are, for the most part, a reserved people who value their privacy. Having lived among them on and off for almost twenty years and having during that time reported to America mostly about impersonal aspects of British life—politics, economic developments and such stuff—I was nagged by the suspicion that I would be violating confidences by publicly exploring their more intimate ways and whims, manners and motives, pleasures and imperfections, aspirations and hang-ups. It seems perfectly reasonable to analyze what Americans are up to, to dissect the character of the Russians, or to scrutinize French patterns of behavior. But as an outsider doing the same for the British, I had to overcome the feeling that I was behaving in an ungracious fashion, like whistling in a cathedral or looking a gift horse in the mouth.

To those among the British who find reason to be riled by details of some of the observations which appear in this book, or by the fact that they appear at all, let me say that I have been motivated by affection rather than spleen. These are a special people. Their strengths far outweigh their shortcomings.

In writing about the British, terminology is not generally a problem, except when it comes to what to call them. They are usually called the English, but that's not absolutely correct. It's a little like saying all Americans are Californians or Texans. Scotland and Wales, which are definitely *not* part of England, are very much part of Britain. The proper collective name for the people of Britain is *Britons.*

Nevertheless, the English do make up 90 percent of the population. English characteristics and institutions are the most dominant and influential virtually throughout the country and are growing more pervasive all the time despite defiant national feelings in Scotland and Wales. There are places in this book where references are made to English rather than British ways. It is usually for convenience and in accordance with common usage, or in quoting others. But it only occurs where there is no likelihood of confusion and never when the reference is specifically to non-English parts of Britain.

It is impossible for me to list all the people from whom I have learned who and what the British are. I would, however, like to record my particular thanks to Barbara Gelb, Scott James, Ivan Kingston, and William Rawlinson CBE for reading the manuscript of this book and offering their criticism and wise counsel, though the opinions expressed in the following chapters are not necessarily shared by them.   —NORMAN GELB

THE
BRITISH

ONE

The Island People

THERE'S NOTHING shallow about the British. Their offerings to the rest of us have been momentous and profuse. They gave the world Shakespeare and the Beatles, the Rolls-Royce and Monty Python, the theory of evolution and the Salvation Army, Dracula and Winnie the Pooh. Their imagination has been rich enough to accomodate both sartorial elegance and the mini-skirt, to place Alice in her Wonderland and James Bond in his, to bring forth both radar and the test-tube baby.

They were the first to codify the laws of gravity and the rules of boxing. They taught the Western world how to make tea drinking a ritual and whiskey drinking a dignified pastime. They are unflappable, eccentric, and intensely private. And though their climate is reputed far and wide to be dreary, disagreeable, and demoralizing, millions of visitors pour into their realm every year to try to capture by osmosis a taste of culture and a touch of class.

Foreigners converge in droves on London's theaters. They haunt the halls of the British Museum. They venture into the provinces—to the rolling Yorkshire moors where the Brontë sisters set their magnificently mannered, highly charged fantasies; to the lush Dorset landscape which Thomas Hardy immortalized in his soul-wrenching rags-to-riches tragedies; to the serene Lake District where William Wordsworth "wandered lonely as a cloud"; to the fairytale backdrop of the villages of the Cotswold Hills; to the craggy splendor of the Scottish Highlands; to the bucolic charm of backwoods Wales.

For a country so rich in scenic beauty and so blessed with spectacular accomplishment, Britain is a surprisingly small place. In total acreage it is less than half as big as France and smaller than the state of Oregon. Between a late breakfast and an early lunch, you can easily drive clear across the British midsection—from Liverpool on the Irish Sea to Grimsby on the North Sea. Britain's furthest reaches—windswept Land's End nosing out into the Atlantic in southwest England and remote, desolate John O'Groats in northeast Scotland—are nearer to each other than Chicago is to New York or Phoenix is to San Francisco. But though the country they inhabit is a smallish speck on the map of the world, a geographical afterthought shaped like a deformed comma, the British are intriguing, indomitable people who, until not long ago, ruled the most far-flung empire the world has ever known.

An advantage of smallness is the historical or cultural signifi-cance of practically every place in Britain. Here is a spot where prehistoric inhabitants erected still-standing circles of stone to worship the sun. Here are the remains of a Roman villa, a Saxon church, a Norman castle. Here is where the Magna Carta was signed; where Henvy VIII honeymooned with the fifth of his six wives; where Anne Shakespeare was left behind when the Bard of Avon drifted on to make something of himself in London Town; from whence the Pilgrims set sail for the New World; where a king was beheaded by his people (long before the much more hot-blooded French thought of the idea); where the Campbell clan lured the trusting MacDonalds into a trap and slaughtered them; where steam engine ran a train for the first time; where Mary Shelley, the creator of the immortal Frankenstein (the novelist daughter of one of the world's earliest feminists), lived; where Karl Marx is buried; where the mysteries of DNA were unraveled; where Dwight David Eisenhower organized the liberation of Europe. Everywhere you look is a landmark—meaning, tradition, occurrence, and a con-vincing reason for being intrigued by being there and for experienc-ing a sense of occasion.

For visiting foreigners, there are added dimensions to the British experience. Men of the world wing in to London from Los Angeles and Tokyo, from Rio and Dusseldorf to drop a thousand dollars on a Savile Row suit and to get measured for a dozen Turnbull & Asser shirts at a hundred dollars a throw. Cool, with-it women, otherwise attuned only to the most sophisticated of fashions, make for Laura Ashley's to sigh shamelessly over and accumulate totally un-sophisticated frocks gushing with romantic sentimentality and nostalgia. Harrods' vast department store arranges to stay open at night for Middle Eastern oil sheiks to have their private run of the place and come away with thousands of dollars worth of goodies. People from all over arrive hankering after cashmere sweaters, Wedgwood china, Liberty prints, most of all craving a taste of the unique atmosphere of polish, propriety, and decorum with which Britain is said, far and wide, to be graced and which, indeed, it boasts in greater measure than anywhere else.

"Civilized" is the overused tribute employed by visitors to describe Britain, as if their own usual haunts are barbaric and madcap. What people mean is that they are less likely to be treated rudely there than in other places, less likely to be ogled by the natives as if they were creatures from alien worlds, more likely, if addressed at all, to be spoken to courteously.

To visitors, things in Britain generally seem admirably tidy and in place. Nor is this impression deceptive. There is nothing disjointed about most Britons. Even those among them who are eccentric, frivolous, or misanthropic tend to be methodical, as might be expected in an atmosphere where propriety is a persistent consideration and where "shipshape" has long been high-caliber praise. Though no longer as numerous as they once were, it is still possible to encounter those fastidious eccentrics in Britain who make neat bundles of their garbage before depositing it outside for the "dust men" ("garbage men" has a deprecating ring to it) to haul away.

There was talk a little while back of "swinging London" where no holds were barred. But Britain doesn't really swing in the accepted sense of the notion. With some pointed exceptions to prove the rule (City of London merchant bankers, Strategic Air Service commandoes), the British are a people of style rather than action. Their eccentricities are quaint and curious rather than flip and far-out; fads in fashions rather than lifestyle convulsions. Procedures are more important than perpetrations. It's not whether you win or lose; it's how you run the race.

There's magic to this special British formula, enough to dazzle and impress a lot of other people in a lot of other places. It's what keeps the annual London Wimbledon contests the high point of world tennis competition, even though it's been a long time since Britain has itself produced a convincing string of tennis champions. Henley remains the international mecca of rowing competition, though the British have long been outclassed on the river. There's the right mood, attitude, and sleight-of-hand to sustain Lord's Stadium in the British capital as the central world shrine of cricket, though the West Indians and Australians have had much more impact on the game than the British for many years now.

British history is, in fact, laced with greatly acclaimed, much-honored heroic losers: Hereward the Wake, the Saxon warrior remembered for his bold, futile rebellion against Norman conquerors; Welsh and Scottish chieftains who resisted English domination but also went down to ultimate defeat; General Gordon who, with his men, was slaughtered by Moslem insurgents in Sudan while defending an outpost of the British Empire he had been sent to abandon; the "600" who galloped gallantly to waiting disaster in the "Valley of Death" in the Crimean War, insanely but characteristically not breaking ranks even when catastrophe could have been foretold because of their impeccable discipline; the commandoes whose raid on Nazi-held Dieppe in the Second World War turned into a cruel misfortune. Failures they may have been but they all performed creditably and with style. With heroes like that, a cult of the "good loser" is inevitable.

When Julius Caesar—a general in the field but not yet an emperor—passed word along some 2,000 years ago from his base in France that he intended to invade a land called Britannia, a small-minded rival back home in Rome contemptuously insisted there was no such place. Caesar was accused of concocting this Britannia of his simply so he could later fabricate equally phony triumphs over its fictitious warriors. He would thus win himself new laurels and boost himself a few more rungs up the ladder of power and influence in the Roman Empire. But when the inhabitants of that supposedly imaginary country perversely foiled the first attempt of Caesar's seasoned legionnaires to tame them, no one could ever again doubt the existence of the British.

Questions have, however, regularly been raised about who and what the British are. In recent years, when they have been deep in the doldrums, bathed with gloom and doubt and battered and baffled by the cold facts of modern economics ("If God is an Englishman, why is the country in such a mess?"), those questions have been particularly pointed.

Are the British exquisitely well-mannered, impeccably attired, unflappable people who have bestowed upon the world incontest-

able standards of civilized behavior or are they shabby, shiftless
charlatans who have shamelessly squandered a rich legacy be-
queathed by their forebears? Are they a tough, sturdy breed who
have, time and time again, proved their mettle on fields of combat
and who once efficiently governed a sizable chunk of the world or
are they snooty and self-admiring, so confident of the superiority of
British ways that they are incapable of learning from others, even
when their own shortcomings are devastatingly conspicuous? Are
they gentle folk who, having once been preeminent among the
peoples of the world, graciously stepped aside to let others take a
turn at the top of the heap or do they obstinately cling to images of
the past because they are too stubborn to look reality in the face?
Will their downhill slide, so glaring in recent times, continue until
their glorious past mocks at them from their history books or will
British ingenuity, once proverbial, be revived, reviving Britain
itself?

There is recurring talk of how the British are adopting new
values, new morals, and new manners. An ongoing process of
development and adjustment is undeniably at play. Who would
have believed twenty-five years ago that Margaret Thatcher would
be prime minister and the dominant personality in such an
overwhelmingly male-oriented country? Who would have thought
it possible then that the leading political figures in what was not
too long ago so straitlaced a land would submit to being uncer-
emoniously grilled on television by aggressive interrogators half
their age who don't even wear neckties? Who would have imagined
that the main distinguishing feature of the best-selling newspaper
in the country where Victorian prudishness was invented would be
a daily fix of topless cheesecake and that the newspaper's owner,
Rupert Murdoch, having perfected so infamous a journalistic
practice, would then also be permitted to become the owner of the
illustrious, eminently respectable London *Times?*

Changes take place all the time. But the British, no more than
any other people, do not keep switching off old lifestyles and
switching new ones on like moulting lizards flaunting fresh skins
each year. A brief binge a few years back did not turn imperturbable
London into a perpetually swinging city. A row in Parliament over
Queen Elizabeth and her family costing the taxpayer a hefty sum to
support in regal fashion did not herald the beginning of the end of
the thousand-year monarchy. The native-born punk culture did not

signal the advent of cultural chaos. Fashions come; fashions go. But durable threads are woven through the fabric of British life and are not easily unraveled to be chucked blithely away.

Generalizations, like those made in the following pages, are of course fragile things. Once, while chauffering a visiting American through London, and having just told him that the British are the most courteous drivers in all of Europe, even-tempered, patient, and considerate (they are!), we suddenly found ourselves in an ugly, inexplicable fracas with the driver of another car. He turned out to be drunk but sober exceptions are by no means rare. There are, however, enduring British traits which survive spasmodic, transient fads and fancies.

Though courteous by inclination (not to be would be in bad taste), the British are fiercely independent. They react to pressure with an obstinate pride which probably is not much different from that exhibited by predecessors on their island who, though overwhelmed and subdued, never really accepted the gift of civilization that the invading Romans thrust upon them in ancient times. They still absolutely refuse to be hounded, harried, hurried, pressed to the wall, or told what to do. When actor Peter O'Toole's interpretation of *Macbeth* was unanimously savaged by London newspaper critics (the kindest of whom called it ludicrous), instead of closing the next night, as a play so mauled by the press would usually do in New York, the theater was besieged the next morning by long lines of defiant Londoners trying to get tickets, and the play later went on to a hugely successful tour of the English provinces. (A critic's suggestion that audiences turned up only because they longed to see both Shakespeare's immortal tragedy and O'Toole's reputation simultaneously butchered sounded like sour grapes.)

Not long ago in Liverpool, in an uncharacteristic act of strike-breaking, workers at a factory, bridling at inept union leadership, defied a walk-out call and showed up at work. When the surprised and delighted personnel manager suggested that a new, harmonious era had thereby dawned for the strike-battered plant, the workers immediately put their tools down and went out on strike, managing with mischievous serenity to demonstrate their independence and to outrage both union and employer before tea time that day.

Such defiance of what is expected of them isn't confined to group behavior. When a London baker who runs a small bakery decided to stop making a delicious black rye bread—so good that some gourmets traveled great distances for it—the baker blithely explained, "Too many people wanted it." When a clerk in a British store tells a customer that the item he wants is "on order," it often means only that the clerk is disinclined to go poking tediously around in the storeroom for it.

The British magazine *Business Traveller* ran a check on the services of a series of prominent London travel agents, sending reporters in to pretend to be contemplating journeys and asking for advice and assistance. They emerged from only one of the travel agencies they tested with "a sense that the journey might be enjoyable." In the closing stages of a protracted real estate transaction, a British real estate agent lost his fee by telling a foreign client, who had called for information about how things were progressing, that it was about time he did some of his own work on the deal. At a time when there was much anguish about privately-owned art in Britain being sold to rich collectors in other countries, and thus lost to the nation forever, trustees of a leading British museum kept cancelling meetings with an Englishman who wanted to donate a priceless painting to them until, in frustration, he profitably disposed of it overseas.

British writer Denzil Batchelor, spoiled by exposure to more compliant attitudes in different countries and vexed by the indifference of many waiters he encountered in eating establishments on home ground, complained, "There is in England no tradition of service . . . as there is in many [other] countries where it is not considered a degrading occupation to satisfy a fellow human being's needs."

There is nothing deliberately malicious or contrary in the British approach, galling and even offensive though it may sometimes be. It is not an ingrained compulsion to rile or trouble others. Britons can be enormously accommodating and helpful. Many visiting foreigners come away bubbling with praise for the cordiality of those they encountered. There are countless stories of exceedingly obliging people like the Englishman (a stranger) who, when we both arrived at a suburban London airport very late one midwinter's night after a long, tiring flight, stayed around (without being asked to do so) for almost an hour helping me try to get my frozen car started in the airport parking lot and then, when it couldn't be done, insisted on driving an hour out of his way in his own car to deliver my family and me to our London home.

Recalcitrance and bloody-mindedness arise when Britons are required to perform tasks they find distasteful or when their individuality is belittled. Both those wearisome conditions are, almost by definition, rampant in any society. Not many of us are spared having to cope with them. But few people react as reflexively or as strongly as the island people of Britain. Ralph Waldo Emerson noticed this quality more than a century ago and wrote that the English "have that nervous bilious temperament which is known by medical men to resist every means employed to make its possessors subservient to the will of others."

More recently, Arthur Koestler noted that "the same bloke who unhesitatingly risked his life at Alamein (in the Second World War) to 'keep Britain free' would not lift a finger at Dagenham (a car factory outside London) to save Britain from bankruptcy." Most other people can be induced or intimidated to do what is required of them. Most other people will bow to rewards, threats, or cajolery. But though the British will uncomplainingly perform the most onerous and thankless tasks if they think they ought to, they have to be in truly desperate straits before they are prepared to succumb to pressure to do things they don't want to do.

Popular impressions to the contrary, many of the strikes which plagued the country in recent years were not fundamentally about getting higher pay, though pay invariably was the major talking point. A lot of Britain's most serious labor difficulties involved workers who were among the highest paid in the country. Their strikes were, as often as not, eruptions of bitterness, petulance, or just plain cussedness. Big annual pay raises were gradually built into the system to try to dispel discontent but it couldn't be bought off.

Workers elsewhere, contemplating new cars, more spectacular vacations, and home improvements, were willing to work harder and longer for productivity bonuses. Their British counterparts thought of the bonuses simply as their due. They took the money but productivity showed little improvement. It remained cheaper in Britain to buy American coal and pay the shipping costs than to buy the home-mined variety. It remained cheaper to turn a cargo ship around in the port of Rotterdam across the North Sea than in

London. Britain's nationalized steel industry lost money on every ton of steel produced.

It's not that apathetic and strike-prone British workers were unaware of the damage done to Britain's prospects by their actions or that they were not interested in the more substantial rewards that might accrue to them as they had accrued to American, German, and Japanese workers. Before soaring unemployment levels made many of them more willing to give ground on principles, it was more a case of simply not accepting the time-honored fact that desired ends sometimes can only be achieved through dreary means.

As a philosophy, the means-to-an-end approach sounds crass to the British. It seems degradingly calculating. "I've got my pride, you know," is regularly uttered by genuinely modest, unpretentious Britons to explain self-defeating actions or attitudes. Many see no reason to dredge up any explanation whatsoever. After all, cutting off noses to spite faces has heroic dimensions and true heroes don't have to broadcast their heroism to the world, especially if they're heroic losers.

As if consistency is too confining for the likes of them, the British—despite the tenacity of their spirit and the sturdiness of their character—exhibit a multitude of contradictions. Though disdainful of those in authority and profoundly conscious of their rights and privileges, they reflexively form orderly queues at bus stops and box offices and would rather suffer in silence than make unseemly scenes in restaurants. They are firm believers in democracy but highly esteem their queen who, with a typical British concession to the gulf between form and substance, reigns but does not rule. No Briton will concede that someone else is better than he is, but blueblooded aristocrats retain privileged positions in British society. The British commitment to equality is confused and befuddled by anachronistic habits and attitudes which make class advantages and handicaps still very real and meaningful. There is much truth to John Stuart Mill's observation about his compatriots, that they "do not dislike to have people above them as long as they have some below them."

British stiff-upper-lip unflappability is neatly expressed in Rudyard Kipling's admonition to "meet disaster and triumph and treat both those imposters just the same." But alone among the countries where soccer is popular, Britain suffers interminably from ugly crowd violence at soccer matches. Riot police are alerted in European cities when British fans arrive to cheer on their teams in international matches.

The British are noted for their tact and discretion but see nothing peculiar about calling a north England hospital the "Hospice for the Terminally Ill" or in having London establishments officially named the "Hospital for the Incurables" and "Hospital for Sick Children." It would seem likely, to foreigners at least, that descriptions like that billboarded around those hospitals might upset patients at those otherwise excellent institutions. Along the same lines, the British commonly call hearing aids "deaf aids."

Slovenly speech on British radio and television can unleash a deluge of outrage but a stock British comic figure is a Colonel Blimp-Doctor Watson character (his kind really exists) so full of nasal pomposity, mental confusion, and verbal constipation that he can barely get a recognizable word out. Britons note with quiet satisfaction that the first words on the moon, albeit from an American, were spoken in English but deride what they consider unrelenting American abuse of the mother tongue. However, when Secretary of State Alexander Haig was taken to task in American newspapers for playing fast and loose with the language—turning nouns into verbs, etc.—letters were hurriedly dispatched to the editor of the London *Times* testifying that such a seemingly cavalier treatment of the language was in fact a venerable English tradition.

The British taught the world the benefits of capitalism and then proceeded to construct an intricate cradle-to-grave welfare state. They pioneered the industrial revolution, but let the more impetuously industrious Americans, Germans, and Japanese steal their lead. They erected and efficiently governed an elaborate empire over which the sun never set—until it sank like a stone after World War Two. And though the imperial past is now relegated to the history books, they take quiet satisfaction from the fact that the American Founding Fathers, though rebels, were British through-and-through, and that the legacy of British imperial rule promises a fair trial to accused men in places as far apart as Australia and India, Singapore and Kenya, Jamaica and Hong Kong, Boston and Santa Barbara.

. . . this scepter'd isle . . .
this fortress built by Nature for herself
against infection and the hand of war. . . .
WILLIAM SHAKESPEARE
Richard II

It is almost a thousand years since anyone has invaded Britain and vanquished the British. The Spanish tried and failed disastrously before they even hit the beaches, their magnificent Armada savaged by the intrepid seadogs of the Virgin Queen, Elizabeth I (after whom the state of Virginia was named). Napoleon and Hitler were held off as well. Not since William the Conqueror crossed over from Normandy in 1066 to seize the English crown has any invader been able to penetrate the British island fortress. It remains almost as hard to penetrate the protective insularity of the people who inhabit that fortress. They are honorable, loyal, considerate, trustworthy—it's all there in the oath of the Boy Scouts, an organization founded by an Englishman, Sir Robert Stephenson Smythe Baden-Powell. But their island mentality strongly colors British attitudes.

They scrupulously guard their personal privacy, preferring to mind their own business and for others to do the same. The Duke of Wellington was expressing a preference to which his compatriots are still partial when, in reply to a question about what he liked most, he said he liked to walk alone. When the British say of a person, "He kept himself to himself," it is said admiringly, even if they're talking about someone discovered to have been a dangerous maniac. They find chit-chat of a personal nature extremely awkward and grow queasy when confronted with the American habit of trying to find out what they do for a living. Asking where they went to school—an important indicator of class status—can also make them feel awkward.

Like primitive people who refuse to allow themselves to be photographed for fear of having their souls stolen by the camera, many Britons act as though their names are magical code words which should preferably be withheld to prevent others from extracting occult significance from their identities and thus leave them exposed and vulnerable to a mocking world. For a foreigner to seize the initiative and introduce himself can prove a social blunder because it amounts to premature, excessive intimacy. For courtesy's sake, it also seems to require reciprocal disclosure. There's no telling where it all might end!

It is not unusual for a foreigner to feel exasperated and bewildered at a party in Britain when he engages in an enjoyable give-and-take with someone, senses the warm glow that comes from making contact with an agreeable stranger, only to hear that stranger wind up the encounter—before a subsequent get-together can even be hinted at—with, "It was terribly nice meeting you. Maybe we'll meet again sometime." A young Canadian exposed to that kind of treatment at three successive London parties spent a long time trying to figure out for what gaucheries (excessive familiarity, dirty language) he was held accountable to deserve such a brush-off. He could not be convinced that it wasn't his fault.

People who go to parties expect to talk to guests. It's the "done thing," pleasant, diverting, even scintillating—*in its place.* Such casual intercourse is, however, not necessarily appropriate at other times or in other circumstances. An Irishman will spill out his life story to a stranger during a chance encounter in a bar. A German will seek to impress that stranger with an account of his talents and accomplishments. An American will invite him home to meet the wife and kids. But people in Britain can take the same train to work every morning for years without knowing each other's name and without exchanging more than a few words, usually about the weather—a device for short-circuiting more substantial talk. It was a contention of Emily Hahn, who undertook an examination of the British character thirty years ago, that "serious discussion gives most Englishmen gooseflesh." Things haven't changed much. A visiting English friend grew visibly alarmed at the conflict of views strongly expressed at my dinner table by myself and an American friend. He stayed carefully clear himself and was relieved when he saw that friendship had not been endangered by the exchange and that no one's dignity had been trifled with.

On a questionnaire about friendship in a study of personal relationships in Britain, a number of people replied, "I have no friends." The survey said "distant cordiality" was the best way to describe the typical relationship of neighbors: "Not one in twenty knew [their neighbors] well enough to drop in on them without an invitation and it is very exceptional for neighbors to entertain one another for a meal or to spend an evening together." Such deliberate seclusion was once generally considered a middle- or upper-class preference but Geoffrey Moorhouse, who wrote about *Britain in the Sixties*, found "a staggering lack of community, even of elementary contacts" in working-class parts of London.

Years ago, people from elsewhere living in Britain assumed they were not invited home by their British neighbors because most foreigners, employed by foreign firms, were better off than most British. People in Britain were still painfully extracting themselves from a protracted siege of austerity stretching back to the Second World War. It was thought that the British feared being humiliated because their homes and the hospitality they could offer could not match those of their more solvent foreign neighbors. But as living standards improved in Britain, they still rarely extended hospitality to their neighbors—native or foreign—and it was clear the reasons were more fundamental.

That the British are reserved by nature is proverbial. But it is not because of haughtiness or insensitivity to the existence of others. Most Britons are profoundly sensitive. There is, however, a sharp contrast between them and, for example, the Italians and French, who seem to thrive on excitement. For those others, practically all emotional storms soon blow over and are forgotten. But the British, who dread emotional commotion, do not let go that easily. If they gave themselves half a chance, they would cultivate and cling endlessly to whatever personal exasperations crop up as devotedly as they treasure and cultivate the strips of backyard they invariably call their gardens.

For the British, personal complications, if permitted to develop, endure endlessly because they are not the fleeting nuisances they are to some people. They are intolerable intrusions. They tempt people to contemplate, to say and do reckless, inappropriate things. They have the effect of mutilating standards of composure and control the British want desperately to maintain. When they do let loose, they often discover later to their chagrin that they've exploded over trivial, unworthy annoyances. It's too much trouble. It's far too upsetting. A curtain of privacy, studiously but effortlessly maintained, serves them as a portable moat, warding off awkward entanglements that might take forever to sort out and put straight. Why bother? "Better safe than sorry."

At his home—"his castle"—an Englishman is addicted to hedges, walls, and other property demarcations. This strategic seclusion shields him from troublesome misunderstandings which haunt the British imagination. It provides the fabric from which such play- wrights as Harold Pinter and Tom Stoppard have woven their bewitching dramatic extravaganzas.

If an American can be said to wear his heart on his sleeve and to telegraph his feelings with reflexive smiles or grimaces, Britons can be said to keep their hearts buried deep in their inside pockets and to convey their feelings in codes which are not readily decipherable to the uninitiated. They do not tip their hands. Margaret Halsey suggested that "English life is seven-eighths below the surface, like an iceberg, and living in England for a year constitutes merely an introduction to an introduction to an introduction to it."

Nor is British self-control, and the overpowering element of propriety it contains, something of which only foreigners are keenly aware. The novelist E.M. Forster noted, "It's not that the Englishman can't feel—it is that he is afraid to feel. He has been taught that feeling is bad form. He must not express great joy or sorrow, or even open his mouth too wide when he talks—his pipe might fall out if he did."

This was a reference to the tradition of rigid social indoctrination at Britain's private schools, which are perversely called "public schools" and which have for a long time turned out products—like former prime minister Lord Home—who barely part their lips when they talk. (There's a joke about a stranger trying to decipher the nationalities of various people, the punch line of which is, "If I were anymore English, I wouldn't be able to speak!")

But a cool, unemotional stance is not confined exclusively to the upper classes. A climate of unruffled seclusion, of refraining from individual public displays of feeling, pervades all of British society and is sometimes expressed in curious ways. Shoppers in street markets, which thrive in British cities, will meekly accept damaged fruit from pushcart vendors (the good stuff is only for display) rather than exhibit their displeasure at being so blatantly cheated. Though sympathetic to the troubles of others, no expression changed among passengers in a London subway train when one of their number suddenly began vomiting blood. Though their feelings of kinship and love are strong, the British don't cuddle their children, not even at home. It has been pointed out that the word "nursery" is commonly used in England as the place where both children and plants are reared, as if both needed similar control and isolation during formative stages.

Personal privacy is also the stuff which spawns the climate of eccentricity for which Britain is renowned—the lady living with forty-seven cats, the man so enamored of the tales of King Arthur that he clangs down to breakfast in armor each morning, Sir Francis Chichester sailing solo around the world past retirement age. Unconventional maybe, but no one's business but their own. The actress Beatrice Campbell contended, "You can do what you like in London so long as you don't do it in the street and don't frighten the horses." She was wrong. Unless it is particularly offensive, you can do it in the street as well. George Orwell noted that one of the differences between being down-and-out in Paris and London was that in London the cops didn't always keep moving derelicts on when they loitered in the streets.

Britain is the home of the stiff upper lip (which, according to one wit, may be another reason so many English people barely open their mouths when they speak). It is the home of the ability to cope with adversity without flinching, whining, or getting flustered. A classic example was the Marquess of Anglesey who, when the commanding general noted at the Battle of Waterloo, "By God, sir, you've lost your leg!," calmly replied: "By God, sir, so I have." Such composure captivated philosopher George Santayana who said, "These self-sufficing Englishmen, in their reserve and decision, seemed to me truly men. . . . The low pressure at which their minds seemed to work showed how little they were alarmed about anything. Things would be managed somehow. They were good company even when they said nothing."

It would be a mistake, of course, to imagine that, as individuals, all Britons are strong and silent, are living in a perpetual state of siege or endlessly primed to scramble out of range of entanglements. There are those among them who are hospitable, accessible, friendly, garrulous, excitable, and nosy as anyone anywhere. There are specific characteristics and nuances of behavior which tend to distinguish people of one class from those of another and those in different regions of the country. People in northern England tend to be more blunt and less sophisticated than those in the south, and sometimes embarrass southerners with effusive friendliness. People in Wales tend to be more articulate than other Britons. People in Scotland have a justifiable reputation for being dour and

obstinate. But those are not the predominant British characteristics; they do not reflect the essence of the British character. Nor do
they fit into the catalog of idealized British virtues, not like pluck
and fortitude of the kind exhibited by Captain Lawrence Oates.

A place is reserved in the pantheon of British heroes for Captain
Oates. Sick, frost-bitten, wanting no longer to be a dangerous
burden to the hard-pressed Antarctic expedition of which he was a
member, Oates deliberately slipped away into frozen oblivion one
night, casually telling his shivering tent mates as he left, "I'm
stepping outside. I may be sometime." A superbly British gesture, it
was tidy and uncomplicated—no fuss, no bother, no mess to clean
up afterwards. A subsequent claim that the letters of a survivor of
the expedition indicated that Oates had made his heroic sacrifice
only after repeated hints and nudges from the expedition leader was
too painful to receive wide notice in Britain.

For self-control to survive as a national trait, there must be a
reassuring crutch of continuity and stability. If bragging were not
undignified, modern Britain—where self-control is second nature—
could boast of more than its fair share of both. It has been spared
violent revolutions of the kind which convulsed Russia and France.
Many centuries have passed since the country was last torn by
chaos and anarchy. Its civil war was bloody and bitter but was
fought out and done with more than 300 years ago. Since then,
outbursts of civil strife in the country, though sometimes dramatic
and destructive, have been comparatively brief, pretty well isolated,
and capable of being digested by the community without widespread upheaval. The General Strike of 1926, which partly paralyzed the country and which elsewhere would have been marked by
eruptions of violence, passed with a minimum of disorder, to the
confusion of revolutionaries baffled by the sight of strikers playing
soccer in the street with policemen on picket line duty. The recent
spate of street riots, triggered by hostility between police and black
youths in Britain, was serious. But those outbursts were not nearly
as devastating, protracted, or bloody as riots in such European
centers as Berlin, Amsterdam, or Zurich.

Not that Britain has been graced with fewer reasons for civil
unrest than other places. Poverty and urban squalor have by no
means been missing from the British landscape. Provocative upper-
class privilege and lower-class exploitation have been persistent

themes across the length and breadth of the country. Opportunities for personal advancement based exclusively on talent and diligence have, until very recently, been virtually nonexistent and even now are not much to write home about.

But whatever provocative impulses and urges have surged through British veins, restraining influences have been powerful enough to dampen down earthly expectations and aspirations of the kind which once prodded Parisians off to storm the Bastille and which drove American Southerners to take arms against Northern supremacy in the War Between the States. The British countryside was once the scene of periodic unrest, fueled by injustice and deprivation. In more recent times, the British have displayed a talent for throwing picket lines around factories, organizing rallies to protest government policies, and getting local government bodies to defy the wishes and instructions of the prime minister and Parliament. But such outbursts are simply not in the same class as incidents of historic turbulence which changed the course of history in other countries.

The origin of British restraint is not easy to pinpoint. A contributing factor is the traditional method (now in the process of serious change) of rearing children both at home and in school not to be disobedient or rash and to know their places. Some contend that the British have shied clear of upheaval or insurrection of late simply because, despite obvious problems and shortcomings, they have convinced themselves that they, at root, have it far better than anyone else. They are, after all, British! But probably the most important component of British restraint is an enduring Puritan influence, a product of sterner aspects of the country's early Protestant heritage.

Puritans were strict on matters of morals (and everything else). They were morose when it came to life's possible pleasures and satisfactions. According to the Puritan ethic, those who shunned such frivolous indulgences as zest, gusto, and excessive comfort, those who ungrudgingly endured the vale of tears into which we were born, were deemed worthy and admirable. Such calculated self-denial, methodically disguised, was absorbed into the British subconscious long ago. It still permits Britons to consider things to be virtuous or proper only because they are joyless and dreary. George Bernard Shaw suggested cynically, "An Englishman thinks he is moral when he is only uncomfortable."

He was, as the British say, "spot on." Having fun is in fact not very high on their list of priorities. The Spanish historian Salvador da Madariaga, who lived many years in Britain, chided that while the Puritan influence has not prevented the British from sinning, it has kept them from enjoying it. A French visitor once marveled, "The English amuse themselves sadly, as is the custom in their country." Erotic masochistic flagellation—deriving sexual pleasure from being beaten—was once known throughout Europe as "the English disease," a name later given to general economic malaise.

Puritanical influences are detectable in attitudes towards food in Britain, where it is rarely prepared to standards of excellence. Not often enough does British cooking even rank as particularly good. Too often it is remarkably drab, with spices remaining an unexplored mystery and garlic a crime. The British were the last of the industrialized peoples to install central heating in their homes and even now many Britons, while tolerating the intrusion and use of heating devices in their living rooms, keep the radiators in their bedrooms firmly turned off and their bedroom windows open at night the chill winter through.

On winter days, an extraordinary number of young Britons venture outside with light jackets or sweaters as their heaviest protection against the elements and seemingly relish the thrill of being cold enough for their teeth to chatter. Men who know better swelter in respectable woolen suits on days warm enough for shirt sleeves.

The British suffer inordinately from what George Orwell called "artistic insensibility." The vast majority of them who are not partial to serious music or art ridicule such things. The contrast between the architectural inspiration of European showplace office buildings and housing projects and the equivalent in Britain reveals how far the British have clamped the lid on their aesthetic imagination. British architects working abroad tend to show far greater flair than those working at home, as if they are in on secrets their homebound colleagues are not permitted to share. British life generally retains many bracing elements, physical and moral, which would have found favor among those Puritans of times past who chose to fast on Christmas Day rather than desecrate the Yuletide by feasting and making merry, and who saw little reason for enjoying life on any other day of the year either.

Julius Caesar reported that ancient Britons extracted a dye from a plant substance and painted themselves blue with it. Caesar suspected it was done to make them look ferocious in the eyes of their enemies, though it may have been an obscure form of religious observance. Possibly it was considered the appropriate color in which respectable folk were to be seen in public—in the same category as the suit jackets Britons were later to inflict on properly attired men around the world.

Though central to the British image today, the emphasis on respectability is of only recent vintage. The early history of Britain is laced with unabashed, undisguised brutality. It may well be that today's much-admired, self-imposed layer of decorum and the blue veneer favored by their early forebears serve and served the very same purpose—to restrain and mask fierce aspects of character which were so relentlessly exhibited in former times and which may still lurk not far beneath the British skin. Anyone who has seen a riot at a soccer match in Leeds, or is familiar with the testimony in trials of south London strong-arm criminal gangs, or knows about the cruel bullying of young boys in schools ("It builds their character"), or has heard of the Italian ski resort which has banned parties of British school children because of fighting and vandalism, or has taken part in the opening day rush at the summer sale at Harrods knows there is much more to Britain than good manners and fair play. Those admirable characteristics may be only a thick outer facade, like the crust of the earth which covers, contains, and controls a turbulent, fiery interior whose existence is confirmed by periodic volcanic eruptions.

The Puritan code originally kindled devotion to duty and work and a commitment to achievement. The hard-working, useful laborer, like the village blacksmith or stonemason, was greatly respected. He did his work uncomplainingly with dedication and skill and was content with his station in life. He was contaminated neither by crude ambition nor a craving for great wealth.

The Puritan ethic also produced one of Britain's most enduring folk heroes—the clever amateur. By definition, an amateur is an enthusiast, someone who does what he does because he is good at it (or would like to be). In the last analysis, unlike a professional, he is answerable only to himself. Who can remember Sherlock Holmes ever accepting a telling-off from a dissatisfied client or, for that matter, ever submitting a bill for his services which might have empowered his client to get uppity? An honorarium was slipped his way now and again, but Holmes didn't really care. He was in it only for the fun of playing his sleuthing games and cavorting through the fog in his cape-coat and deer-stalker hat, with his trusty magnifying glass in his pocket. The same sort of thing was true for a long list of other fictional detectives, empire builders, heroic spies, and daring explorers—men who penetrated the perilous unknown equipped only with the natural talent for survival that came with being British and for whom being British was reward enough.

However, just as the advent of the assembly line and other dehumanizing contrivances were to demolish the tradition of uncomplaining, undemanding dedication to hard work, the bitter facts of economic survival were destined to demolish the dream of untarnished, uncorrupted amateurism. The cold, hard world intruded on visions of the dashing adventurer having the time of his life (and endless resources) pursuing noble tasks as and when it suited his whims. Suddenly cash had to be on the barrelhead or the assignment couldn't even be contemplated. And then there were cost overruns and miscalculations which had to be taken into account. Accountants and solicitors had to be consulted. It was all very boring.

The virtues of amateurism were, however, too deeply ingrained simply to be chucked away. A new type of amateurism sprouted. By necessity, sums were involved. But "amateurs" clung to a revulsion against professionalism. They continued to dabble at their calling while earning their livings through such dabbling, but they steadfastly refused to be subject to outside quality control and value judgments.

A foreign businessman working on a tight schedule got to know better than to assume that his British counterpart would forego Saturday morning golf simply to negotiate a contract. Hard-driving businessmen were considered boorish. There was something shifty about someone who succeeded after starting from scratch. Those who flaunted their authority rather than wielding it subtly, if at all, were deemed vulgar.

This was a revised form of amateurism. It was quaint, civilized, and colorful. But it has a lot to answer for because amateurs weren't always up to the jobs they undertook. Senior British civil servants, rather than aviation experts, were the ones who made decisions on the hugely profitless supersonic Anglo-French Concorde airliner. Despite the excellence of British stagecraft, many of the plays opening in London's West End could benefit greatly from another two weeks in rehearsal. Most of the effigies of famous personalities in a well-known London wax museum would be unrecognizable without their labels. A popular British television mimic has to name the celebrities he is mimicking or no one would know who they are. *Trying* is as virtuous as succeeding and often draws the same rewards. That's what British amateurism is about.

There are various benefits which result from such an undemanding approach to life. Psychosomatic ulcers are much less common in Britain than they are in high-pressured American environments. Comparatively few Britons have ever felt the need to call on the services of a psychologist. Built-in restraint promotes a softer approach to life. There are other benefits as well. When, in recent years, Germany and Italy were plagued by a rash of terrorist bombings and assassinations and when America had to cope with a bout of "Weathermen" troubles, Britain's anarchistic "Angry Brigade" was speedily brought to heel by the authorities before they could do any damage worth mentioning. Though the incidence of street crime has been rising in Britain, as it has in many other parts of the world, and though an occasional frenzy of fear might be stirred by such felons as the "Yorkshire Ripper" who murdered several women in northern England in the late 1970s, there are still not that many places in the country where a person would have to think twice before strolling about alone, unarmed and unafraid even in the dead of night.

It is impossible to determine what shapes the character of a people. No doubt climate is a factor. Aside from being Britain's favorite topic of conversation, its weather is famous for being mischievous and troublesome. It is unpredictable, not in the sense of "who knows what tomorrow will bring" but in relation to whether it will be "pouring down buckets" by lunchtime. This is less true for parts of Britain where people can generally be confident of bad weather—if it's not raining there now, it soon will be. According to an old English gag, "You can tell when summer's here; the rain gets warmer." It is said of Scotland that if you look across Loch Lomond (the lake) and can see Ben Lomond (the mountain) on the other side, that means it's going to rain; if you look across the loch and cannot see Ben Lomond, that means it *is* raining. Even in the less disagreeable climate of southern England, mornings, afternoons, and nights of a single day can be graced (or cursed) with different elemental conditions.

It was late spring when I first came to Britain and through some quirk, perhaps related to getting used to a new bed, I awoke before five each morning to see a glorious, bright dawn with the sun just beginning to make its promise teasingly clear. I would then go back to sleep each morning and wake to the plop of raindrops on my window two hours later. Fortunately, I soon got used to the bed and stopped waking for those counterfeit dawns and fake promises. In time, there were mornings without rain. Sometimes they were sunny; sometimes they were cloudy. Invariably, the one became the other before midday and sometimes changed back again in the afternoon.

At least that's my recollection because the climate of London, if not of all the rest of the country, has changed noticeably of late. Clean air laws permitting only smokeless fuels to be burnt appear to have had the effect of helping to clear the skies so that rain, though still a regular feature of the London scene, is less frequent. As a matter of fact, whatever the reasons, the statistics indicate that soggy London now usually gets less rain than sunny Rome. It would come as a humiliating shock to the historian Tacitus who, during the Roman occupation of Britain, dismissed its climate as "horrid because of the frequency of rain and mist."

During winter, London daytime temperatures rarely fall below freezing and drop only a few degrees under during winter nights. The suburbs and exposed areas are a touch colder. Though trees shed their leaves come autumn, the grass remains green the year round (a pleasing touch) and flowers begin poking up out of the ground well before winter is officially done with. But there have been winters long ago when the Thames froze so hard that booths and tents were set up on the river's thick, solid surface and horses and carriages were driven across it. London rarely gets much snow to speak of, though Scotland and the English west country usually can count on at least a partially white winter.

During English summers, temperatures rarely climb more than a degree or two above eighty. When things get warmer than that, newspapers begin speculating about the causes of the "heat wave" and make puns about the "London Riviera." But a freak summer spell a few years back was sizzling enough to turn even the green, usually well-watered moors of northern England a lifeless brown and forced the inhabitants of this normally dampish island to engage in the foreign habit of conserving water.

Spring and autumn are generally gentle times of the year. Either wet or cold, winters tend to be dim and dismal, though there are occasional compensating moments: While writing this on a January day in London, I broke off for a walk in a park and was treated to the surrealist vision of two young women, decked out as if for Wimbledon in June, playing first-rate tennis with a gentle mist wrapped around them.

Though usually pleasant, British summers are really anyone's guess. But unlike other places where suicide rates are linked to climatic conditions, British moods and character do not vary with the seasons. There's no opening up in springtime and closing down as autumn fizzles out. The summer has long been marked by a "silly season" with people doing strange things at the seaside, rolling up their trouser legs and wading into the water and donning paper hats made of newspaper to fend off the sun. But such flightiness is due more to the summer being vacation time than to the weather. The British have thought things out. For the sake of balance and proportion, they generally allow the weather little influence on their attitudes and habits.

Many a sandwich planned for a sunny countryside picnic has been contentedly gobbled down inside the car on a country road, with the rain battering down outside. It is not considered foolish to lug along an umbrella on a bright, cloudless morning. Still to be deciphered is the significance of the casual, frequently heard comment, "Turning out fine." It is usually accompanied by a suspicious glance toward the heavens and is usually uttered regardless of which way the weather is turning.

The Tribes of Britain

HE WAS A BRIGHT, articulate twenty-year-old
Cambridge University student who was applying for
unemployment insurance during the summer vacation because
he hadn't been able to find a suitable job to tide him over till
classes began again. He said manual labor was beneath him.
Questioned, he confessed regretfully that he considered those
who performed such labor beneath him as well.

The elderly woman spoke with the posh intonations of the
British upper classes. She was not impolite but sounded
accustomed to being catered to. She had to ask three times
where she might find light bulbs before the girl behind the
counter in a London Woolworth's, who had just agreeably
served a visiting American, motioned her dismissively to the
wrong section of the store.

Only after he was safely buried and had revealed all in a
scandalous posthumous autobiography did members of the
House of Commons suggest they had known all along that one
of their number had considered his homosexual adventures—
some of them within the Houses of Parliament—far more
important than the affairs of state.

The British have no identity crisis. They know precisely who
they are and who they are not. More by instinct than calculation,
they know to which of the many British tribes they belong. And
they know exactly what sort of behavior their tribal membership

requires of them. Though the good, the wise, and the enlightened among them condemn divisive influences as a social disease, and though tribal lines are crossed or blurred more often now than ever before, the "us-and-them" syndrome is tenacious, enduring, and as British as the Union Jack.

A scene in the hilarious English movie *The Man in the White Suit* tells the whole story. In this cinematic moment of truth, quarrelsome union people and snooty industrialists simultaneously make the astounding discovery that they have a common interest (to squelch a stupendous invention that would end up costing both profits and jobs). The scene was memorable because of how glaringly it cut against the grain. It was the exception driving home the truth.

The fact is, recognition of common interest among its tribes is simply not easy to come by in Britain. Though theirs is for the most part an orderly society and though they can pull together in times of national crisis, the British are relentlessly committed to group and class loyalties. They know exactly who is "us" and who is "them."

Whatever else they do, those identities and loyalties promote a reassuring sense of belonging: soldiers to their regiments (long after they have turned civilian); working men and women to their union (even when they object to union policy); "public" school boys to their schools (even when they are old men); soccer fans to the teams they support; gentlemen to their clubs; mods, rockers, skinheads, and punks to their respective gang affiliations; barristers, solicitors, surgeons, and other professionals to their professions, jealously guarding their secrets and prerogatives from outsiders with the vigilance of medieval guildsmen. A London doctor, asked by a patient to tell him what was in the medicine he had just prescribed, replied sharply, "None of your business!"

A City of London businessman knows he can rely on others like himself to adhere to accepted City codes and practices. His word is his bond. He will risk millions on verbal deals within The City—contracts to be signed later. Members of the House of Commons, disdainful of the House of Lords, refer to it ritualistically as "the other place" and erupt in fury if a lord dares to step into their chamber. Within the British Establishment, consideration for Establishment figures is so reflexive that when art historian Anthony

Blunt was exposed as having been a Soviet spy years before (he had been granted immunity from prosecution by British intelligence!) he was courteously received in the London *Times* dining room after being grilled about his treachery by *Times* reporters. He was fed smoked trout. In addition to being scooped, the non-Establishment *Daily Express* was outraged by the treatment accorded Blunt and declared that it wouldn't have offered the ex-spy so much as a kipper.

Resolute us-and-them commitments contribute mightily to the perpetuation of the most unyielding and most important of British tribal distinctions, those of class. "To be classless," wrote a prominent British newspaper columnist, "is to be an alien, rootless, cut off from any truly intimate and satisfactory communion with any section of society." Though such words may sound antediluvian to people (including many Britons) who abhor class distinctions, they are not a distortion of British circumstances.

It is true that Prime Minister Thatcher's father was a grocer, that the father of the editor of the *Times* was an engine driver, and that actor Michael Caine's father was a fish market porter. It is also true that the facts of present-day economic existence have dramatically altered many of the traditional trappings of class status. Skilled and semi-skilled working men are now highly paid while many aristocrats have to scrounge for the wherewithal of financial survival. It is not unusual for unskilled people to command wages which permit them to spend reasonably freely while many with middle-class identities, roles, standards, and aspirations have to count pennies. But such developments have had little impact on social mobility. By the tacit consent of practically everyone in Britain, that remains virtually nonexistent.

Class identity is defined by habits and values rather than by earning power. The "genteel" poor in a countryside cottage badly in need of repair and the working-class poor in a Liverpool slum consider themselves a world apart, having only their poverty in common. The Manchester machinist and the Leeds business executive, earning roughly the same wages, share little other than an interest in keeping their taxes down.

When Britons of different classes find themselves affording and taking the same package vacations abroad, they also find the inevitable mixing and mingling with each other awkward and uncomfortable. A social mobility survey carried out under the direction of Oxford University sociologists concluded that there has been no change at all in recent times in the relative chances of reaching the top for those born into different social classes. For the most part, the top continues to be hereditarily self-perpetuating, and so do the other levels of society.

In the land where Adam Smith first defined the doctrine of free enterprise and the contribution it could make to the community as a whole, the idea that a skilled mechanic, for example, might leave the garage for which he works to set up and own a garage of his own—making him an entrepreneur rather than a worker—is totally foreign. Someone actually seeking to shift from working class to middle class through initiative or education, or to have his children do so, is deemed by others in the working class to be a turncoat, a sellout, an apostate who has put himself beyond the embrace of traditional British tolerance. That's not considered eccentricity; that amounts to trying to belittle all others of the same background who are, after all, just as good as the person putting on "la-di-da" airs.

Only a meager one-quarter of British sixteen-to-nineteen-year-olds (the ending high school/starting college ages) whose fathers are unskilled workers are in full-time or part-time school. The lines are set early. Not long ago, a thirteen-year-old London girl was so tormented by her working-class schoolmates because she spoke "too posh" that her working-class parents felt obliged to find another school for her.

The middle classes are no less defensive in their attitudes. A middle-class spokesman for working-class objectives is written off by others in the middle class not only as a villain but as probably unhinged as well. A middle-class son bringing home a Cockney lass to meet his folks would fill them with despair and intimations of disgrace. A middle-class English girl working as a waitress in Los Angeles said it would have ben socially impossible for her to have taken such a job at home.

The British-Hungarian humorist George Mikes observed, "Britain has a working class which does not work; a ruling class which does not rule; and a middle class which is not in the middle but is sliding fast to the bottom." Nevertheless, they all remain reflexively aware of their tribal identities, the "sliding" middle class as obstinately as working-class people and aristocrats. Despite inflationary pressures which confuse and unnerve them, members of the middle class strive to fulfill a tribal role as guardians of standards of respectability and rectitude—not easy to do these days when hippies and squatters radiate a kind of raffish charm. Ironically, their dedication does not spare them being troubled by persisting uncertainties which transcend current fashions. Those uncertainties are part of their heritage and probably part of their role as well, keeping them on their toes. Lower class and upper class seem unequivocal, firm, certain, while middle class too often seems neither here nor there, occupying a limbo of perpetually imminent social gaffes, gaucheries, and crassness. The "people-in-between" poet Hilaire Belloc called them:

> The People in Between
> Looked underdone and harassed
> And out of place and mean,
> And horribly embarrassed.

With a frigid, dismissive "How very interesting," conspicuous middle-class efforts to attain social distinction are spurned by the upper class as vulgarly presumptuous, like cheap red wines masquerading as vintage claret. At the same time, such middle-class maneuvers to climb a rung up the class ladder are ridiculed by working-class people as an empty facade—"all show and no breakfast."

Ambition sounds too virtuous not to be praised in theory, but in practice it is frowned upon by the British as tawdry. Still popular is the pretty Anglican hymn *All Things Bright and Beautiful* which tells of:

> The rich man in his castle,
> The poor man at his gate,
> God made them high or lowly,
> And ordered their estate.

No mention there of merchants or industrialists whose energy and imagination kindled the Industrial Revolution which Britain pioneered, and whose ingenuity and enterprise founded the British Empire. No mention there of the doctors or scientists through whose vision British genius had its richest expression. It is as if what comes between "high" and "lowly" is disreputable and best ignored both by the man in the castle and the one at the gate.

Meek middle-class concepts of propriety tend to encourage such an implied slur. Talk of money is shunned by proper middle-class people in Britain as boorish and "terribly middle class." They prefer not to talk about schools or education if it would reveal that they did not attend high-status educational establishments. They tend to be apologetic when they discuss their jobs because it underscores their class identity. Come summertime, money problems sometimes compel them to make do with a fortnight at a cheap working-class vacation spot, like a seaside camp-styled colony in southern England, but those are holidays which they feel called upon to describe disapprovingly (not really worthy of their sort of people) if they can't manage to avoid mentioning them at all.

Yet middle-class objectives—equality before the law, independence, respectability, tolerance, homeowning ("safe as houses"), possessions generally—are among the dominant values of Britain. They have been impressed upon the British imagination by those selfsame merchants, managers, civil servants, and other middle-class activists who, despite their achievements, continue to harbor misgivings about their attitudes and actions. They have been unable to accept or alter the fact that they are being economically overtaken by an aggressive, confident working class which knows exactly what it wants: good pay, decent places to live, cars, clothes, and vacations—no agonizing over status, image, or similar codswallop. They have tried to reinforce their socially elevated position with all sorts of silly gimmicks at work, like having tea served to them in china cups while working men in the same company are required to make do with metal mugs, and company cars for a large portion of non-working-class employees. (The British Road Federation estimates that 60 to 70 percent of new cars registered in the country are company-owned.) And to show their respect for status, middle-class executives and civil servants still frequently choose not particularly qualified aristocrats to sit on the boards of their companies and public institutions simply because of the grandness of their titles.

Most of the leaders of Britain's Labor Party, some of the country's unions, and many of its diminutive radical socialist factions are of middle-class origin. But that cannot be taken as evidence that class lines are being dissolved. Those people belong to a tribe all their own—the *would-be working class*, which even includes an aristocrat or two. Member of Parliament Anthony Wedgwood Benn spurned the title of Lord Stansgate, which he inherited from his father, and chose to be called simply Tony Benn (even having *Who's Who in Britain* omit details of his privileged Establishment education from its listing on him) as he pursued titular leadership of the country's leftwing political forces. Katherine Whitehorn, a perceptive columnist for the London *Observer*, noted, "Fleet Street [the British capital's newspaper district] is full of people who hiss 'middle class' with the intonation of 'nigger,' who nonetheless pull in high salaries and own houses full of interestingly expensive objects; obviously they feel themselves working class in the sight of God."

The youngsters who attend Britain's private schools generally feel themselves something completely different in the sight of both God and their fellow mortals. These schools, now virtually the exclusive preserve of the upper middle class which vastly outnumbers the aristocracy, produce the most polished, the most poised young men in Britain. Unless a boy is particularly unlucky, graduating from Winchester or Eton provides credentials and style which amount to an enormous head start. It opens doors, promotes acceptance by better universities, pins down good jobs, and generates respect, except from a handful of neanderthal aristocrats who, blinking at training in such schools for some young nobles, consider middle-class upstarts "too clever by half."

Nor is the working class, which has no trouble spotting a patrician-in-the-making, overly sympathetic to the product of private educational institutions from which, with very few exceptions, its sons and daughters are in effect barred. An Eton accent and tone of voice, which is excellent for selling British products to foreigners, is also enough to inflame a tricky labor-management situation on a factory floor in Wolverhampton. Wiser company directors know enough to keep private school graduates far away from such potentially explosive environments.

Eton, Winchester, Westminster (which are academically, perhaps, the finest high schools in the world) and some other British institutions have centuries of tradition upon which to draw. But even less famous boarding schools, including those which are weak on academic pursuits and accept youngsters of limited intelligence, also specialize in molding self-assured, self-respecting, unflappable young men, often starting when they are only eight years old. It is startling to encounter a well-spoken, courteous eighteen-year-old in complete control of both himself and the situation he finds himself in who nevertheless suggests, "I'm not really very clever"—and to realize that he's telling the truth!

Ironically, it's not often you can meet products of those extraordinary schools who, despite the fact that they might still don the school tie, recall their school days with anything more than distaste, often with loathing. One such graduate suggested that the social and professional rewards they accrue from having attended such illustrious establishments is payment for the torment they endured in those places: the bullying (still evident though somewhat toned down these days); the emphasis on rough-and-tumble sports even for the fragile and the disinclined; the often cold, uncomfortable dormitories; and the exclusion from the bosom of their families except for a few weeks each year of their school careers. World War Two hero Field Marshall Sir Bernard Montgomery said, "By the time I left school, a very important principle had begun to penetrate my brain . . . that life is a stern struggle and a boy has to be able to stand up to the buffetings and setbacks." In *The Blood of a Britishman*, Anthony Glyn wrote, "A boy's first week at his preparatory school is likely to be the most traumatic experience of his life, one for which he is, at the age of eight, totally unprepared. Until that moment, he has not realized that there are so many people in the world who wish to hit and hurt him." Historian Robert Kee said that going to a private school "was quite a good training" for when he became a German prisoner of war.

The private schools of Britain have traditionally been hothouses of character development. It is where boys learned to command by learning to obey. And though in keeping with contemporary trends they have loosened up a bit, they remain far more rigid and disciplined than other schools. Boys at those schools who make a practice of stepping out of line are soon sent packing.

They are comparatively expensive establishments, capable of setting fees amounting to one-quarter the take-home pay of middle-class fathers, some of whom start saving up for them as soon as their wives give birth. Families with two or more children enrolled often have to struggle to make ends meet.

The excellent, academically selective grammar schools of Britain have, on the other hand, been free of tuition charges. They have catered largely to the offspring of less well-to-do middle-class families. But they have also provided a channel for brighter working-class youngsters to escape narrow class confines which restricted their educational opportunities and ultimate job prospects.

Many of the grammar schools have, however, now been closed or forced to go private as a result of a move by the last Labor government. It sought to eliminate class distinctions in education by ending subsidies to schools which served only the academic (mostly middle class) elite. The strategy was to channel all government high school funds into "comprehensive" schools. These would become melting pots for pupils of various educational abilities and class origins and then send them forth into a brave new world reasonably equal in educational background. The achievement of social equality would not be too far behind.

It was a high-minded undertaking. It could, however, only work if sufficient funds and imagination were available to make the "comprehensives" capable of meeting the needs of the bright as well as the average and less bright students, and if the teachers were adequately trained to cope effectively with the new educational atmosphere. Some excellent comprehensive schools were built with superb laboratories and gymnasiums and all sorts of modern educational aids.

Many middle-class parents worried that the new system would expose their offspring to undesirable influences and might lead to a collapse of their class advantages. But many who did not share those concerns still saw the comprehensives as a risky experiment and were disinclined to permit their children to be the guinea pigs. They feared that those schools would be directed primarily at downplaying and discouraging academic achievement because, in big, unwieldy classes, such achievement would be considered divisive. They feared the aim would turn out to be a common educational denominator for all and that the system would end up churning out only mediocrities. Less-than-promising early experiences of many of the comprehensives fueled their anxieties.

As a result, the experiment never really got off the ground. Those parents who could afford to, and some who couldn't, turned instead to the long-standing private schools or to grammar schools which had just gone private to avoid being comprehensivized. Despite their substantial fees, most of them quickly acquired waiting lists as increasing numbers of middle-class parents sought the long-term advantages for their children which education at such schools could offer. Though scholarship places have now been provided at many of the private schools, the failure of the comprehensives to do what was expected of them has produced a situation in which fewer bright, poorer children have access to high-caliber, disciplined, academically oriented education. Instead of narrowing the insidious gap between the tribes, the assault on the grammar schools widened it.

A problem Britain faces is the reluctance of better-educated youngsters to go into the productive industry so important to Britain's future. Such jobs are not highly regarded by those youngsters. In a bid to escape the stigma of what they see as middle-class sordidness, they have increasingly opted for more reputable careers, going into television, becoming lawyers, journalists, teachers, merchant bankers, musicians, civil servants. More than a century ago, Lord Macaulay complained about a similar problem: "The curse of England is the obstinate determination of the middle classes to make their sons what they call gentlemen. So we are overrun by clergymen without livings, lawyers without briefs, physicians without patients, authors without readers. . . ."

A worrying consequence for present-day Britain has been a shortfall of talent in business middle management. In one of the country's largest companies, with multinational aspirations, it was discovered that executives in other departments had only the vaguest idea of the valuable advice and assistance they could call upon from the firm's crackerjack but vastly underused research division. The enterprise and imagination of those executives was just not good enough to make use of what was available to them.

It is not altogether their fault. Restrictive and discouraging class divisions between those who occupy the most senior positions in companies and those in middle management have traditionally been insurmountable. For an enterprising underling to presume to tell his betters in senior management how to do their jobs was an invitation for a frosty suggestion that he take his talents, such as they were, to another firm where they might be better appreciated.

Some years ago, a bright young chemical engineer I knew fled to America in disgust after being unable to get a serious hearing from his company's top officials—the ones empowered to make the necessary decisions—on proposals for improving the company's efficiency and output. He was rewarded for his initiative by being made to feel like a nuisance.

Though that sort of top-level narrowness has begun to give way to a measure of flexibility, there's still a lot of it about. A recent study by a University of Sheffield occupational psychologist indicated that as the latest slump hit Britain and many executives started losing their jobs, it was the brightest and most enterprising among them who were the first to be shown the door.

A formidable array of codes distinguish the dominant British tribes from one another—the way people speak and dress, the houses they live in, the way they raise their children, the stores they buy in, how and what they eat, what schools they go to, and the sports they indulge in. Even the kinds of dogs they keep can be telltale clues. The upper class leans towards pure-bred hunting hounds, less ostentatious terriers and spaniels, and corgies like those belonging to the queen. The middle class tends to opt for handsome or cuddly creatures—dalmations, setters, collies, tiny Yorkshire terriers and other lap dogs, and such noble looking canines as afghans. Among the more popular working-class dogs are fierce things like dobermans and alsatians, swift beauties like greyhounds and whippets, poodles for some strange reason and, scorning the hokum of pure breeding, the working class takes kindly to mongrels.

Class distinctions are also evident in eating styles, though generally the British and truly good food remain obstinately irreconcilable. With the current chic emphasis on cuisine on television and in magazines, newspapers, and books, many British home cooks now produce an eminently satisfying meal—a clever veal dish, a tasty chicken pie, a decent stew, and of course that pride of the British kitchen, the Sunday lunchtime joint (usually roast beef if they're flush; shoulder of pork if they're not).

There has been something of an effort to revive and smarten up traditional dishes like steak-and-kidney pudding and jugged hare. Recipes for local specialties like Lancashire hotpot, Norfolk par-

tridge stew, Yorkshire goose pie, and even more daring concotions
have begun appearing in newspaper cooking columns. A major
campaign has been launched to popularize such neglected English
cheeses as Wensleydale and Double Gloucester. Generally,
however, the overall effect is not convincing.

The food is often interesting and sometimes generous doses of
tender loving care go into its preparation. But it is rarely really
delicious or memorable. If you have a truly memorable meal in
Britain, as sublime as the ones you can expect to encounter in
central Italy or in just about any district of France, it is likely to be
at the home of a cook attuned to continental culinary nuances or in
one of the mere handful of truly first-rate restaurants in the
country, like the Box Tree in Yorkshire, the Miller Howe in the
Lake District, and the Tante Claire in London. Inspectors for the
French *Michelin* food guide have only just unearthed a British
restaurant, Le Gavroche in London, which they consider worthy of
their supreme three-star rating. Its cuisine is, of course, French.
This indication of haughty culinary discrimination may result from
the long-standing French conviction that the British couldn't so
much as scramble an egg properly even if the greatest chef in the
world stood by directing their every move. But it is true that British
restaurant guides have to make enormous allowances as they go
about drawing up their listings and making their recommend-
ations. If they didn't, those guides would be among the slimmest
volumes in the world.

It is possible to tour the east of England whose coastal waters
teem with fish and be able to order no other seafood but canned
tuna in most restaurants. In Kent, the fertile garden province of the
country, most vegetables available to local people are pre-
posterously shipped in by way of the Nine Elms central market in
London where nothing is grown. Scottish beef can be magnificent—
"incomparable" according to some gourmets—but it is hard for a
visitor to find a truly superb steak in Scotland outside a handful of
the best (and most expensive) restaurants in its major cities. As a
guest in the dining room of one of London's most exclusive
gentlemen's clubs, whose members include some of the most
distinguished personalities in the country, I was presented with a
portion of poached salmon (in theory a British delicacy) which
looked and tasted like a small chunk of pink rubber and which was

accompanied by hollandaise sauce which resembled a two-day-old omelet. The much-traveled club member who was my host apologetically explained that the quality of the cuisine was not one of the club's strong points.

It hasn't always been like that. Forebears of modern Britons—Saxons, Vikings, Normans—all were trenchermen of distinction. The Saxons were said to be "accustomed to eat until they were surfeited and to drink until they were sick." In times past, corpulence was considered a virtue, generally because slenderness could be deemed a sign of straitened circumstances. In Georgian times, gentlemen who were unfortunate enough to be thin wore cushion-like supports underneath their shirts to give the impression of the bulk normally associated with extravagant gastronomical indulgence. Gold watch chains were draped across the bulging bellies of successful men to highlight those proud protuberances.

Extraordinary menus can be found in the records of bygone times. It is true that they do not always testify to fine palates. ("The English," a Frenchman once mocked, "have 60 religions and only one sauce!") But they told of dining tables groaning under the weight of tempting edibles:

> We had [wrote diarist Samuel Pepys] a fricassee of rabbits, and chickens, a leg of mutton boiled, three carps in a dish, a great dish of side of lamb, a dish of roasted pigeons, a dish of four lobsters, three tarts, a lamprey pie, a most rare pie, a dish of anchovies, good wine of several sorts, and all things mighty and noble, and to my great content.

A country gentlewoman recorded that her dinner table display

> . . . consisted of three boiled chickens at top, a very fine haunch of venison at bottom, ham on one side, a flour pudding on the other, and beans in the middle. After the cloth was removed, we had gooseberries, and a remarkably fine dish of apricots.

Those days are gone, perhaps for good. Now well-off Britons indulge at home in several courses at each meal but they tend to be modest sorts of dishes: consommés, poached fish, roasts; high quality ingredients with few pretensions and fewer aspirations in preparation. Nothing showy. Nothing garish. Nothing exciting or unseemly. Their only culinary peculiarities result from the influence of working-class nannies on upper-class children so that they retain throughout their lives a pathological fondness for such pedestrian delicacies as bread pudding, jam roly-poly and toad-in-the-hole (sausage in pastry).

Working-class British cafes (deliberately mispronounced *caffs*) do a land-office lunchtime business in beans-on-toast, spaghetti-and-chips (chips being French fried potatoes), eggs-and-chips, greasy sausages-and-chips, canned pasta, packaged rice stews, and various other concoctions which would make working men in other countries howl in outrage but which millions of Britons like—or tolerate—well enough to fancy for the evening meal as well. Heavy bottled sauces are kept handy to obliterate whatever distinctive tastes might survive.

McDonalds and other outfits churning out mass-produced fast food have found a lucrative market in Britain. They provide stiff competition for fish-and-chips. Fish prices have soared in recent years and the prevalence of stale frozen fish and cheap frying oils make that old British standby less appetizing than it once was, for those who care about such things. The precious few who do care converge whenever possible on the handful of places which still serve only high-quality fresh fish fried in decent-quality oil.

In parts of England, fish-and-chip establishments do a roaring trade in "chip butties"—homespun sandwiches of French fried potatoes with maybe a dash of vinegar sprinkled over them to provide a touch of pizazz. It's almost as if the countless Britons who crave such stuff were gluttonous adolescents or pregnant women with lunatic food cravings.

Many Britons who reject such exotic fare prefer to settle instead at lunchtime for white bread sandwiches of dry cheese, cheese and chutney, or deflavored packaged ham. According to a British expert on nutrition, "Most foods don't really taste of anything." He meant that it's the methods of preparation of raw ingredients which lend foods most of their distinctive flavors. But his comment might just as easily have been an explanation for the prevailing lack of food discrimination in his country.

There probably is an explanation. The devastating impact of two world wars, a series of numbing depressions and recessions this century, plus recurring bouts of government-imposed austerity have contributed to turning Britain into the culinary desert it now resembles. No doubt long-term Puritanical traditions, which deemed enjoyment of food to be frivolous at least and wicked at worst, played a part as well. When Lord Snowden, Queen Elizabeth's former brother-in-law, making no bones about it, said simply, "I don't care much for food," he was speaking for a goodly number of his compatriots. They eat, but with neither enthusiasm nor care. Before he was married, the next king of England, Prince Charles, who could have dined on anything he fancied, liked to settle for an egg-on-toast for dinner in front of the television set if he wasn't obliged to attend an official function.

With sports, as with food and dogs and all things British, individual eccentricities allow for the occasional uncharacteristic preferences—like golf, normally a middle-class diversion, but classless in Scotland. But soccer, with its letting-off-steam enthusiasms and its unabashed team allegiances, is the primary spectator sport of working-class fans. For major professional matches, thousands of them stand jammed together on the seatless stadium "terraces" for hours, cheering on their teams. A core of middle-class devotees looks on in more relaxed fashion from seats in the grandstand but generally the sport is too plebeian for the tastes of others in Britain. For many of those others, the habit players on the soccer field have of ecstatically embracing goal scorers is far too unrestrained.

Middle-class sports enthusiasts tend to opt instead for the rough-and-tumble of rugby, a game ("for gentlemen played by ruffians") much promoted in private and grammar schools because getting roughed up on the field of play is supposed to build backbone. Other bones might be broken in the process. When it happens, the player may grit his teeth in pain. But crying out in agony or just plain crying is frowned upon.

Except in Yorkshire, where appreciation of the game transcends class tastes, the middle classes also furnish most of the devotees of cricket. The British are often unnerved by how excited West Indian and Australian cricket fans get at international matches. According to the British cricket ritual—magnificently enacted on delightful village greens on sleepy Sunday afternoons—polite applause, moderate cheers, and not overly loud declarations of "Well played!" are the proper accolade for superior performance on the pitch. An occasional, not excessively exuberant roar of approval from the crowd when something truly spectacular happens is permissible. But sustained vehement acclaim is unseemly.

After cataloging the superior skills of players about to compete in a cricket match, and being told that it sounded therefore as though it was going to be an exciting contest, an Englishman is reported to have murmured in horror, "Good grief, I hope not!" When a team captain and an umpire were jostled by vexed fans at London's Lord's Cricket Ground because a match was delayed, the London *Times* asked only half-jokingly, "Has civilization as we know it ended?"

Wimbledon international tennis competition, televised for hours on end every summer, brings members of the middle classes of virtually all ages, sizes, and descriptions out onto courts in gleaming whites. But the upper class generally confines itself to the traditional survival sports of hunting and shooting. These pastimes are also related to the soldierly function from which the aristocracy and country gentry originally sprang. No longer, however, are those activities the monstrous diversions they once were, marked by the mass slaughter of animals, with armies of beaters driving the prey toward waiting patrician hunters while gun loaders stood ready to replace and reload their spent weapons.

The Marquess of Ripon claimed to have accounted for a half million head of game by the time his shooting days ended some sixty years ago. Now the cost of beaters and loaders, the decimation of wild herds, and the inroads of anti-blood sports protesters make such a deed impossible. But the "glorious 12th" (August 12th) when the grouse shooting season begins remains a major event on high society calendars. A shoot, with the Prince of Wales dropping by to bag a few brace on the country holding of this or that noble lord, or joining his mother for shooting on a royal estate, is an enduring throwback to days when monarchs had huge private game reserves at their exclusive disposal, like London's Richmond Park which is still roamed by royally owned, but now legally protected, wild deer.

The Hunt—fox hunting—is even more strongly derived from the martial inclinations of early aristocrats. Pursuing on horseback a fleeing creature across open fields was the way knights often rushed into battle. The thrill of pursuit remains a driving compulsion among those dedicated to the hunt. Lady Augusta Fane defined the lure:

Not for the lust of killing,
Not for the places of pride,
Not for the hate of the hunted,
We English saddle and ride,
But because in the gift of our fathers
The blood in our veins that flows,
Must answer for ever and ever
The challenge of "Yonder He Goes."

The British who "saddle and ride" these days are no longer drawn exclusively from the aristocracy and the gentry. Among the most ostentatious claims to enhanced social status to be made by merchants and businessmen when they can afford it are the hunt and the shoot. Their undisguisable presence among traditional, effortless practitioners of those sports has had a demoralizing effect on some of the more haughty patricians. They fear that the commoners trespassing on noble pastures are another signal that the old order in which people knew their proper station is swiftly, irredeemably slipping away. However, their less fussy blood-brothers are perfectly willing to welcome initiates of humbler rank, renting out places in the shoot for respectable monetary considerations and charging by the pound for the birds those guests bring down and would like to carry away.

Remnants of different vocabularies continue to be indicators of British class identity. The middle classes, for example, say "wealthy" to mean affluent. Having fewer hang-ups about money, the upper and working classes say "rich." While others in Britain tend to say "Pardon?" when they haven't heard what someone has said, the upper class, making no bones about it, spurts out "What?" The upper class also says "false" teeth while others euphemistically refer to "dentures" (of which there are a lot about in Britain because of neglect of proper nutrition.)

Working class people use the toilet, the upper classes prefer the lavatory (pronounced *la-va-try*), while the middle classes commonly call it "the loo" (believed to derive from *l'eau*—French for water, referring to "water closet.").

The working class still often refers to the midday meal as "dinner" and the evening meal as "tea." Working-class people frequently address strangers as "dear," "love," or, jokingly as "squire." The middle class, and often the working class as well, refer to strangers as "that gentleman" or "that lady" while the upper class—much more choosey—says "that man" or "that woman." The upper class has an appalling inability in overcoming an antique gentility in speech; they avoid growing excessively intimate by not using the words "I" or "you" if they can help it. Instead they say "one," even when the result sounds fatuous. A politician, asked if he had been telephoned by the prime minister, retorted, "The prime minister doesn't telephone *one*. *One* telephones the prime minister." When Queen Elizabeth gave Princess Anne a Gloucestershire house as a wedding present, a London newspaper, mocking the princess's speech affectations, headlined the story ONE'S COUNTRY PLACE.

Transatlantic linguistic differences can cause misunderstandings in terminology. Tasteless, improper behavior or speech is commonly reviled as "common" by middle- and working-class people. The American glorification of "the common man" can be a little baffling to the British.

Not only words serve to identify a person's tribe in Britain. There are distinctive working-, middle- and upper-class accents, usually tinged with regional features as well, except that the upper class tends to have the same speech inflections and mannerisms throughout the country.

A series of controlled tests carried out by a University of Bristol psychologist indicates that British people in general are prepared to make far-reaching value judgments about others based exclusively on their accents. In one of these tests, high school seniors were asked to comment on the opinions of people presenting identical arguments with identical choices of words but with different accents. The students deemed those with "proper" accents to be more persuasive than those with Cockney or other regional accents normally associated with the working class. The tests indicated that those with "correct" accents were generally considered by the students to be more intelligent, competent, self-confident, ambitious, and industrious. The report based on the test results claimed "there is concrete evidence that in Britain today the 'wrong' accent is an impediment to progress in—or entry to—certain professions." It said that without seeing them, the students even appeared to believe that men with "correct" accents were handsomer and taller.

Television is the most effective leveler in history, in speech as in other things. People tend increasingly to employ the same vernaculars across class and regional lines. Often more revealing is the manner of speaking and the things people talk about. Viscount Weymouth, for example, could casually and with dignity reveal in a newspaper article, on how he spends a typical day, that he and his wife live apart most of the year, a matter which would be cheap newspaper gossip if a celebrity of lesser social standing were involved. Lord de L'Isle, custodian of his magnificent ancestral estate, Penshurst Place in southern England, once candidly explained that the charge of admission to his home, paid by day-trip visitors, was influenced by "as much as we can extract from them without actually being dishonest." It was said with all the disarming, ingenuous confidence for which the British aristocracy has established a firm reputation. Charming, droll, it was nevertheless the kind of remark which could easily have sounded money-grubbing.

There aren't all that many hereditary aristocrats in Britain—only about 900 in all. Unlike the practice in some continental countries where princes and counts abound (the postage stamp principality of Liechtenstein, only sixty-five square miles big, boasts dozens of princes and princesses), the British peerage has been limited by primogeniture. Only the eldest son of an aristocrat inherits both his title and his property. Other offspring either live off lesser legacies or fend for themselves. The effect has been to keep the estates of aristocrats intact from generation to generation. In parts of Europe, where estates have been split up and parceled out each generation to the various heirs, many present-day nobles have ended up owning little more than their illustrious titles.

There are five orders of peerage in Britain. Dukes are the most senior, then marquesses, earls, viscounts, and barons. Once upon a time, the higher the rank the greater the family fortune. But times have changed since the days when a marquess apologetically declined elevation to a dukedom by the king because he couldn't afford the promotion. Now a baron might outshine a duke when it comes to calculating personal wealth, though you would have to go far to find a duke living anywhere near the shadow of poverty.

Some peers have proved better than others at conserving their inheritances or generating new wealth. British peers used to look down on people in "trade" unless they were involved in commerce themselves. But unlike their European counterparts, they never insisted that only "old money" was good money. Only one peer out of five can trace his peerage back past 1800 and only one aristocratic title out of every two dates back to before the twentieth century.

The peerage has always needed transfusions of outside resources to foot the bills for the maintenance of aristocratic pomp and luxury. From time to time, there was talk that "the order of nobility" serves to prevent the rule of vulgar wealth and the establishment of a religion of money in Britain. But one of the secrets of the survival of the British aristocracy has been the willingness of its men (and sometimes their desperate longing) to marry the daughters of rich commoners. No excessive patrician pride was trotted out when chances materialized for acquiring the wherewithal to guard the family name from financial embarrassment and possibly pay off gambling debts in the process. A clutch of young American heiresses descended on London around the turn of the century intent on becoming duchesses, countesses, or even just Ladies. Many were not disappointed. In her book *The Dollar Princesses*, Ruth Brandon quotes an advertisement placed by "An English peer of very old title . . . desirous of marrying at once a very wealthy lady. Her age and looks are immaterial." What was required of her was £25,000 paid in cash to her future husband. Most peers were much more discriminating but they were not uninterested in the dowry their commoner brides might bring with them.

Several British aristocrats have enormous fortunes. In addition to extensive holdings in the English hinterland, the Duke of Westminster owns some 300 choice acres of central London. His family name is Grosvenor, as in Grosvenor Square where the American Embassy, which pays ground rent to the duke, is located. The Duke of Buccleuch owns more than 200,000 acres of Scotland.

But property is only one dimension of aristocratic affluence. The walls of the rooms of the Earl of Pembroke's Wilton House, outside the pleasant cathedral town of Salisbury, are lined with Rembrandts and other masterpieces, including a room full of Van Dykes. The state rooms of the Duke of Marlborough's Blenheim Palace sparkle with priceless paintings and furniture. Though some may have been put on the block by now, Nancy Mitford, herself of aristocratic origin, some years ago quoted a jeweler as saying that of the 100 finest diamonds in the world, sixty are owned by English families.

Nevertheless, many aristocrats have felt the chill winds of austerity—or at least what they consider austerity—wafting through the corridors of their stately homes. A butler interviewed for a job at a ducal palace which once might have boasted a staff of forty complained that he would have been expected to make do with but a half dozen servants if he had taken the job, and *foreign* servants at that. There were once about 30,000 butlers in Britain. Now there are fewer than a hundred.

Gone are the days when the numerous members of the domestic staff of one country home were required to stop, turn, and face the wall when they encountered a member of the family on the stairs or in the hallway so as not to give offense by always getting underfoot. A stately ancestral residence might have come equipped with a staff of fifty or more. Cutting back on servants was not easy. After being advised to reduce expenses and told that one way to do so would be to have fewer than six courses at dinner each night, one aristocrat protested that, after all, he took only a mouthful of each. Another complained that with things developing as they were, he was really worse off than the poor who weren't obliged to find the money to pay any servants at all. A third aristocrat, when advised that having a pastry chef on his kitchen staff was perhaps an unnecessary luxury, moaned, "Can't a fellow have a biscuit when he wants one?"

The fact is that inflation, death duties, and other taxes have made it increasingly uncomfortable for the noble lords of Britain to maintain their magnificent country estates and their patrician lifestyles. Not averse to crass mercantile adventures, many of them have converted their stately homes into business operations, opening them to paying visitors and tacking on wildlife parks, children's zoos, toy museums, old car museums, all sorts of sideshows, cafes, and souvenir boutiques to lure in the love-a-lord public and extract ready cash.

It might be considered quite a comedown for aristocrats to transform their exquisite country holdings into circuses to turn some fast money. But they have done all this with elegance and panache and sometimes with considerable commercial savvy involving large investments and long-term planning. Most of all, they have done it with absolute confidence, remaining about as concerned about the judgment of others as their forebears were about the opinions of serfs and servants. It is the same sort of obliviousness which permits upper-class Englishmen and English-women to sound off at the top of their voices in public places about personal matters as if no one who might overhear could possibly be of any significance—the servants who waited at table at home never were and nobody ever lowered a voice simply because the soup was being served.

Oscar Wilde's wry contention that "a gentleman never offends unintentionally" was mistaken. So reflexive are the ways and habits of British patricians that they do not know when their manners rub others the wrong way, though probably most would not be overly distressed if they did. Much of the very real built-in antagonism felt by the working class for people who speak with pukka accents derives from the inveterate indifference of those people to the feelings and attitudes of those they deemed their social inferiors.

Only in middle-class homes did servants have to knock before entering bedchambers or sitting rooms of their employers. Such advance notice was not required by the lord or lady who couldn't care less what the servants might think if, barging in unannounced, they stumbled upon behavior which others might consider im-proper or private. No worry was wasted on what the butler saw. A female foreign commoner who married into a British noble family disclosed that it took her a long time to recover from the recurring shock of servants just entering without knocking.

Arrogance in public was once the hallmark of a certain type of British patrician. There was a notoriously crabby aristocrat who used to sit with his cane at the entrance of his exclusive London club and strike any member he disliked who presumed to enter. Another peer of the realm, famous for his bumptiousness, used to call in regularly at another such London club only to use the toilet there. Finally approached one day by a porter who had worked up the courage to ask, "Is your lordship a member?", he replied in astonishment, "Good God, man, do you mean this is a club as well?" Caught out like that, a member of the middle classes would have lied about an appointment in the club lounge for which he was already a half hour late,and he would have had a name ready if asked with whom that fictitious appointment was to have been.

Though obstinate relics of high-and-mighty patrician behavior are sprinkled around the British countryside, guarding the flanks of the upper classes against excessive intrusion by newly moneyed *hoi polloi*, most aristocrats take very well to swimming unabashedly with the tide of change. Not for nothing does the British aristocracy sustain a reputation for dignified endurance when surviving aristocrats elsewhere are usually thought of as jokes or gigolos. The British patrician class has for the most part never been fully wedged in and confined by the kind of social rigidity which inhibits Britain's other tribes. It has always been prepared to give some ground, permitting a selected corps of others to cross the class divide, adopt its values and habits and share its social supremacy. In keeping with current democratic fashions, the number of admissibles is much larger now than ever before.

The country gentry has always been on the fringe of the aristocracy. Some country families have been planted where they are and riding to hounds there for centuries. But the wider patrician class is something else. It draws its non-aristocratic recruits from among that same crowd of newly affluent individuals who are still shunned as johnnies-come-latley by the smallish clique of more demanding, fossilized senior bluebloods who have lost touch with reality.

However, not everyone with financial credentials is eligible for acceptance into highest society. Candidates for the rank of gentleman or the female equivalent must have that certain style, a patrician way of doing and saying things, sharply defined patterns of speech and behavior, to distinguish them from the herd. A suitably molded Eton graduate who is heir to a department store fortune might be acceptable for a weekend stay at a stately home or to participate in a non-paying shoot with a covey of nobles. His father probably would not.

Fairytales to the contrary, the distance between Henry Higgins (with his aristocratic bearing) and Liza Doolittle (the daughter of a garbage collector) remains unbridgeable except perhaps for a night out on the town or a dirty weekend in Torquay, provided she keeps her mouth shut in public and doesn't cling embarrassingly to his arm in the nightclub or hotel lobby. The chasm between Higgins and the local supermarket manager or town hall functionary would be even more gaping. Of the fifty-five million Britons, only a few thousand at most have been permitted to cross over, first to attend and then to join the patricians.

Is newfound aristocratic flexibility all a hoax then? Is it, as some might be led to believe, really only a subtle conspiracy, with the cries of poverty emanating from a number of aristocratic throats part of the same fraud? Are aristocrats lying low until circumstances permit them to shoo away the unworthies they now pretend to accept and remount their inviolate pedestals? While rejecting this conspiracy theory as fantasy, Evelyn Waugh neatly diagrammed it: "[The aristocrat] is biding his time until the present craze for equality has passed, when he will reemerge in all his finery to claim all his privileges, to ravish brides." And to ship poachers off to prison colonies in Australia.

It isn't going to happen. There is no conspiracy, though a handful of bluebloods are capable of contemplating such a delicious coup while dozing off in front of blazing fires in the splendid sitting rooms of their stately mansions. There is nothing new to the image of privileged peers dreaming of the good old days before lesser mortals grew uppity. A country gentleman wrote as far back as 1375, ". . . age of ours, whither turnst thou? For the poor and small folk, who should cleave to their labour, demand to be better fed than their masters. Moreover they bedeck themselves in fine colours and fine attire, whereas were it not for their pride and their privy conspiracies they would be clad in sackcloth as of old."

Nevertheless, patrician privileges lingered on and their vestiges probably will continue to do so well into the next century. The British aristocracy is, however, drifting inexorably toward extinction. Not by choice. Not out of generous recognition of the folderol of class pretensions. The British aristocracy is going suavely, unflappably to the wall because their lordships really don't have anything special to do anymore. They are redundant, obsolete, ineffectual.

There was once an empire they could administer. Lord Mountbatten, Queen Elizabeth's "Uncle Dickie" (assassinated by the Irish Republican Army in 1980), did a superb job as viceroy of India. But India no longer needs, nor would it tolerate, viceroys. The last British governor-general of Australia flew home in 1965. Now

Australia picks from among its own ranks a dignitary to fill this largely ceremonial job. British aristocrats on ritual diplomatic missions to former colonies in Africa usually seem totally irrelevant, as if dispatched only to provide picturesque light relief footage at the tag end of gloomy television news roundups at home. Lord Harlech was such a successful ambassador to Washington in the early 1960s not because of his distinguished ancestry but because he personally slotted neatly into the Kennedy clan's White House Camelot.

The British military, where aristocrats once thrived, is now the province of specialists in strategic planning, modern weaponry, and geopolitics. Trimmed to the core, it has few openings at the top for those who offer none of those skills, and not many aristocrats do. Politics is also closed to them. They are required to renounce their titles if they want to sit in the predominant House of Commons from which the prime minister and the cabinet govern the country. With taxes making stern demands, particularly on unearned income, even the option of just sitting back and vegetating at the family seat in the shires is being undermined.

The new breed of English aristocrat—the men who have made the emergence of the new, wider patrician class possible—have looked elsewhere for their careers. Viscount Newport runs restaurants selling delicacies to the well-to-do in London's Knightbridge and meat pies to tourists in the British capital's Covent Garden district. The Earl of Pembroke is a television director, strong on detective serials. Lord Bethell is a member of the European parliament and a writer specializing in Russian affairs. The Earl of Lichfield is a professional photographer. The Marquess of Hertford runs a public relations firm. A female aristocrat operates a successful catering service. Other nobles are active in book publishing, film production, broadcasting, and other, mostly glamorous professions and pursuits.

There is, as a matter of fact, only one exclusively lordly job— being a member of the House of Lords. All hereditary peers over the age of twenty-one who have not been disqualified as insane, bankrupt, or in prison for criminal convictions may attend the House. In addition to fulfilling a public duty when they do so, it makes them eligible for certain privileges. They cannot be sued for any statements they make in the House. They may claim expense reimbursement if they attend sessions. Some lords have not been above checking in and out just to claim those expenses.

But even the House of Lords has lost most of its exclusive aura. To give the chamber added political significance and legitimacy, the queen, largely at the recommendation of the prime minister, each year appoints distinguished citizens to be "life peers"—their titles are not passed on to their offspring—to sit with the hereditary nobles. The appointments are for life. There are recurring demands from leftwing politicians that the House of Lords be abolished as undemocratic. But the Lords must agree for this to happen and it seems very unwilling to do so.

Suggestions have been made that a Labor Party prime minister should use his powers to require the queen to pack the chamber with specially selected life peers who would provide a majority prepared to vote the upper house out of existence. Such a development is, however, unlikely in the foreseeable future. The Lords do not have much political muscle but they do prove occasionally useful in slowing down passage of controversial legislation so that it can be more carefully considered and perhaps subsequently amended by the House of Commons. The upper house is also an admirable place in which to shift aging politicians out to pasture in an atmosphere where they can still make speeches and contribute to the political life of the country. There is respect and kindness in that practice, as well as occasional usefulness.

More than a century ago, Benjamin Disraeli, a mediocre novelist who was to become founder of the modern British Conservative Party, deplored the existence of "two nations" in Britain—the rich and the poor "between whom there is no intercourse or sympathy; who are as ignorant of each other's habits, thoughts and feelings as if they were dwellers in different zones, or inhabitants of different planets; who were formed by a different breeding, are fed by a different food, are ordered by different manners, and are not governed by the same laws."

But even then there were more than two divisions. Even then they included an array of nuances and shadings—lower upper class, middle middle, upper lower, etc. Though crusading egalitarians have come and gone since Disraeli's days, and though the major divisive barriers are sometimes vaulted by the exceptionally gifted or irrepressibly determined, those barriers remain essentially intact.

Up they stay despite a meaningful improvement in working men's living standards. Such an improvement has been recorded in all industrial nations but the British are unique in permitting what is normally a leveling development to sharpen class hostilities. The better off the British working man has grown, the more convinced he has become that the us-against-them confrontation is here to stay. He has also come to accept that the trade unions, whose membership has increased significantly in recent years, provide the battalions for his ongoing tussle with "them."

It's not political. Countless dedicated union members regularly defy the advice of their leaders and vote against the Labor Party. Conservative Prime Minister Thatcher could not have been elected without their support. However, loyalty to the union is a fundamental fact of working-class life in Britain and a strike with "Everybody out!" is the key ritual testifying to that solidarity.

This is true whether the walkout is called (understandably) after a breakdown in pay negotiations or a slowdown is imposed (absurdly) because a foreman is rude to an assembly line fitter. Otherwise sensible, upright union members faithfully observed a strike called by their shop steward because the management of a company refused to fire a security guard who had prevented some workers from pilfering tools. Glasgow Airport was closed by a strike after a baggage handler was denied permission to swap shifts to participate in a darts contest. A British Ford factory was closed by a walkout called over an argument about where workers were supposed to hang their coats. Reflexive identification with the union cause is the name of the game, even when it's union against union in a jurisdictional dispute.

Those firm allegiances have grown out of the success the unions have had in improving pay and working conditions. But there is a more subtle, historic source of working-class solidarity with the unions in Britain. Those unions restored a sense of worth and significance to the descendants of the hordes of rural folk who had been wrenched from a comparatively slow-paced existence by the industrial revolution generations ago.

They had been drawn from farming areas to factory cities and mining towns by the prospect of otherwise unavailable jobs. They had been held in contempt in the squalid ghettoes in which they had to live. And they had been savagely exploited by employers who could draw from an immense pool of dirt-cheap labor at their doorsteps. To stir up class solidarity and class hostility, some labor leaders at meetings today still invoke the "Tolpuddle Martyrs" who were banished as convicts to Australia 150 years ago for getting others to take union oaths. It is hardly the emotional climate for getting people to pull together.

Statistics contradict the conventional belief that the British are more strike-prone than others. Even during the worst of their strike epidemics, other countries, including the United States, out-matched Britain in workdays lost through official industrial action. But official strikes in Britain are only part of the story. Wildcat walkouts and unofficial go-slows are still as British as fish-and-chips. Nor do the statistics reveal much about the effect of extensive layoffs which take place in heavy industry when one union among many (a big car firm might have to deal with sixteen of them) brings a company's activities to a complete standstill.

Sluggish productivity has been plaguing most industrial nations as the world cautiously moves toward a post-industrial age. But few countries are burdened by the "export or die" requirement which rules Britain's economic existence. Able to produce only a little more than half the food its people eat, the country must sell enough manufactured goods in other countries to pay for the enormous quantity of edibles it must import.

Therefore, strikes which cramp productivity are undeniably against the national interest. But national interest and the argument that "the country cannot pay itself more than it earns" have been hammered at the unions so often that they simply are not taken seriously by union negotiators. Nor do they make much impact on individual union members for whom tribal solidarity and the obsession with protecting "us" against "them" is the first priority.

Mutual interest across class lines has been a fantasy invoked by politicians and newspapers and sabotaged by virtually everybody else. Only the impact of industrial impotence, leading to the stone-cold reality of massive unemployment, toned down the strike craze which was so much a part of British life in the 1970s.

An examination of such an intriguing people cannot be adequately undertaken without dwelling on the changes continually at play. Not long ago, a British judge could say that "a bit of wife-thumping on a Saturday night may not amount to cruelty in some [working-class] parts of England, but a bit of thumping in Cheltenham [a middle-class preserve] may be cruelty. The social background counts." No British judge could now accept that wife-beating anywhere in the country is tolerable.

Not long ago, the pattern of activities and interests of a member of the royal family was carefully charted along lines of social superiority. Now not even an eyebrow was raised when it was disclosed that Princess Margaret's son, the nephew of the queen, intended to be trained in woodworking. No one expected him to become a gainfully employed carpenter, toiling for a living and hauling a lunch pail to the job each morning. But it was accepted that a bit of royal family contact with "the people" and the things they do couldn't be bad.

Ideas have changed about what makes people what they are. Not long ago, deliberate frugality, diligence, and enterprise were believed to be what turned the middle classes into solid citizens. Now respectability and self-control are dissected and suggestions are made that, "The middle class child was weaned earlier. . . . This early training in control over basic drives contributed to the middle class personality's ability to defer gratification and to channel aggression into socially acceptable forms later in life."

Whatever the reasons, and taking account of changes and adaptations, distinctive ways and habits of the various British tribes have proved remarkably durable. In a country where privacy is much treasured and jealously guarded, and where propriety tends to keep individuals from unloading their problems and worries on the shoulders of others, such group identity has proved an important crutch. But it also has a squelching effect, discouraging the development of new attitudes and hampering British efforts to adjust to the requirements of the world as it is today.

The divisions which mark life in Britain are compounded by another, comparatively new but already explosive conundrum—racial disharmony. Britain's "colored" population consists of Blacks and "Asians" (who are people of Indian, Pakistani, or Bangladeshi origin). They are all immigrants or the descendants or offspring of immigrants from remote corners of the British Empire.

Each group has distinctive characteristics of its own though there are efforts to focus on common ground within the country's non-white community to further its interests and cope with its adjustment problems. Mostly through immigration (now sharply restricted), the non-white British population has increased sixfold in the last two decades. Of no significance in social terms not long ago, it now amounts to more than four percent of the population (a proportion that continues to grow) and it now demands great attention.

The country's leading cities have suddenly acquired restless ghettoes with substantial non-white communities fitted out with all the antagonisms, injustices, and disorders that accompany racial strain, particularly in times of economic hardship. Organizations in Britain like the National Front and the British Movement, which promote racial hatred, have been particularly active during outbursts of social unrest. They know that when unemployment levels soar, many people thrown out of work seek scapegoats, and that non-whites are easy targets for prejudice. Nevertheless, racist organizations in Britain can claim little success and less popularity.

However, many whites, particularly the elderly, for whom even the sight of a non-white was once a rare experience, are vexed and vulnerable to racial prejudice when confronted with unBritish behavior on home ground. Many have been alarmed and angered by the unprecedented chain reaction of street-riot eruptions which recently plagued parts of several British cities. Many white youths participated in those disturbances, and were primarily responsible for some of them. But they were originally initiated by (and copied from) aggrieved black youngsters and they occurred almost exclusively in areas in which there are large resident black communities, like Brixton in London, Toxteth in Liverpool, and Moss Side in Manchester.

Groups of young blacks, who believe themselves to be victims of police harassment and who are unquestionably the worst victims of the country's demoralizing unemployment problems, attacked the police with bricks, bottles, and Molotov cocktails and engaged in bouts of looting and destruction. The riots were confined to just a few streets in each incident. But they prompted many store owners in nearby unaffected districts to board up their display windows as a precaution, giving the impression that larger parts of British cities were under siege, an impression magnified by some sensationalized news reporting. MOB RULE GRIPS THE CITIES screamed one London newspaper headline. BRITAIN'S NIGHT OF ANARCHY, proclaimed another.

But though the riots were serious and their underlying causes required urgent examination, compared to earlier riots in Detroit, Los Angeles, and other American cities—in which at least 125 persons were killed—the British riots were, in fact, brief, isolated, and quickly brought under control. There was, remarkably, only one reported death, an innocent young man caught up in the trouble by accident and run down by a police vehicle which had charged in to disperse a group of Liverpool rioters.

Though blanket charges of police harassment of blacks are exaggerated, they are not completely without foundation. Countless black youths complain of being stopped and questioned in the street by police for no reason at all and often taken back to the police station for more intensive grilling. A boy was so intimidated that he confessed to stealing two toy cars even though his receipt for payment was in his pocket all the time. The black gardener of my local park in London was hauled in for rough questioning by a police officer who simply could not believe that the sportscar he was driving was his own. That sort of humiliating treatment inevitably nourishes a volatile sense of outrage, undiminished by police claims that the undeniably high crime rate in the ghettoes is responsible for their heavy policing of those areas.

Some people in Britain object to the failure of non-whites to adjust to general British patterns of behavior. They object to all-night parties in residential communities with music blaring deafeningly till dawn and to jostling on bus queues. Many white store owners are outmaneuvered and outraged by non-white competitors who, in keeping with practices in their countries of origin, offer customers better service by keeping open late at night and on Sundays, contrary to normal British procedures in which customer convenience has low priority.

Though Britain has provided a safe haven for immigrants in the past (Protestants escaping religious persecution in France, Jews and other fleeing the Nazis in Europe, Poles and others fleeing Communism), it has never received so many immigrants in so short a time, and never so many with different racial identities. Many non-whites, and especially the 40 percent who are native-born Britons and speak with Cockney and other regional British accents, have adopted British ways. But most do not yet consider themselves English (or Scottish or Welsh).

It will be a long time before the country adjusts to its latest batch of newcomers and the newcomers adjust to the country. There is likely to be a lot of anguish and frustration, and probably more trouble in the streets, before that happens. Tolerance remains a predominant British characteristic. But it will be sorely tested over the next few years.

THREE

A Woman's Place— a Man's World

THERE'S A QUEEN on the throne. There's a formidable female prime minister at 10 Downing Street. And there's a covey of female celebrities whose doings regularly feature in the columns of London's newspapers and magazines. From a distance it might appear as though sexual equality is thriving in the hardy British climate. But despite the emergence of a number of notable female public figures, Britain really remains essentially a man's country. The fuss over a best-selling authoress, glittering actress, or television news commentatress is deceptive. Women occupy very few positions of responsibility or authority in the British government, professions, business, or media. "Where would they go to the loo?" a senior businessman said when asked why none of his executives are women.

Preparing his son for the trials and tribulations of life, the eighteenth-century statesman the Earl of Chesterfield advised him, "A man of sense only trifles [with women], plays with them, humors and flatters them as he does a sprightly forward child, but he neither consults them about, nor trusts them with serious matters." The advice was taken as gospel not only by Chesterfield's male offspring but by most other Englishmen as well. It is advice most of them still take.

It is true that women have the same legal rights as men in Britain. They can acquire, own, and dispose of property. They can enter into contracts, sue, and be sued. They can give evidence in court and serve on juries. But despite a law which forbids sexual discrimination, an energetic Equal Opportunities Commission, organizations designed to promote and protect women's rights, and an endless stream of newspaper and magazine articles touting sexual equality, the women's liberation movement in Britain has been little more than a flop.

A respected columnist in one of the country's leading Sunday newspapers invoked the code of chivalry to insist "women will always need men's protection, which can best be gained, now as ever, not by challenging his power but by exploiting her weakness." A recent British textbook on banking noted, "Notwithstanding the enlargement of women's status . . . the presumption in law is that she is incapable of understanding business transaction by the exercise of her own wit." According to statute, a married British women's earnings are "deemed for income tax purposes" to be her husband's.

A tribunal deciding whether a young woman had been unfairly fired from a job awarded her compensation from the company which had sent her packing because of her tantrums and sulks. It ruled that "No amount of legislation can alter the fact that there are physiological and psychological differences between the sexes." In a recent court case, a judge commenting on the testimony of a witness, observed, "It is well known that by nature women are inclined to be rather personal. They attach themselves to persons." At the newly constructed main office of a north country English bank, the cleaners' broom closet was built inside the ladies' toilet, thus putting the women in their place.

When other British book publishers were struggling to survive economic recession, a London firm which churned out endless streams of gushing romantic novels, featuring "manly" men and "feminine" women, could count on a seemingly inexhaustible and highly lucrative female market which gobbled up everything that came off the presses. When Simone de Beauvoir wrote that women are "in the process of demolishing the myth of femininity," she must have been looking somewhere else.

Even in royal realms, a British woman is inferior to a man. When Prince Charles succeeds his mother and becomes king, his wife will become queen of England. But Queen Elizabeth's husband, Charles's father, who was born a prince of Greece, did not become king of England. Only the royal male can pass on the highest rank and title of all to the royal spouse.

Although British women outnumber British men by about

thirteen to twelve, only three percent of the members of Parliament are women. In many local political party branches, a woman's only role is serving tea at meetings, doing the secretarial chores, and arranging fund raising fêtes. Though about half the adult women in Britain work (most of them to help balance the family budget), a woman's status is still largely associated with that of members of her family—her husband's job and earning power, her son's education or career, her daughter's marriage prospects.

The tradition of male dominance and female fragility and ineptitude is so entrenched in the country that women's lib has made only slightly more headway among British women than it has among British men—which means practically no headway at all, although official action has had some effect. A court of appeals ruled that a Leicester furniture store could not decide that a woman must list her husband as a certified guarantor before it was prepared to extend credit to her unless it required husbands to list their wives the same way. Another court ruled that a woman has a right to a share of the matrimonial home even if it is registered exclusively in her husband's name. But feminists have no guarantee that the law will always act the way they would like it to. Though further legal challenges are to be made in the case, a court declined, for example, to compel El Vino's, a famous journalists' hang-out in London's Fleet Street, to terminate its long-established practice of serving only men at its bar. Women still have to be seated at one of the tables if they wish to be served.

All that is, however, small potatoes compared to the much more pertinent question of job opportunities for women—the only real route to sexual equality. British women have managed to make some headway in penetrating job areas previously reserved only for men. There's now a British woman pilot or two, a woman railway station manager, a soccer club secretary, an auctioneer, a high-ranking police officer, a disc jockey, television producers and camera operators, and women competently holding down a variety of other "male" jobs. But the pioneers remain so few in number that they are really only token indications of a chink in the armor of male supremacy.

Some companies claim trade union shop stewards have made it clear there would be trouble among the men if women were put in positions of authority over them. An equal pay law was largely sabotaged by reclassifying the jobs women held to keep them from getting the same pay as men for the same sort of work. Again, management blamed the male-dominated unions for insisting that this be done. There are virtually no senior female union officials in Britain, not even in unions whose members are mostly women.

A survey by one of the country's leading employment agencies says one in five men in Britain would turn down a job rather than work under a woman. The men questioned contended that women are too emotional, inefficient, and anti-male to be put in positions in which they could order men about. Half of them said men should automatically be given promotion preference over women, regardless of qualifications.

It's not only the men who cling to such attitudes. Some company managers claim they would like to promote women to more responsible jobs but that likely candidates for such promotion just aren't interested. An investigation by a British women's magazine concluded that most women in the country do not want to enter what they regard as male-oriented careers. It found that "marriage, children, and the family ethos are still preferred by most women over jostling for promotion on a perhaps endless ladder to success."

Women's liberation in Britain has been consistently undermined by conditions built into the country's economic life. Whatever injustices are thereby perpetrated, Britain on the whole might be considered fortunate that the feminine breakthrough has not yet occurred and that it shows little sign of materializing in the immediate future. Aside from a few brief intervals, unemployment has for many decades been a persistent or potential threat to much of the country's male population. But if it is to mean anything, women's liberation must include a vastly increased number of skilled and responsible jobs for women. Those job opportunities could only be won at the expense of male breadwinners because Britain already has far more civil servants, teachers, administrators, and specialists in most professions than it needs. It is actively engaged in trying to train unemployed persons, mostly men, in skills that might find them jobs and take them off the social security handout rolls. Eliminating existing prejudices against women taking responsible jobs in a society which has more women than men could disastrously complicate the country's already chronic unemployment problem.

That may be why many outspoken British feminists are ide-
ologically committed to a form of radical socialism which promises
full employment regardless of prevailing economic conditions or
job requirements. It is also why many of them consider marriage
and the family—both of which would be transformed by genuine
women's liberation—oppressive and insidious institutions designed
to keep women in their place.

The British feminist movement has been handicapped in recent
years by neglect of its formidable roots. Perhaps out of desperation
at making so little headway, it has reached across the Atlantic for
much of its stimulus, to the much more high-powered and effective
American feminist movement. That movement drew much of its
initial modern momentum, strategy, and many of its cadre from the
American civil rights campaigns of the 1960s, campaigns which
were only vicariously part of the British experience. It still sounds
contrived when Britons, protesting this or that, chant the American
civil rights movement anthem, "We Shall Overcome."

There's really no need for British feminists to look elsewhere for
moral support. As long ago as 1675, in *The Gentlewoman's
Companion*, Englishwoman Hannah Woolley condemned "the
great negligence of parents in letting the fertile ground of their
daughters lie fallow, yet send the barren noddles of their sons to the
University, where they stay for no other purpose than to fill their
empty sconces with idle notions to make a noise in the country."
It's been almost 200 years since Mary Wolstonecraft (mother of
Mary Shelley who wrote *Frankenstein*) published her *Vindication
of the Rights of Women* in which she urged, "Consider . . .
whether, when men contend for their freedom . . . it is not incon-
sistent and unjust to subjugate women."

The great nineteenth century philosopher of liberty John Stuart
Mill meant his treatise *On the Subjection of Women* to be a device
for shaming men into recognizing the iniquity of keeping women
locked in subservience. At the beginning of the twentieth century,
a campaign to gain the vote for women moved into high gear in
Britain. Suffragettes engaged in various militant activities, including street marches, heckling public speakers, getting themselves
thrown in jail, chaining themselves to the gates of Parliament and
going on hunger strikes to make their point. One suffragette threw
herself in front of the King's racehorse at the 1913 Derby and was
trampled to death for the cause.

But it was the advent of the First World War which provided the conditions for easing discrimination against women. When men were called to arms, women were needed in the factories to maintain war production and in various other civilian jobs vacated by the men called to duty in the bloody trenches of Europe. That a woman could make a perfectly competent bus conductor or handle gun powder in a war munitions plant made nonsense of earlier attitudes which confined females to the kitchen or the nursery or to maid's work.

Nevertheless, it was clearly understood that the women were only keeping the home fires burning till the boys came home. They were granted the right to vote after the war and after a woman (American-born Nancy Astor) entered Parliament in 1919. But not until the Second World War were they again called upon in any great numbers to take on jobs and assume roles which allowed them a measure of responsibility and initiative. However, war's end again meant a step back for feminism, though sturdier seeds had now been planted and soon some began to sprout, or at least tried to.

In her book, *A Woman's Place*, Ruth Adam describes the impact of changing social attitudes to women in Britain: "A woman born at the turn of the century could have lived through two periods when it was her moral duty to devote herself, obsessively, to her children; three when it was her duty to society to neglect them; two when it was right to be seductively 'feminine,' and three when it was a pressing social obligation to be the reverse; three separate periods in which she was a bad wife, mother, and citizen for wanting to go out and earn her own living, and three others when she was an even worse wife, mother, and citizen for not being eager to do so."

Such confusion is understandable in a movement which has had many eloquent and determined advocates but which, nevertheless, has repeatedly failed to get off the ground. A stereotype persists in Britain of the working-class woman as a feeble drudge, capable only of unskilled work if employed at all. The popular image of the professional woman is of a curiosity, maybe talented but, if so, unique among women and probably subject to unpredictable emotional outbursts and unbalanced judgments.

British observers endlessly deride what they see as the inordinate importance of females in American life—"Momism," wifely dominance over the husband, glorification of the female generally.

Whatever the real situation in America, such female influence simply does not exist on the British scene where neither Mom nor the wife occupies a central position. Recent research among leading British businessmen indicated that they dismissed their wives as "useful but not essential" in getting where they were. They placed them only thirteenth among the reasons for their success (first was their own ability to work with a variety of people).

The incidence of divorce—the fate of one out of five marriages in Britain—adds a special dimension to the problem of sexual inequality. Less able to find suitable jobs, and sometimes jobs of any kind, many single women in Britain are thrown onto the mercies of the welfare state for their survival and the survival of their children. Bulletin boards in civic centers and the offices of National Health Service doctors regularly carry notices of meetings of clubs for unattached women where they might find mutual assistance in this man's world.

Its failures have turned some elements of the British feminist movement frantic, more radical and, in some cases, more deliberately outrageous. The old image of the upright, distinguished feminist has just about faded away. One British feminist wrote in some wonderment how, as a girl, feminism meant to her "shadowy figures in long old-fashioned clothes who were somehow connected with headmistresses [of schools] who said you shouldn't wear high heels or make-up. It was all very prim and stiff and mainly concerned with keeping you away from boys. . . . I had a stereotype of emancipated women: frightening people in tweed suits and horn-rimmed glasses with stem buns at the backs of their heads. Feminism was completely asexual."

The image of the British feminist today is completely different. She may or may not be physically attractive but makes no deliberate effort to make herself unattractive. She is confident in herself and devotes much of her energies to writing about sexism in magazines, books, or talking about it at political meetings. She is generally well-educated and, like in the old days, generally of middle-class origin. She tends to be convinced that only a major social revolution can bring justice to women.

But her impact on Britain's male-oriented society remains minimal. One prominent feminist wrote despairingly, "After ten years of being angry in the face of ridicule and grim resistance, some of us are a bit flaked." She had been looking for "a new generation of feminists to emerge from school, college and early marriage . . . to elbow us veterans out of the way and take up the struggle. There are some, of course, but not the hordes I would like to see."

Her own feminist efforts have continued unabated but they are dwarfed in a country where it is still common for the husband to keep his weekly wages to himself, allotting his wife her weekly "housekeeping" beyond which she cannot spend on the family or herself no matter how much he shells out at the pub.

There's no need to look further than down the street anywhere in Britain to grasp the extent to which females are still relegated to second-class status. Some 70,000 pubs—one of Britain's most distinctive institutions—are dotted across the face of the country and, though the pub rather than the family or the church is the center of British social life, it has always been and still is a distinctly masculine preserve. The climbing price of beer has recently trimmed attendance down somewhat but the men of Britain still spend more time in these "public houses" than they do awake at home with their wives and children.

It is standard behavior for the British male to retreat to his "local," the pub where the bartender is likely to know what his "usual" is without his having to specify, where he feels he belongs, where he is as relaxed and composed as stereotyped Englishmen are supposed to be all the time. Samuel Johnson once cooed, "As soon as I enter the door of a tavern, I experience an oblivion of care and a freedom from solicitude." The closest equivalent British women have to such an establishment is the afternoon bingo hall, an escape venue primarily for lower-class women, less popular now than a few years ago but even then not offering the warming quality of refuge and conviviality of the corner pub.

Women are not expressly barred from pubs. In some pubs, mostly in fashionable or youngish middle-class areas, they form a regular part of the clientele, knocking back best bitter with their male companions or gin-and-orange or settling for a tame glass of Babycham. But it remains unseemly for a female to intrude on this male preserve unless escorted by a man or at least meeting a man inside. It took court action in Cardiff to compel a pub there to permit even suitably escorted women to order "unladylike" pints rather than half-pints of beer. There are countless pubs where, despite the presence of the barmaid (buxom by tradition), a woman would feel as distinctly out of place as she would at a stag party.

As galling to feminists as the virtual exclusion of unaccompanied women from pubs is the fact that these temples of masculine sway tend to be cozy, inviting, congenial establishments. Most of them are completely free of the sense of brooding or menace found in bars in many other parts of the world. They tend to be so addictive that it is only foreigners who go on "pub crawls" (visits to a series of pubs on a rambling night's carouse). A native remains loyal to his local even though a dozen other equally agreeable pubs might be sprinkled about within strolling distance of his home.

Pubs are landmarks. People locate other places according to their distance from the Crown and Anchor or the Pig and Whistle. Strangers seeking directions are told how far past the Three Bells or the King's Arms to take a turning off the road to get where they are going. Pubs in both cities and countryside are often stops or destinations for public buses and are listed as such on official bus timetables. Local history is often based on the annals of the local pub. The Rose and Crown at Dartford was the rendezvous of the rebels in the Peasants' Revolt in the fourteenth century, and the place to which they scrambled back in despair after their uprising collapsed. The Sun, in the town of Hitchin, served for a while as headquarters for Oliver Cromwell's army during the English civil war. Thomas Paine, who called the English pub "the cradle of American independence," wrote "The Rights of Man" at the Old Red Lion in Clerkenwell.

But the chief significance of the pub, and of its tavern predecessor, has always been its calling as a club, a hangout, a home away from home. The English poet, George Crabbe, knew it for what it was:

> 'Tis his home who possesses not one of his own;
> And to him who has rather too much of that one,
> 'Tis the house of a friend where he's welcome to run.

One of the first English settlers in the untamed region that was to become the state of Virginia noted morosely that his new homeland provided "neither taverne, beer house, nor place of reliefe." More recently, Michael Jackson, in his book *The English Pub*, called the pub "neutral ground" where "the reticent Englishman can invite an acquaintance for a drink. . . . without any risk that the style of his home life will be found wanting. . . . Nor will there be any problem in getting rid of a tiresome guest—the person who issued the invitation in the first place is at liberty to excuse himself when he wishes, providing it is not his turn to buy a round of drinks. . . . In a country pub, a poacher can meet a gamekeeper with impunity. In a city pub, a business deal can be transacted without either party having the advantage of home ground."

Organizations and clubs rent out upstairs rooms of pubs for their gatherings. Pubs are a favorite venue for meetings of local union branches and for non-Establishment press conferences. Fox hunts in the shires, with their immaculately liveried horsemen and horsewomen, their hornblowers and their packs of hounds, usually originate and end outside country pubs, as they have for centuries.

Once upon a time, in remote corners of the country, pubs served as part-time court houses for itinerant judges. At the Elm Tree in the Dorset village of Langton Herring and in some other courthouse pubs, men found guilty of capital crimes were hanged on the spot from pub beams. In London, St. Stephen's Tavern across the street from the houses of Parliament is frequented by members of the House of Commons who know that when their presence is required on the floor of the House to vote on legislation, a bell especially installed for the purpose will sound off to send them scurrying off to do their duty for party and country.

Pubs have been intimately connected with the development of sports in Britain. The game of cricket was originally devised at the Ball and Bat in a small Hampshire village. A variation on the cricket theme, called bat-and-trap, never successfully captured the British imagination but is still played on village greens outside pubs in parts of southern England. Many of the great bare-knuckle fights of the early days of boxing took place in pubs or behind them. Some pubs still feature boxing. The Thomas à Beckett in south London has its own gymnasium and ring. Muhammad Ali trained for his heavyweight championship title fight in Britain in 1968 at the gym of the Load of Hay in north London.

In less tender-hearted times, pub landlords arranged cock fights, matched bulldogs against tethered bulls, and staged bear-baiting and badger-baiting displays. Like the lunchtime striptease in some pubs these days, the object was to attract and entertain clients. Now various other gimmicks are also in order. Music pubs specialize in traditional jazz, old English music hall fare, rock-and-roll, the sounds of punk, country-and-western—whatever might attract a loyal following. The Widow's Son in London's East End retains a gaslight atmosphere to make it distinctive. The Rose Revived is a riverside antique, tucked in beside an ancient Thames bridge at Newbridge in Oxfordshire. The Orange Tree in the London suburb of Richmond, like several other big city pubs, offers performances of plays, sometimes good enough to move on to London's West End. There is a rich variety of pub attractions. But the basic attraction is the pub's get-away-from-it-all atmosphere.

The British pub of today is a descendant of the inns which sprang up hundreds of years ago to provide rest, refreshment, and safety for pilgrims and other travelers traversing the countryside alone or in small groups, on foot or horseback. These inns were generally situated at crossroads, ferry crossings, at the edge of towns and cities, and on the fringes of forbidding forests where entry as nightfall approached was inadvisable for peaceful wayfarers.

Travelers taking advantage of the facilities of inns could expect to be refreshed with stimulating beverage and fed for a modest price. Sleeping accomodations generally amounted only to straw pallets on hard floors but were nevertheless welcome after a long day on the road. Many inns had large courtyards where carriages could be safely entrusted to stable boys overnight and horses fed and rested without danger of being rustled by highwaymen, against whom the gates and doors were closed and bolted at bedtime. An Elizabethan traveler noted:

> In all our inns we have plenty of ale, beer and sundry kinds of wine, and such is the capacity of some of them that they are able to lodge two hundred or three hundred persons and their horses at ease, and thereto with a very short warning make such provision for their diet as to him that is unacquainted withall may seem to be incredible.

In addition to catering to wayfarers, the inns soon became neighborhood hangouts where local men congregated most evenings, then as now leaving their wives at home. Many inns became gathering places for thieves, smugglers, ruffians, hellraisers, and other reprobates. Some served as brothels. Parliament felt obliged in 1604 to pass a law defining taverns, alehouses, and inns as places "for the Receipt, Relief and Lodging of Wayfaring People travelling from Place to Place and not meant for the entertainment and harbouring of Lewd and Idle People to spend and consume their Money and Time in Lewd and Drunken Manner."

Pubs in cities also began as travelers' rests. Some older city pubs still offer modest sleeping accomodations. But the tremendous influx of country folk into the cities in the seventeenth and eighteenth centuries to man the Industrial Revolution, to take factory and mining jobs, and to settle permanently in their new, congested habitats turned most public houses into places where men merely gathered to drink and to try to purge themselves of the drudgery of their jobs before going home to bed.

Pubs were never hangouts for the upper classes, except those of its members who had a penchant for slumming. Nevertheless, the British compulsion to erect class divisions has long been on display in public houses, many of which retain partitions to separate "saloon bars" (which are frequented by those pubgoers who prefer not to mingle with riffraff even if it means paying a bit more for their drinks) and the "public bars" (where the clientele is made up of blue collar workers or, in the countryside, farm laborers.) Furnishings, glasses, and service in the saloon bars are generally more elaborate; the atmosphere is more refined. Some of the fancier pubs have "lounge bars" with waiter service.

There are several types of pubs, each of which is distinct in atmosphere and clientele. The most common are the quiet pubs, the lively pubs, and the country pubs. Quiet pubs are usually situated on back streets of cities or towns, though they sometimes can be encountered also in poorer rural regions. Women are very rarely to be found in them, and never young women. Strangers are almost as scarce. Regulars sit at small, beer-stained tables or stand, leaning on their elbows, at the bar. There is a wordless communion among them. Occasionally someone lets slip a comment. Rarely does it require, or elicit, a response.

The drinking—generally beer—is steady and serious but not in great volume. It is slow and deliberate, as if each pint were the last the drinker would have the privilege of downing before being

ousted from this comforting, dimly-lit, languid limbo and cast into
some sort of equally low-keyed hell. A careful game of dominoes
might be in progress in a corner, or darts with the thud of those
missiles slipping through the stillness like the pop of a slow-
dripping faucet. Behind the bar, "mine host" (though it would be
laughable to call him that today), as solid and noncommital as a
robot, straightens glasses. A stranger could walk in, order a beer,
pour it over his own head, do a handstand in the middle of the floor,
yodel, and make a soft-shoe exit and nobody would even look his
way. Several minutes after he had left, one of the regulars might
mutter, "Queer bloke, that," wonder what on earth was happening
to the quality of his pub and that would be the end of that. It is a
great place to be alone with your thoughts, though someone
unfamiliar with the scene, and bewildered by it, might be led to
suspect that others in this hushed enclosure must be up to more
than they are letting on, that camouflaged wickedness or at least
conspiracies are afoot. The quiet villain is as much a favorite of the
British imagination as the unflappable hero.

The goings-on in a lively pub differ wildly from those in a quiet
pub. It is just as distinctively British though its atmosphere would
be hard to duplicate under other circumstances in the British Isles.
The lively pub is frequented mostly by young people, including a
fair number of women. It is crowded, noisy, and vibrant. People are
jammed uncomplainingly together, shoulder to shoulder, buttock
to buttock. Others make their way through the crush to and from
the bar. Room is made for them with good grace. There is much
camaraderie. Conversation and laughter is easy, though words
aren't always easy to make out above the din. Strangers are
painlessly absorbed into group exuberance. In warm weather, the
crowd overflows onto the streets and even into nearby parks. At
closing time, barmen go around collecting glasses from the sills and
benches of the immediate neighborhood.

Most Britons would find the unrestrained good fellowship on
display in lively pubs—the banter, the casual shoulder-rubbing, the
give-and-take with strangers—ill-advised and improbable in other
settings (except perhaps young people's parties). But there seems to
be a hunger for this kind of informal carousing. Why else would
many people spend their brief lunch hours, standing up in crowded
bunches in pubs near where they work, sipping at drinks and

munching on tired pub sandwiches, having a wonderful time. It is not uncommon for people playing truant from work to show up only to share lunchtime with their mates in jammed pubs across the street from their offices. It can't be the food. In his *Pub Guide*, Egon Ronay described the search for good food by his pub inspectors as "a nightmare" in which they encountered such stuff as "inedible travesties of sandwiches" and "shriveled bread sausages."

There are also halfway-house pubs, midway between the quiet and lively varieties. These are places where there can be a certain amount of good cheer but where an explosion of mirth would be frowned upon; places where a measure of solemnity would be tolerated, but within reason.

The third major category of pub is, however, the country pub, an establishment which occupies a special niche in the British scene. For many who live in the country, these are the only places where they encounter their neighbors. The country pub is often the center of community activities—local politics, community fund raising campaigns, local sports. The courtyards of many old country inns, where once horsedrawn carriages stood, have now been converted into parking lots for patrons and on weekends they are jammed to overflowing. Though country pubs of ancient vintage have had to be refurbished, they tend to reflect the old-time architectural styles of their respective neighborhoods. More often than not, the windows of village pubs look out on village greens where, on sleepy summer Sunday afternoons, local men partake of slow-paced cricket matches, after which they repair to the pub for an ale or two before heading home.

In recent years, to the regret and often the outrage of those who cherish British traditions, many pubs have been decked out with a modern, glittering image or redecorated in a false antique one. Some pub managers have devoutly clung to the genuine old-time flavor, retaining Victorian-etched mirrors, cubical screens, and even sawdust on the floor. But in too many places, fine old oak tables have been replaced by formica-topped, easy-wipe substitutes, and bentwood chairs have made way for seats draped with glossy velveteen. Concealed lighting has also been installed for effect and to keep the transformation from being too obviously depressing to traditionalists.

Most British are no more discriminating about their beer than they are about their food. Many a foreigner has been convinced that anyone who is addicted to tepid, bitter beer will drink anything. But there *are* British beer connoisseurs. They are part of a movement launched to promote the survival of old British brewing standards at a time when the big brewing companies have swung over to the economical production of keg beer, impregnated with carbon dioxide gas to do what the more expensive, much slower maturing process does. The result, says the Campaign for Real Ale (CAMRA) "is a bland, sweet, fizzy concoction that is as much like real beer as vinegar is like wine." CAMRA periodically publishes a *Good Beer Guide* identifying the pubs across the country which have shunned brewers employing such speeded-up production methods and which serve what discriminating British beer drinkers consider a properly brewed brew.

In recent years, there's been a growth in popularity for American and continental-style beers, called lager in Britain but not very different from some traditional British light ales. Ordering lager in pubs in some parts of the country once had sissy overtones. But extensive he-man-type television advertising by lager brewers has managed to change that.

So-called working men's clubs, mostly in the north of England, have always been as male-oriented as pubs. They originated in the nineteenth century as temperance after-hours sanctuaries for poor working men who otherwise would have had no place to go other than taverns and gin mills. Now they are mostly working-class hangouts for drinking (beer mostly), socializing, and entertainment. Many British singers and comedians served their apprenticeship playing the working men's clubs circuit. Most of the clubs retain "men only" sections but many now have lounges where women are welcome, usually as guests (and usually the wives) of male members.

Though pubs are the main centers of social life in Britain, the country is famous for another social arena even more devotedly dedicated to perpetuating masculine privacy and privilege. Men of rank and position in London who find popping down to the local for a leisurely pint with the lads, and maybe a game of darts, insufficiently genteel, and who would be totally out of place in such a setting, go elsewhere. They retire instead to masculine

retreats of their own come pub time. They make for the rarefied
atmosphere of their gentlemen's clubs, known the world over for
their exclusivity, and some of them for their stuffiness. These clubs
are the off-duty haunts of the British Establishment where, as an
eminent clergyman once put it, "Women ceased from troubling and
the weary are at rest." Less high-flown was the quip of a London
wit who said, "A club is a weapon used by savages to keep the
white woman at a distance." Efforts to mimic the London phenomenon and establish a club environment in New York, Philadelphia, Boston, Paris, and other cities never quite got it right. It's a
London thing.

As might be expected, members of clubs tend to be birds of a
feather. Socially prominent Tory politicians join various bluebloods
at White's, the oldest of London's gentlemen's clubs. It was
founded in 1697 and became a fashionable retreat practically from
the start. It has been described as an oasis of civilization in a desert
of democracy. Prince Charles had his pre-wedding stag party there.

Senior clergymen and judges, literary personalities, and eminent
scientists converge on the Athenaeum, some seventy of whose past
members are buried with honor in Westminster Abbey. Boodles is a
hangout for country gentlemen and the London horsey set. Upon
joining Boodles, the late Ian Fleming, creator of James Bond,
explained that he expressly wanted to belong to a dull club, though
cynics might suggest his problem would have been to find one
where anything really happened. When a member was discovered
dead, propped up in an easy chair in his club lounge, it was believed
he might have been lying there lifeless, his newspaper covering his
face, for several days without anyone noticing.

Brook's has traditionally been a gathering place for intellectual
politicians, men with ideas but also with the good sense not to go
spouting them aloud at every provocation to befuddle the occasional artist and aristocrat also in attendance there. At Brook's,
porters once boiled coins to decontaminate them and ironed folding
money and newspapers to make them neat. Businessmen, lawyers,
bankers, and professional pundits are among the members of the
Reform from which the fictional Phileas Fogg set off on his journey
of *Around the World in Eighty Days.* Many a club would never
have permitted so loud-mouthed a showoff to cross its portals.

The Royal Automobile Club was founded in 1897 "for the

protection, encouragement, and development of automobiles." It has an excellent swimming pool and squash courts. It is believed that, expecting imminent exposure and arrest, Russian spies Guy Burgess and Donald Maclean, both employed by the British Foreign Office, took lunch at the RAC as their last leisurely glimpse of the Britain they were forsaking before fleeing to sanctuary in Moscow in the 1950s.

The Travellers' was established in 1819 at a time before just about everybody indulged in foreign travel "to form a point of reunion for gentlemen who have travelled abroad." Among its members these days are foreign ambassadors, Foreign Office factotums, and even the occasional genuine explorer. It is rumored that the Travellers' is also where British spy chiefs do their more important conferring, away from the less reassuring atmospheres of their offices. The Garrick claims to be immune to the stuffiness of other clubs, having among its members some of Britain's leading journalists, broadcasters, actors, and others who are glamorously employed.

The gentlemen's clubs have their origins in the London coffee houses which began to be frequented by men of fashion, the professions, and business toward the end of the seventeenth century. King Charles II, whose father had been overthrown and who feared a conspiracy against himself, tried to suppress the coffee houses but had little success. They increasingly attracted groups of devoted regulars. In time, membership arrangements were devised by some of them and only carefully selected members were admitted. New premises were found as the establishments took on more defined club identities. Some began occupying the mansion residences in which they are housed today, most notably in "clubland" along Pall Mall and St. James's Street in central London.

The clubs gradually developed the character they still retain, grandly defined by one commentator as "a sort of defensive alliance tacitly concluded between a number of individuals, all moving in the same sphere of life, against the troubles and perturbations by which humanity is assailed." In fact, they were gathering places for privileged men with time on their hands and an aversion to people who were not like themselves.

There were all sorts of clubs—for scholars and writers, for

politicians and businessmen, for aristocrats, court officials, and church dignitaries, for wits and jokers. There was a Liars's Club whose members were dedicated to telling tall tales. There was a club in which members were identified only by assumed names reflecting their personalities—garrulous Sir Talkative Doolittle and grumpy Sir Gregory Growler. There were clubs of high-spirited, trouble-making young nobs. In time, sets of rules were devised to govern the behavior of members in good standing. In one club, frequented by some of the most distinguished and powerful men in the land, a member deemed to have behaved improperly could be made to sit draped in a tablecloth like a dunce and lectured at as if he were a naughty boy. A proper gentleman had learned during his formative days at school to take his medicine like a man, even if it seemed humiliating or silly.

Sometimes even applicants with impeccable social credentials were required to apply twice or three times before being accepted as members. Though too proud to tolerate snubs in other nooks and crannies of society, they willingly exposed themselves to rejection by members of clubs they wanted to join. The expression *black-balled* grew from the procedure one of the clubs initiated for permitting an existing member to veto the membership application of an outsider of whom he disapproved by dropping a black rather than a white ball into the ballot box when his application was considered. It was generally accepted that it was preferable for a dozen suitable applicants to be turned down than for one unsuitable would-be member to be accepted.

Membership in a better club could be an important step in a young man's career. A junior official in a government office could find himself hobnobbing with a minister. A youngish executive could find himself occupying a chair in the lounge next to that of the chairman of the board of his company and perhaps even exchange a word with him about how damnably deaf the drinks waiter was getting. But there was a time when many of the clubs were the province of "true gentlemen" who lived off independent incomes, usually derived from property holdings. These men had no occupation and considered those who had to work for a living a lesser breed.

Such a gentleman was likely to sleep late into the morning, putter around till it was time for a pre-lunch drink or two at the club, where he then would take lunch and spend most of the midday. During the late afternoon, he might fulfill a social obligation, or see his solicitor about overdue funds he was expecting or wander about till it was time to go home to dress for dinner, taken at the club as well. In his study of London clubs, Ralph Neville summed up the life of this sort of clubman: "He lunches and dines, dines and lunches, till the sands of the hourglass have run out, and the moment comes for him to enter that great club of which all humanity must perforce become members." So defined, the hereafter doesn't sound like the sort of club to which that sort of gentleman would have cared to belong.

Those were the days before (suitable) restaurants, (respectable) nightlife, or cars for spins into the countryside. Unless he was inclined to visit a brothel, of which London had a goodly number, there was very little for a highborn gentleman to do but sip away at brandy-and-soda well into the night, deep in a comfortable armchair in a lounge peopled by other highborn gentlemen similarly engaged. One was with one's own kind, which was the only environment British gentlemen would tolerate. It was said of one club that it was so congested with aristocrats that if a porter paged "Sir John" in its lounge, a dozen men so named would reply. It was in Boodles that an elderly aristocrat used to sit in a chair by the window because he liked "watching the damned people get wet" outside. In another club, a member, annoyed by the slowness of the drinks waiter, pushed him through a window into the street and then told other staff who rushed to see what the commotion was to "put him on my bill."

In the old days, members were haughty about their club membership. They expected those who were unfortunate enough not to belong to appreciate how far they stood at a disadvantage. The secretary of one club wrote to the secretary of another in a remote corner of the British Empire that some of his members were on a visit there and he "would appreciate it if you would show them every hospitality. We cannot, of course, reciprocate, as you will readily understand."

But times have changed and are changing still. The clubs have depended for survival on two things—a plentiful supply of well-heeled members of the right sort and a plentiful supply of cheap labor. Now porters and waiters can earn more and need work fewer hours at hotels and in other jobs. Clubs are hard put to provide the service their members expect, and virtually all have been forced to violate custom and tradition and hire waitresses and other female staff. All have been compelled to increase their subscription charges and most now do so every year in line with the rate of inflation. At the more exclusive clubs, an applicant must still join a waiting list or might be blackballed. But some clubs will now accept virtually any male applicant who is prepared to pay his initiation fee and subscription and who manages to drum up a sponsor who is already a member.

Another part of the problem for the clubs is the dramatic change in the habits of members since the good old days. Once upon a time, most members had houses or pied-à-terres in central London. They could and did easily reach their clubs both day and night to lunch, dine and sit around imbibing into the wee hours. Now many clubable men are comfortably ensconced with their families in fashionable commuter-belt suburbs and exurbs to which they generally repair after work each day, perhaps having time for a quick whiskey at their clubs before fulfilling family commitments their predecessors scoffed at. There are now fewer "country members" who use overnight accomodations available at the larger clubs, once a meaningful source of club income. Financial pressures are unrelenting. One club secretary tells of a long-standing race-horse-owning member who came into his office one day to announce, "Don't know whether I can afford to come here anymore. I've been living off the immoral earnings of my stallion for years and the poor old bugger is wearing out!"

Notwithstanding these difficulties, the gentlemen's clubs remain the retreats of cliques of the most important men in British government, business and the professions. It is standard for large companies to require their executives to belong (at company expense) to at least one of the more prestigious clubs (some belong to several), to establish the company's credentials, and to meet informally with people it is important to know. Government ministers and senior civil servants are more likely to exchange useful information over lunch or drinks at their clubs than in the corridors of power. The introduction of commercial television in Britain to supplement the noncommercial BBC—a revolutionary development—was plotted in one of the more distinguished clubs.

Enormous business deals are wrapped up in club lounges with not a pen or contract in sight. But such proceedings have done little to transform the club atmosphere. Though not quite as somber as they once were, Rudyard Kipling's description of the mood of the Athenaeum as resembling that of a cathedral between services is still not far wide of the mark for many of them.

Money problems have induced some clubs to modify their attitude towards women. Some years ago, a few of them opened their doors to female guests of members at lunchtime and sometimes at dinner too. Now some clubs have begun accepting women members though deeply-rooted misogynistic prejudices die hard. At one club which now accepts women, the club chairman expressed the hope that "they will be persuaded not to use the bar at lunchtime" and a leading member warned that women members would be tolerated "as long as they haven't got shrill voices." He need have few fears about being deafened by the ululations of females. To the regret of many club treasurers, but to the satisfaction of most members, the austere chambers and deep leather chairs of clubland are still rarely graced by a feminine presence.

Early this century, several women's clubs—modeled on the gentlemen's variety—were launched by feminists who refused to accept that only men should have such stamping grounds. But those clubs all soon went under. Women did not have the resources to maintain clubs that could rival those of gentlemen and perhaps, then, they also did not have the desire to inhabit such sexual ghettoes. In any case, women's clubs have not been revived.

Present-day feminists have formed a variety of exclusive women's groups and associations but none yet exhibits the distinguished, durable, and recognizable trappings which only time, tradition, and a certain form of dignified zaniness can provide. If they prove to have staying power, perhaps they will develop such characteristics in days to come. But as things now stand, they make little impact on the man's world of Britain.

FOUR

To Love or Not to Love

BRITISH ATTITUDES toward love and sex are complicated and convoluted even though there are good reasons why they shouldn't be. The greatest love story of all time, *Romeo and Juliet*, was written by an Englishman. King Henry VIII renounced the Catholic Church and founded the Church of England when a pope declined to sanction his divorce from a woman he didn't love and his marriage to a woman he did. Love precipitated a monarchical crisis in Britain in 1936 when Edward VIII insisted on marrying a twice-divorced American woman (later to become the Duchess of Windsor) and was willing to abdicate the throne to do so. As far back as it goes, English poetry is laced with both blunt and tender expressions of romantic sentiment, comparing love to summer days, moonlit nights, newfound worlds, and paradise itself. Yet, at a time when romantic love is commonly cherished, openly admired, and even cooed over, the British remarkably manage to sustain a reputation for being unmoved by affairs of the heart.

Suggestive humor on prime-time British television today is far more blue than the American climate would tolerate. No other mass-sales daily newspapers in the world are as punctuated with topless cheesecake as the British press. Sexual innuendo predominates in the series of hilarious and enormously popular British *Carry On* movies—*Carry On, Sailor; Carry On, Doctor; Carry On Up the Khyber*. The arrival of video recorders in Britain led to "erotic entertainment" featuring among the biggest selling video cassettes in the country. Candy-store window bulletin boards throughout London carry barely disguised advertisements from prostitutes—"French Lessons from an Expert" or "Model Seeks

New Position." Such British classics as *Fanny Hill* and *Tom Jones* pioneered the link between literary imagination and pornography in the modern novel. The British were among the forerunners in the development of contraceptive methods—the sheath is named after its inventor, a certain Dr. Condom, believed to have been a physician at the court of King Charles II. Yet, at a time when erotic indulgence is increasingly respectable and even fashionable in many parts of the world, the British are commonly thought to be passionless "cold fish."

The foreign stereotype of an Englishwoman is of a formidable female who harbors warmer feelings for animals (horses, dogs, cats) than for men. She is either full-voiced, tweedy, and athletically gaited, accustomed to having her way and about as desirable as an oak tree, or she is a Vogue-model-type, pretty as the sunrise, slender as a standing lamp, and as frigid as a January day on the Northumberland moor.

The equivalent picture of an Englishman is just a touch more flattering. He is a well-poised male chauvinist, trim and impeccably attired (even when his clothes are fashionably shabby), courteous to women but considering their company a tedious waste of time when there's good brandy or beer to knock back. Or he is a tireless devotee of cricket, soccer, or business, boring when at all comprehensible, as interested in either a romantic attachment with a soul mate or a roll in the hay as he is in the hibernation habits of snails. While other Europeans are said to lead normal sex lives, the British are said to make do with hot water bottles. One European observer, commenting on the sex life of the British, suggested "they reproduce themselves by a form of spontaneous generation not yet fully known to biologists."

These stock portrayals are, of course, unjust and untrue. Britain has its fair share of attractive, sexy, charming, and interesting men and women. Despite the recent advent of the test-tube baby, the British birth rate does not indicate that standard procedures for the perpetuation of the species are being ignored, nor is the rate of illegitimate births substantially lower in Britain than it is in the rest of the Western world. Sexual attractions and impulses are as animated and compelling in the British Isles as they are elsewhere. High school age students receive lectures on sex. Family planning centers in all major cities are kept busy dispensing advice. British journals carry "lonely hearts" advertisements from those seeking romantic and/or sexual companionship. Girls have boyfriends and boys have girlfriends. There's prestige attached in both cases. In new school and work situations, there's regularly a rush to find a "friend" of the other sex.

It is true that boys in Britain are generally less willing than in the United States to lavish attention on their dates, to pick them up from their homes, or deliver them there. But the difficulties and expense of erratic, costly public transportation in a culture where comparatively few youngsters have cars may have been partly responsible for establishing these patterns. Girls are more often expected to pay their own way, though perennial cash shortages among the young in Britain and the influence of Women's Lib may be a cause. On Valentine's Day, newspapers are full of openly proclaimed, paid announcements of love. Flower shops generally do well—it is not uncommon to see a man carrying flowers intended for the current love of his life or his wife.

Of a less romantic nature, sex manuals sell briskly in Britain and stores peddling "sexual aids" do not do badly, in some places having branched out from back-street locations in seedy sections of town into more respectable neighborhoods (where they often have their windows shattered by outraged or tipsy imbibers after the pubs close on Saturday nights). "Adult" movies of *The Stud* or *Diary of a Window Cleaner* variety are shown in neighborhood movie houses.

All things considered, the British are not as sexually backward as they are pictured as being. Nevertheless, their reputation for being uninterested in matters of sex and romance is not really undeserved. The past, as novelist L.P. Hartley suggested, may be a different country where things are done differently, but flirtation is not a natural British skill or pastime these days. Neither is subtle courtship or blunt seduction. The sight of public smooching, even by courting couples, is hard to come by in Britain. Nor do married couples indulge openly in displays of affection. Romantic dalliance is considered something for the capricious French or volatile Italians. Americans are thought of as being adolescently oversexed. *No Sex, Please; We're British* is the ironic title of a comedy of erotic bungling which has run successfully on the London stage for many years. Such sexual bungling, comic or not, is a favorite theme of the

British theater as if adolescent gawkiness has hurdled the generation gap to infect Britons of all ages and thus warn people away
from the real thing.

Market research seems to confirm an asexual, unromantic image.
A leading British beer company settled for a television commercial
which featured a young man ducking into the refuge of a pub for a
pick-me-up with his macho mates in order to stave off the nagging
advances of his girlfriend. The ad was considered so successful that
it was followed by another featuring a man sneaking into a pub to
escape from his wife. The director of a London computer dating
agency said his experience has indicated that though British men
choose down-to-earth British women for their real-life relationships, they prefer exotic foreign females for their fantasies.

People see nothing extraordinary in joint honeymoons for two or
more couples, designed to save brides and grooms from having to
face up to seclusion with one another in remote, romantic corners.
A survey conducted on behalf of a paint manufacturing company
indicated that the British believe pink, red, and black color schemes
help make a bedroom more sexy and that, therefore, most of them
take great care not to paint their bedrooms in those hues. The
predatory rather than the amorous female, the scold rather than the
siren, feature as characters in popular British culture on television
and in newspaper cartoons. Their masculine counterpart tends to
be pompous, self-centered, a little foolish and often "past it" before
his time.

In his study of *Sex and Marriage in England Today*, Geoffrey
Gorer quotes evidence that about 20 percent of men and women in
England do not believe most people actually fall in love. "England,"
he said furthermore, "still appears to be a very chaste society" with
two-thirds of married women and one-quarter of married men
virgin at the time of their weddings. "One of the most constant
products of the English educational system," he says, "is shyness—
the fear that one will be laughed at or rejected by strangers,
particularly strangers of the opposite sex."

A comparison of "lonely hearts" advertisements in London and
New York seems to bear this out. A not particularly unusual ad in
the *New York Review of Books*: "Small group of highly attractive,
professional women of substance invite male counterparts . . . for
tea, sympathy and whatever comes next. We are winners; no losers,
please." A typical ad in the *New Statesman* in London: "Cultured

woman, 35, attractive (they say), humorous and sincere . . . seeks warm-hearted, thoughtful man for meaningful friendship." Discretion and timidity is as common among young British adults in sexual situations as it is among their seniors. It is not simply shyness; it is a matter of shielding personal dignity against possible assault.

The consequence has been a rash of emotional blockages in relations between men and women, initiated early on in their sexual lives. Mini-skirts, skin-tight jeans, and other provocative fashions which the British did so much to popularize only made things worse, providing form without substance. H.G. Wells was depressed by what he called "the lack of courage to love and the wisdom to love." For many young Britons, marriage is the admission price for sexual life and thus becomes the means to that end. It gives matrimony a lopsided significance. If sex with the chosen spouse subsequently proves joyless or nonexistent (and reams of literature flood the market explaining how exhilirating sex can be for one and all), the price paid gets to seem unforgivably exorbitant.

Trial marriages, before couples become formally locked in wedded bliss, have become increasingly fashionable in sophisticated circles. A commoner, married to a blueblood, who is normally referred to by her aristocratic title (Lady Kitty), informed a host that strictly speaking it wouldn't be Mr. and Mrs. who would be showing up for dinner. He meant to say subtly that his wife was a peeress. The host, a British ambassador on foreign soil, misunderstood and tolerantly replied that there was no need to be concerned—there was a lot of that sort of thing about.

Clinical psychologist Douglas McKay recently told a London conference that the British determination to maintain a front of dignity and keep their feelings under control leads to sexual difficulties which cripple marriages. He said many British couples are "emotionally constipated," having learned from childhood to permit themselves to relax even a little only in "safe" situations. They might, for example, be sexually aroused on the dance floor where the presence of others inhibits rash behavior and saves them from worrying about the necessity or desirability of letting go all the way.

In 1973, Australian newspaper magnate Rupert Murdoch, having acquired a subtle insight into the British character, bought a struggling London newspaper, *The Sun*, and within a few years converted it into the best-selling newspaper in the country. His editors did the job by putting the photograph of a seductive, bare-breasted girl on page three each day and offering regular center-spread advice on how best to develop a livelier and more enjoyable sex life.

The success of *The Sun*, among both men and women, was an extraordinary revelation. The British were exposed as a nation of voyeurs, anxious to examine the forbidden fruit they were reluctant to taste. A London jury had already ruled some years earlier that D.H. Lawrence's novel *Lady Chatterley's Lover*, with its explicit descriptions of sexual desire (which the prosecution had suggested no right-minded man would allow his "wife or servant" to read), was not obscene. John Profumo, a government minister, was disgraced and compelled to resign, not because he had cavorted with a prostitute, but because he had lied to Parliament about it when rumors had first begun circulating. In many ways, the British swam with the tide of sexual permissiveness—or at least treaded water. But implicit in the dichotomy between their attitudes and actions has been the belief that though sex is no longer necessarily indecent, it remains a worrying business.

Unlike most other aspects of British life, current attitudes about love and erotic behavior are not a legacy handed down by Britons of long ago. It is of more recent vintage. Unabashed, romantic inclinations, as well as sheer lust, are entrenched in the earlier chronology of British fortunes. There were moments long ago which make our own permissive age seem only mildly unrestrained.

Once upon a time, the pleasure gardens of London, much frequented by the citizens of the capital, were notorious for the libidinous pleasures many of those citizens chose to pursue there. There were times when the language of love was the preeminent enriching element in British prose and poetry. T.H. White wrote that beauties of eighteenth-century Britain "lived through romances of such intricacy and splendor that Hollywood in delirium would scarcely do them justice." Dedicated guardians of public morals have come and gone but not as frequently as those men and women for whom romantic sentiment or sexual drive were of compulsive significance.

Knights like those placed by legend around King Arthur's famous roundtable actually existed even if a genuine Galahad and Arthur himself possibly did not. But instead of being profoundly virtuous gallants, as people were led to believe, they were described by contemporary chroniclers as shamelessly lustful rogues, given more to lechery than chivalry. "Fornicators and adulterers" is what the sixth-century monk Gildas called them. That description can hardly be affixed to the current flower of British manhood who are not commonly seen as being either salacious or wanton.

Nor is it the image subsequently fabricated in Britain later on during the Middle Ages when tales of the exploits of King Arthur and his warriors were first widely disseminated by nimble-witted storytellers. The reputation of those randy footloose horsemen was thoroughly laundered by them. They were transformed into high-minded, fearless knights for whom the love of a woman was a pure and noble commitment, as profound as life itself. The licentious-ness of the impetuous, roguish horseman and the helplessness of the unprotected females they fancied were studiously masked. It was not unknown for a woman, going about her business in the countryside, to hide in fear in ditches when the clatter of hooves signalled the approach of a "gallant" knight. Nor was it unknown for not-always-reluctant women to be called upon to comfort such knights as best they could after rousing jousting contests.

But the new age of the storytellers required that at least the reputation of womanhood be inviolate and respected, that it be fashioned in a way consistent with prevailing religious codes which scorned promiscuity and libertine antics. The graven image of woman—comely, worthy, frail—was hoisted up onto a pedestal (to which it would from time to time be returned by the whims of fashion). Idealized women were glorified by the balladeers of the day, as they often are today.

Men were lowered into their armor where, it was made to seem, they could do no harm except to rivals on the jousting field, wicked adversaries they encountered in battle, or occasional dragons they met along the way. It was no more true to life than a commercially successful, sybaritic pop singer crooning these days about the poverty he would be willing to endure to win the heart of his one true love. But it was an elegant vision.

By the time songs were being sung about purer-than-pure, love-sick knights combing the earth for good deeds to perform to prove their worth to their ladies fair, brothels where clients had to prove nothing more than ability to pay had long been established and thriving in London. In 1116, such houses were even licensed by the king. His purpose was neither to promote moral degeneracy, which required no royal assistance, nor to provide premises for sexual release for the ruttish burghers of London Town, who did well enough, thank you. His Majesty's purpose was to introduce law, order and, above all, taxes into an expanding moral underworld concentrated at the time in Southwark, south of the Thames. Among other things, the law sought to make certain that clients of brothels were not shortchanged by the ladies who practiced their trade in such houses. It was decreed that "no woman is to take money to lie with a man but she lie with him all night till the morrow."

Though royal decrees had little noticeable impact, they demonstrated the extent of intermittent concern. In 1483, Henry V, best known for his battlefield victories over the French, issued an order to his people to "Eschewe the Stynkynge and Orrible Synne of Lechery" which was said to be encouraged by "mysguyded and idil women . . . walkynge aboute by the stretes and lanes of this Citee of London." Such streets were well known throughout London. The females who paraded along Maiden Lane (which still bears that name though not the same reputation) were hardly maidens. Nor was there any secret about the commodity available for a price on Love Lane, commonly known as a "street of wantons."

There was, however, a widespread, well-founded impression that unrestrained and uncontrolled whoring bred disease and mayhem. A complaint against brothels asserted:

> Here 'tis that Impudent Harlots by their Antick Dresses,
> Painted Faces and Whorish Insinuations Allure and tempt our
> Sons and Servants to Debauchery, and consequently to embezel
> and steal from us, to maintain their strumpets. Here 'tis that
> Bodies are Poxed and Pockets are picked of considerable sums,
> the Revenge of which Injuries have frequently occasioned
> Quarrellings, Fightings, Bloodshed, Clamours of Murther . . .
> pulling down of signs and parts of houses, breaking of windows,
> also other tumultuous Routs, Riots and Uproars. . . . Here 'tis

that many a Housekeeper is infected with a venomous Plague, which he communicates to his Honest and Innocent Wife. . . . Here 'tis that Multitudes of Soldiers and Seamen get such bane that effeminates their spirits and soon rots their bodies. . . .

The rich, evocative wordplay of the poets and playwrights of Elizabethan England throbbed unashamedly with pangs of love and passion. John Donne, who told the world that "no man is an island, entire of its self," had earlier eloquently invoked an image of an exciting new discovery far away to show that he did not exclude females from that enduring masculine link with the rest of the world which he so ringingly professed:

> License my roving hand and let them go,
>   [he urged his mistress]
> Before, behind, between, above, below.
> O my America! My new-found-land,
> My kingdom, safeliest when with one man manned.

Bold and forthright, or pale and wan, a lover was prepared, even anxious to exhibit his feelings to the world. In Shakespeare, other characters in the play are made to assume that when Hamlet, contemplating murder, was behaving like a loon, it was because he was in love—and that was okay.

According to Philip Stubbes, a contemporary of Shakespeare, the Elizabethan period was not exclusively a time of pure, deep love, whether romantic or sensual. Stubbes said that theaters, where heart-throbbing scenarios were played out on the stage, were "devourers of maidenly virginity and chastity." Audiences at plays were said to be much given to wanton gestures, bawdy speaking and kissing, not quite what transpires in British theaters today, not even among audiences of striptease shows in London's Soho district.

Changes were, however, in the wind. Developing Puritan ethical standards, a product of the Protestant Reformation, translated uneasiness about improper carryings-on in theaters, and anxiety about the pox (syphilis) and disorder in brothels, into the realm of public and personal morals in general. Local courts tried countless cases of sodomy and other sexual transgressions. A law was passed punishing adultery with death. In parts of Britain, local officials were appointed to track down, shave the heads of, and banish "fornicators and fornicatrixes." Brothels, theaters, and other public places reputed to be hotbeds of immorality were closed. Most of this happened during the so-called "rule of the saints," the short-lived Puritan Commonwealth, after Charles I (loser in the English Civil War and vanquished in his struggle for power with Parliament) had been beheaded, and before Charles II reclaimed the throne. It was a time when even wearing provocative attire could be punished by law. A woman who aroused inordinate desire in men could be formally accused of witchcraft, convicted of the charge, and burnt to death to save her soul.

So repressive did this reign of the Puritans turn out finally to be that the royal Restoration, when it came a decade later, was virtually by popular demand. It was accompanied by a unique and peculiar *political* dimension—libertine permissiveness. Openly maintaining rigid standards of sexual morality laid a person open to charges of lingering loyalty to the deposed and discredited Puritans while less squeamish sexual propensities could be seen as evidence of loyalty to the newly restored monarchy.

The works of such witty Restoration playwrights as Thomas Wycherly and William Congreve (whose plays, still highly polished comedy, are revived periodically at the National Theater in London) bubbled with sexual games and antics. The diaries of Samuel Pepys, which convey a remarkable insight into Restoration moods, treated sexual adventure with great casualness. In high society, flirtation, seduction, and general hanky-panky were standard behavior. Women without lovers and men without mistresses invented exploits so as not to acquire stick-in-the-mud reputations.

The reputations of houses of ill repute, to which reputable men repaired for unrestrained cavorting, was never better. There were to be recurring moralistic backlashes against libertine excesses. A scattering of individuals publicly expressed concern about the shallowness of human desires as reflected in the games men and women played with each other. It had little effect. Physical attractiveness became a compulsive objective.

Women took to elaborate use of cosmetics—rouges, skin lotions, powders, and other concoctions which were prescribed for accentuating their charms. As in the more permissive days of ancient

Rome, women's hairstyles became absurdly intricate (the "bee-hive" was invented) and powdered wigs became mandatory for men. A poet, complaining about female cosmetic trickery, moaned:

> Not ten among ten thousand wear
> Their own complexions nor their hair.

To complement their various facial paints, women grew much addicted to artificial beauty marks, variously shaped black patches which were pasted near the corner of the mouth or eye or on exposed parts of the bosom.

Men in fashionable society were also dolled up, though not quite as intricately. They wore powders and perfumes, partly to mask the consequences of not bathing very often. Sexual attachments were casually made and just as casually dissolved. Fleeting sexual flings were modish, encouraged by the growing respectability of the fashion of women receiving visitors in their bedchambers. Romantic love, maidens innocent and pure, gallants signifying their devotion by galloping off on perilous adventures—all those antiseptic notions and frolics were things of the past. But not for long.

In time, as was inevitable, the pendulum of fad and fashion swung the other way. Prudishness of often grotesque proportions was the most striking feature of nineteenth-century Britain. Queen Victoria sat on the throne; the empire was vast and secure; Britain was truly Great and the British had no doubt that they were God's chosen people. They imposed rigid standards of behavior and morality upon themselves. Those Victorian times were characterized by a deep revulsion against callous sexuality, in fact against sexuality of any kind. The age was marked by sets of priggish attitudes and habits which seem preposterous today.

Respectable women visiting doctors' offices would never think of disrobing—they would use dummies which doctors kept available to point out where on their own bodies they felt pain or discomfort so that the doctor might diagnose their ailments. Women were expected to be shocked and not to be above fainting in public when sexuality reared its vulgar head, even in conversation. Swooning at the slightest risqué provocation was an indication of admirable delicacy and refinement of feeling.

All sorts of linguistic contortions were performed to spare them embarrassment: legs became limbs, even when referring to a piano; chickens had bosoms instead of breasts; the belly was the abdomen; pregnant women were said to be "confined." Shakespeare's plays were rewritten with all suggestive references removed and cleaned up; the resulting "family" edition was enormously popular. Proper young women were regularly escorted by chaperones and were taught to dread what might happen to them on their wedding nights, though they were given no specific idea of the monstrosities that awaited them then. A distinguished Victorian gynecologist announced that "the majority of women, happily for them, are not troubled by sexual feelings of any kind."

Women who were jilted suffered serious disgrace even when no sexual exchange of any kind had occurred; they were expected to suffer nervous breakdowns, if not go altogether insane. Men got off more easily, merely being considered cads, unless the women they jilted were dishonorable or socially beneath them. This masculine advantage might not be enough, however, to offset the punishment inflicted on so many boys and young men who were subject to nocturnal emissions while sleeping. Pointed, trap-like devices were strategically fitted around their genital region to wake them, painfully, before the dreaded deed could perpetrate itself.

A great number of books of etiquette rolled off the presses. The guidelines they contained were scrupulously observed by those who wished to be considered (and to consider themselves) well-mannered. It was an age of stern, inexorable principles of morality. But that was only part of the picture. Beneath layers of meticulously maintained respectability, a totally different world existed.

For all its primness, prudishness, and sexual restraint, Victorian Britain experienced an explosion of sexuality with which it is not commonly associated today. Never before had there been such a flood of pornographic literature—magazines, novels, poems, learned studies, memoirs (one man anonymously wrote and published an eleven-volume description of his sex life). Prostitution was a growth industry. Apprentice prostitutes were called "flappers," a name which came to mean something else decades later. Streetwalkers were called "badgers." Jack Harris's *Whoremonger's Guide*, produced by an employee of a central London hotel, was succeeded by other guides containing the addresses, attractions, and prices of local whores. Different brothels were known for their exotic specialties.

The dazzling contrast between strict Victorian standards of rectitude and the underground erotic permissiveness was also in evidence in parts of America and other places at the time. But nowhere was the clash of motivation and of effect so striking as in Britain. A product of the Victorian legacy was, and is, sexual confusion. Neither prudishness nor eroticism retains a stranglehold on the British imagination. But both are very much in evidence.

The British didn't really know what to think or feel a little while ago when a distinguished public figure was revealed as having been interested in child pornography. They find it very hard to tell where to draw the line. They work their way through a maze in which turning in any of the available directions leads to actions and contemplations which are either excessive or indifferent, either coarse or prim. Sex is a conundrum for many people in many places. For a people as committed to propriety as the British, it is particularly baffling.

London Town

VISITORS FROM other lands are easily seduced by London, especially those who have misgivings about big cities and who come expecting to be assailed by the anonymous hard sell of a gargantuan metropolis. London turns out to be gracious and congenial rather than overwhelming. It is a place whose spectacles and sights call for eyebrows raised in appreciation or surprise rather than for hearty exclamations and elbow nudgings. Its amusements tend to please rather than ravish—there are few belly laughs or excitements here. There's nothing frivolous about London. It has calmly survived plague, conflagration, and bombing as well as power and glory and is not readily given to spasms of hoopla. Whatever shortcomings it has tend to be tedious or morose rather than harsh and repellent.

Despite its size (about thirty miles across in just about every direction) and the density of its population (some seven million souls; twelve million if you count the suburbs), the British capital is neither cluttered nor intimidating. Even in the heart of the city, where glistening glass and steel structures of questionable aesthetic value have sprung up alongside the elegant edifices of old London, claustrophobic pressures are toned down by a measured sense of pace and purpose.

There is no panic, not even at rush hour which, in London, is considerably less frenzied than in other metropolises around the world. Frenzy would seem singularly out of place in this setting. Anyone who has gazed across at the houses of Parliament from the south bank of the Thames can testify that, if you discount the newer high-rise additions (which is not always easy to do), central London's skyline is monumental and stirring. Where it is not, it is comforting and reassuring, with tidy rows of chimney pots atop its Victorian apartment buildings or terraces of trim, tasteful houses, four stories high at most, none presuming to blot out the sky.

There is a dazzling amount of greenery in London, far more than a city of these proportions can rightly expect to enjoy. There's a forest at one end of town, park land colonized by wild deer at the other, and a huge assortment of other woods, parks, commons, "greens," and heathland strewn across the city. There are countless tree-lined streets, carpeted with fallen leaves come autumn, and cultivated front and back yards of the houses in which most Londoners live. Though a visitor may have been carried away when she suggested that someone "so disposed probably could see most of central London by swinging from branch to branch," few and far between are the places in town where a person can wander in any direction for ten minutes without spying nature in the raw—trees, grass, or shrubs.

A broad green belt around the city is stringently guarded by law against "developers." If such generous dosages of nature do not suffice, a person has to travel no more than a half hour out of London from most of the city's six major train stations (a few retain the romantic, shadowy atmosphere of old spy movies) to come across livestock grazing. Foxes romp over suburban open spaces at night and owls hoot from trees there.

London is punctuated with tastefully laid-out squares, each lined with sturdy, tasteful buildings, most of them at least a century old. Neglected or abandoned houses in run-down corners of town are regularly acquired and revitalized by people seeking accommodation they can afford in London's monstrously expensive real estate market. Whole sections of the city are thus gradually reclaimed by an enterprising corps of Londoners who make personalized urban renewal their way of life. This process is not always unanimously applauded. Fancily refurbished houses are sometimes shunted quickly back onto the market but priced out of the reach of poorer, less well-housed locals. They object to this "gentrification" of their previously unfashionable stomping grounds where neighborhood grocery stores and greengrocers make way for chic, useless antique shops and decorator salons.

Nevertheless, the various parts of London remain distinctive. Not the first nor the last to do so, Mark Twain called London a collection of villages. "When you live in one of them," he said, "it is not possible for you to realize that you are in the heart of the greatest city in the world." London has always had a knack for extracting exaggerated accounts of its charms from visitors. But its village aspect does remain real and recognizable.

So many of the places gobbled up by Greater London as the city swelled inexorably beyond the old walled town retain distinctive characteristics of their own, even today—Bloomsbury with its elegant squares; Soho with its porno shops, foreign restaurants, and generally shadowy atmosphere; Hampstead with its sprawling heathland, its quaint, narrow sidestreets and fine Regency houses; Knightsbridge with its elegant stores and discreet ambassadorial residences; Highgate sitting cool and remote on a rising looking down on the rest of London beneath it; Hackney with its lively street markets; Wimbledon with its countrified setting.

The variety of diversions London offers is impressive. It boasts internationally renowned dog shows, cat shows, horse shows, and flower shows. International competition in croquet and lacrosse is featured on London's calendar of events. Displays of jousting were revived not long ago (by British movie stunt men looking for work). More conventional sports—soccer, rugby, cricket, tennis, and even baseball (resident Americans cavorting in Hyde Park and Regents Park)—are among the pastimes of Londoners, permanent or transient. There is horse racing (just outside town), dog racing, stock car racing, and motorcycle racing.

London is justifiably famous for its pageantry—the Lord Mayor's Show, State Opening of Parliament, Trooping the Color—all replete with glittering livery and acts of splendorous courtesy. Judges and barristers in the courts still wear wigs and robes. Horse-drawn carriages are still dispatched into London traffic to bring foreign ambassadors to Buckingham Palace to present themselves to the queen. Uniformed Sheriffs, Swordbearer, Common Crier, and City Marshal escort the Chief Magistrate of the City of London to Old Bailey criminal court for the opening of its session each year. Contrary to the words of the song "A Foggy Day in London Town," the British Museum, an infinite storehouse of wonders and marvels, has not lost its charm and is not likely to do so. London has dozens of other museums worthy of the name, including a Museum of Beer and a magnificent War Museum housed in a stately building

which was appropriately designed as a lunatic asylum called
Bedlam (an abbreviation for Bethlehem).

Nor is London that foggy anymore, not since clean air legislation
a few years back eliminated much of the atmospheric pollution.
Pea-soup fogs, those thick, blinding mists which featured in so
many Hollywood versions of London life, now virtually never
occur. A modern Sherlock Holmes or Bulldog Drummond would
have to seek elsewhere for an appropriate London backdrop for his
atmospheric adventures: perhaps a picturesque street market of
which London has many—Portobello Road with its overpriced
antiques and silver, Chapel Street Market with its big-eyed puppies
and mewing kittens for sale, or perhaps indoors at nightmarish
Smithfield meat market among hulking sides of beef suspended
from rows of hooks for inspection by a dawn patrol of retail
butchers and restaurateurs.

With the comings and goings of newcomers over the ages—Celts,
Romans, Saxons, Vikings, Normans, refugees seeking sanctuary—
London long ago got used to strangers passing through or settling
in. This cosmopolitan aspect remains very much in evidence today.
Chinatown, bombed out of the Limehouse district of east London
during the Second World War, is now snugly ensconced a hop, skip,
and a jump from Piccadilly Circus. Blacks from the West Indies
mostly, but also from Commonwealth nations in Africa, have
congregated in the Brixton and Notting Hill areas. There's a colony
of Cypriots in the Camden town district. London's Poles have their
community center in Hammersmith; the London Ukrainians have
theirs near Holland Park. Substantial numbers of Indians and
Pakistanis have settled in Southall in west London. Many
Bangladeshis live in and around Brick Lane in east London where
once Jewish immigrants from Eastern Europe settled. The Anglicized descendants of those immigrants have scattered around
London, though the suburbs of Stanmore and Golders Green still
contain largish Jewish communities.

A community of relatively newly arrived Irish people has now
settled in Kilburn, north London, but the Irish constitute the
largest minority group by far in Britain and are, for the most part,
not residentially locked into geographic communities. Countless
Irish have been in Britain for many generations so that it was rarely

even noted, for example, that a British prime minister by the name of Callaghan (he was sent to Parliament by a district in Wales) had Irish antecedents. There is a spectacular array of places to worship in London—Anglican, of course (both High Church and Low Church), Methodist, Baptist, Catholic, Church of Scotland, Welsh Presbyterian, Jewish (both orthodox and reform), Mormon, Quaker, Seventh Day Adventist, Shiite Moslem, Sunni Moslem, Ahmadiyya Moslem, Hindu, Sikh, Buddhist, Greek Orthodox, Russian Orthodox, Bahai and others.

Hyde Park Speakers Corner, adjoining Tyburn Hill where, until two centuries ago, crowds of Londoners gleefully congregated to watch highwaymen and other criminals hanged by the neck until dead, or taken down before dying to be drawn and quartered, remains a notable setting for London doings. Every Sunday, self-appointed orators, advocating all sorts of causes, sound out urgently, defiantly, bitterly, cajolingly. An anarchist forecasts an imminent violent uprising of "the people" everywhere. A Moslem urges listeners to ignore the headlines about hostages and assassinations and recognize his faith as the true path to peace, friendship, and heaven. An Irishman defiantly asserts his hatred of all things English, including his audience. A man with a clerical collar warns against conspiracies being hatched in the Vatican. Hecklers are everywhere. Speakers Corner is all talk, a symbol of the ability of the British both to manipulate and withstand the weight of words, and to guard their right to use them. It is indeed remarkable that a people generally so taciturn should place so high a premium on the freedom to sound off when they like.

The novelist Henry James, who foresook his American heritage to become a British subject early this century, had firm opinions about London:

It is not a pleasant place. It is not agreeable, or cheerful, or easy, or exempt from reproach. It is only magnificent. You can draw up a tremendous list of reasons why it should be insupportable. The fogs, the smoke, the dirt, the darkness, the wet, the distances, the ugliness, the brutal size of the place, the horrible numerosity of society, the manner in which this senseless bigness is fatal to amenity, to convenience, to conversation, to good manners. . . . You may call it dreary, heavy, stupid, dull, inhuman, vulgar at heart and tiresome in form. . . . But . . . for one who takes it as I take it, London is on the whole the most possible form of life.

Henry James was of an aristocratic disposition. He was jealous about the niceties and comforts of life. By definition, a throbbing metropolis contained for him more nuisance factors than it does for most people. But others who are less fussy also grumble about certain features of London. Footloose revelers are appalled to find themselves stranded in the early morning hours because London public transportation grinds to a halt at about midnight, by which time most of the city's taxi drivers have also called it a day. The recurring paralysis of city traffic whenever a royal procession is mounted in the center of town to greet a visiting nabob is galling and infuriating. It seems as though one or another of London's major attractions and architectural landmarks is perpetually scaffolded for cleaning or restructuring, giving it a scarred look. Clerks in London stores, bored with their jobs and averse to appearing subservient to equals, often turn surly or frosty when faced with customer requests for the kind of service considered normal elsewhere and adopt a curt take-it-or-leave-it approach when questioned about dubious goods or prices.

Samuel Johnson's incessantly repeated epigram, "When a man is tired of London, he is tired of life," is nonsense. Natives who are nowhere near suicidal frequently grow weary of the city and flee to more exotic, more exuberant locations. Born and bred Londoners are continually turning up and sinking roots in distant, improbable places—in the sands of Arabia, among the honky-tonks of New Orleans, in this or that Shangri-La half a world away.

People in the British hinterland speak disdainfully of London. A north country local government official complained to me that central government officials there with whom he had to deal still acted as if they were administrating an immense empire and couldn't be bothered to look too closely into his trivial problems. "Too sick, too quick, and all sham," is the way a Somerset farmer dismissed the capital city of his country. Lord Byron, a mischief maker if ever one there was, described London admiringly as a place "where every kind of mischief's daily brewing." Nevertheless (or perhaps, therefore), the British capital remains a magnet of

extraordinary power towards which most of the talented, ambitious, and enterprising of the British are inexorably drawn from
all over the country.

London is where the theaters and art galleries are, the gold
market and the gambling casinos, the political hurly-burly and the
big business shenanigans, newspaper gossip foragers gathering and
dispensing scandal and bright young things seeking to provide it,
Lloyds of London—purveyors of high-class insurance to the world—
and less well-known operations capable of drumming up on-the-
double a battalion of go-anywhere mercenaries. "What a place to
plunder," a German general said admiringly of London as he
scanned the city from St. Paul's Cathedral more than a century ago.
Its attractions are still potent enough to keep one-quarter of the
British population living within an hour-and-a-half of Piccadilly
Circus.

To the visitor, many of London's attractions are immediately
evident. Many of them are already familiar from the movies and
television—Big Ben (which is the bell not the clock) sounding out
the hour across Parliament Square; Westminster Abbey's soaring
spires; Tower Bridge squatting over the Thames; a London policeman in his distinctive helmet ambling down the street (now often
whispering strangely into his cupped hand, actually into the
miniature walkie-talkie with which he keeps in touch with the
police station); the toy-soldier spectacular of the changing of the
guard at Buckingham Palace; double-decker buses merging into
wrong-side-of-the-street traffic; bowler-hatted gents strutting along
keeping perfect time with their furled umbrellas (though bowler
hats, if not umbrellas, have been slipping gracefully out of fashion).
But London doesn't disgorge all its secrets so readily. Some of its
elements require and deserve closer scrutiny.

The Thames, which bisects London, is not one of the world's
great rivers. It doesn't meander across continents like the Amazon
or the Mississippi. It doesn't roar through spectacular cataracts or
thunder down giant waterfalls like the Nile or the Zambesi. It is
only about 200 miles long, rising, not in towering ice-capped
mountain ranges like the Ganges, but in some slightly elevated,
drowsy countryside west of London. Nevertheless, John Masefield
was right to call the Thames "a great street paved with water."

It is the artery which made London a major international port
city and commercial hub and thereby gave the British capital its
special character as a cosmopolitan center. The view from its
downriver bridges is of the city's familiar and pleasing skyline. The
upriver stretches glide through idyllic countryside. It may sound
mushily excessive but it's not altogether inappropriate to invoke
William Wordsworth's salute:

> Glide gently, thus for ever glide
> Oh Thames! that other bards may see
> As lovely visions by thy side
> As now, fair river, come to me.

Though much of its dockland area is drab and uninteresting, the
Thames provides the setting for some of London's more memorable
sights. The Royal Naval College at Greenwich, best seen from the
river, is a masterpiece of monumental architecture, a blending of
splendor and simplicity contrived in an age when such things could
be done. Tower Bridge, with its twin citadels rising high above the
Thames, is a vision of strength and harmony. An austere sight is
the bunker-like Thames-side South Bank complex, a cultural
center *par excellence*, housing the Royal Festival Hall, the National
Theater, the National Film Theater, and other institutions dedicated to the various arts.

Further upstream, past Putney Bridge, bucolic tow paths (so
called because horses towing barges up the river once trudged along
these routes), backed by park land, line much of the Thames as it
winds its way into London through the Thames Valley. On a
Saturday midday each spring, thousands of people line the banks of
the river to watch the historic Oxford-Cambridge boat race (the
losers buy the winners dinner at the Savoy). It is a very British, very
snobbish attraction based on the deservedly exalted reputations of
the two universities. But rarely is the contest an extraordinary
event. More exciting are the proceedings on the river on a March
day each year when some 400 long shells, each manned by eight
toiling rowers and a coxswain, knife through the Thames at ten-
second intervals, racing against the clock to become "Head of the
River." Picturesque riverside pubs, notably those in Hammersmith
and Chiswick or further into the Thames Valley, are pleasant

retreats. On summer days, people take their drinks outside to sit at tables, lean against railings, or lounge on the grass by the river.

There are inevitably tales and curiosities connected with the Thames. There is, for example, Cuckold's Point downstream where, it is said, a certain William Cuckold tied his unfaithful wife to a stool fixed to a long seesaw plank and ducked her into the Thames just long enough not to drown her. It turned into a lucrative profession. Other "cuckolded" husbands were prepared to pay as much as a penny a time to expose their own straying wives to watery retribution aboard Cuckold's dunking stool. At Execution Dock, a spot now marked by a warehouse, villains sentenced for crimes committed aboard ship were hanged at low tide and kept on display there till three Thames tides had washed over their corpses as a warning to potential felons on passing vessels. Among them was the notorious Captain Kidd, executed for piracy but possibly framed by disappointed business backers.

Despite its brownish aspect, a product of the tide churning up sand and mud from its banks and river bed, and litter strewn along some stretches of its bank at low tide, the Thames is a comparatively clean river these days. It is probably the least polluted metropolitan waterway in the world.

It wasn't always like that. Not long ago, not even the sturdiest marine creatures were able to survive in its murky broth. It is recorded that a man who fell into the river twenty-five years ago drowned despite the nearness of his rescuers because they were unable to see him through the frothing layer of waste detergent foam on its surface. More than a century of industrial waste and urban filth had fouled the river so badly that it was a danger to the health of Londoners. Cholera and typhoid epidemics during the nineteenth century were attributed to the foulness of Thames water. Fish, which had once been plentiful in the river, were unable to breathe in it and died out. People marveled at the comment of sixteenth-century chronicler Raphael Hollinshead that, "This noble river, the Thames, yields an infinite plenty of excellent sweet and pleasant fish."

But nothing could be done. Expanding industry had no other convenient outlet for its waste. The introduction of the magnificent luxury of a sewage system to service household toilets and drains further aggravated the situation. "May I inquire," Charles Dickens asked Father Thames in his *Household Words*, "what that black, sluggish stream may be which I see pouring into you from a wide bricked archway, yonder?" "Oh, that is one of my sewers." And the steams sending forth "strange, party-colored currents" to mingle wih Thames water were from "a soap boiler and a slaughter house, the gas works, brewhouses, shot-factories, coal wharfs, cow-houses, tan-pits, gut-spinners, fish markets, and other cheerful and odiferous tributaries."

Little of that is true anymore. Aroused finally to action, Parliament and the London authorities ordered a sharp reduction of industrial discharge into the river as well as vastly improved sewage treatment procedures. As a result, fish have now returned to the Thames: smelt, bass, mullet, herring, conger eel, almost one hundred species recorded so far. Hope is nurtured that the tasty salmon, which once frequented the river in great numbers, might be tempted back as well.

The return of the fish has encouraged the return also of the Thames angler. On weekends, and often on other days as well, fishermen can be seen perched on river banks or leaning on balustrades of upstream Thames bridges, away from the midtown hubbub, their lines dangling in the flowing stream. They can sometimes also be seen further down river, even on the bank facing the Tate Gallery, making London the only metropolis where city-center angling is practiced.

Between 8:45 and 9:15 each morning, a half million people converge on a smallish patch of central London crisscrossed by a labyrinth of narrow streets, canyons winding through a forest of tall, somber buildings. At five each evening, that same army of transients, moving a touch more quickly, begins a massive exodus from the area, leaving it largely abandoned overnight. This is "The City," the confusingly nicknamed commercial center of Britain, the "square mile" in which there is the greatest concentration of international money markets, commodity markets, and financial services in the world. The world's leading banks (Moscow Narodny Bank has a staff of more than 200) have offices in The City. So do the major insurance and shipping companies. The Bank of England is here as is the London stock market, the country's major law firms, and everything else which contributes to making London so important a business center.

The City is, in effect, one vast betting parlor where, as one observer noted, "Nothing is made but money." Bets of one kind or another are placed by its banks, in its stock exchange, and through its commodity markets and insurance houses on events occurring everywhere—in the mines and factories or countries the world over, aboard ships on the high seas, on planes in the air, in banks all over the globe. A shortfall or bumper year in copper production in Zambia, a frost-damaged coffee crop in Brazil, or the discovery of a new vein of gold in Transvaal can shift the odds. A tanker breaking apart off the coast of Japan or a Latin American government revising its tariff policies can do the same.

The failure of a bank in Atlanta or Ascona shoots adrenalin through the business veins of The City where specialists are equipped to decide quickly whether to fight or run for cover. The overthrow of a government in the Middle East or a purge of political leaders in an Eastern European country has City pundits reviewing the implications, the investments, the possible losses or gains for their clients, and what their next moves should be.

Bankers, government officials, and business potentates everywhere check developments in The City each morning to see how the world is doing, knowing of course that what might be happening to the British domestic economy does not necessarily reflect what is happening in London's "square mile." At a time when the British economy was under severe strain, with unemployment rolls pushed to their highest levels in five decades and companies forced to the wall all over the country, billions of dollars of "hot" money were flooding into The City in search of profits which City specialists devote their considerable talents and energies to unearthing. Not for nothing was it to The City of London that both the United States and Iran turned when intricate financial details had to be hastily worked out for the release of the American hostages the Iranians had seized in 1979.

The day-to-day activities of The City reflect a strange mélange of moods. In the huge hall which serves as the underwriting room at Lloyd's of London, the largest international insurance market in the world, where almost any conceivable insurance risk can be covered for a price, the atmosphere is of brisk professionalism.

Somberly clad underwriters sit in their "boxes," which are more like pews than desks, examining papers, speaking into telephones, or consulting colleagues with whom they are involved in co-insurance schemes. It is, usually, all very calm and unruffled. In the center of the hall, a clerk records serious marine losses with a quill and sounds a bell (salvaged from a ship that went down 200 years ago) when important information arrives—one strike for bad news, two strikes for good.

Lloyd's clerks, wearing livery, are called *waiters*, a term derived from the origin of the organization, and many other City institutions, in a London coffee house some 300 years ago. In the seventeenth century, marine insurers and shippers gathered to do their deals at Edward Lloyd's Coffee House on Tower Street. Man's Coffee House near Charing Cross was frequented at the time by stockjobbers. Bank clerks met at certain coffee houses to exchange checks, making such establishments the first banking clearing houses of The City. A surviving relic of old-time informal meeting places is Henekey's Long Bar on High Holborn. In its discreet cubicles, lawyers would meet their clients in an age before lawyer's offices became proper and fashionable places for the practice of legal matters.

In contrast to the beehive orderliness of the Lloyd's underwriting hall today, the *ring* at London's Metal Exchange seems utter chaos. Dealers sit at first on benches in what seems to be a magic circle, silently examining their notes, conferring quietly with colleagues, or slipping briefly away to check facts and figures over the phone. But when dealing begins, pandemonium erupts. These highly skilled metal merchants (employing professional codes and code signs) shout and gesticulate at each other like lunatics as they go about buying and selling zinc, copper, and other non-ferrous metals. In the process, they set the world prices for these metals.

The twice-daily London "gold fixing" is still another contrasting image in the workings of The City. In a tasteful, wood-panelled room at Rothschild's Bank, five dapper gold dealers, representing London's five major gold dealing companies, meet at mid-morning and mid-afternoon. They sit at separate desks facing each other. Each holds a telephone with which he determines from his company's dealers the latest selling and buying action elsewhere. With this information, the five men agree on a gold price, then return to their own offices until the next fixing. Voices are not raised. No serious negotiation is involved. They are simply using their experience to "fix" what the market has already recorded in a less organized fashion.

It has been charged that The City, with its countless daily transactions involving hundreds of millions and sometimes billions of dollars, is vulnerable to all sorts of unethical and even unlawful practices. A Takeover and Mergers Panel was established a little more than a decade ago to deal with possible improprieties in big stock market transactions. The City police force has a highly professional fraud squad continually engaged in seeking out illegal behavior in other aspects of City activity. The London stock exchange has rules and regulations and there are codes of practice to which City men are expected to adhere and to which, for the most part, they do adhere. But there is no equivalent to the American Securities and Exchange Commission to guard investors and the general public against the danger of hocus-pocus in the world of high finance in London even though the sums involved might be astronomical.

Nor is there any formal mechanism, other than the courts, for dealing with possible transgressions in The City, and the courts rarely can call in financial minds of sufficient expertise to understand exactly what has transpired. The City prefers to deal with such situations itself but its methods of doing so are open to criticism. While it will methodically freeze out a financial newcomer who has engaged in sharp or shady practice, an established City operator who steps out of line can usually avoid unpleasant repercussions provided he makes good his transgressions and doesn't make a habit of it. The City has closed ranks more than once around its own in recent times. More than one City man who has tried to play fast and loose in London's corridors of finance has reemerged like a phoenix to become a worthy and influential pillar of financial respectability, prepared to come to the aid of other established City men who have momentarily transgressed. It's who you are that counts in such circumstances.

Company take-over irregularities in the past, the damaging, speculative buying and selling of companies, false prospectuses, and other questionable, though sometimes legal activities today seem to call for the establishment of a watchdog body to guarantee against improprieties. City men insist, however, that no such thing is needed, not in London. They say tighter procedures and scrutiny would damage The City which functions so well partly because of the speed and informality of its dealings.

If a City man's words were no longer enough to guarantee a deal, if presentations always had to be made to boards of directors and credit facilities had to be checked, if motives had to be examined, time would be consumed and the projected deal would often no longer be worth making. City men claim that if those tighter restrictions were imposed, London would lose its wheeler-dealer facilities which, despite Britain's declining status among the nations of the world, sustains the capital city's position as a vibrant force in international finance and commerce. City men concede that their influence depends as much on world confidence in them as it does in their skills. They warn that excessive meddling by a watchdog outside their control might prod irresponsible people into saying things about them which could undermine that confidence. The less said by outsiders, the better.

Maybe; maybe not!

The City is where London began. In 43 A.D., invading Romans, having landed on England's southeast coast, pinpointed a place where they could negotiate a comparatively easy crossing of the Thames to continue their conquest of Britain and their triumph over its Celtic inhabitants. They built a settlement there and that settlement soon grew into the thriving town of Londinium which the historian Tacitus described as a "busy emporium for trade and traders." It had its Roman temples, basilicas, forums, bath houses, and neatly laid-out streets. It had its Roman officials and Romanized Britons and remained a major imperial center the better part of four centuries.

Bits and pieces of the formidable wall the Romans built around Londinium remain. But little is known of the fate of the city after the Roman withdrawal, when the Roman Empire was disintegrating, until the Vikings showed up to sack London about five centuries later. It seems likely, however, that if the city had been abandoned and left to decay, it was also subsequently rebuilt into something marauding Vikings considered worth burning down.

By the time William the Conquerer beat the Anglo-Saxon rulers of Britain into submission in the eleventh century, the people of London had developed the impressive reputation for independence and defiance they have regularly exhibited since then. ("London can take it!" was the answer to German bombers which blasted the city in the Second World War.) Among William's first acts was to assure Londoners that their existing rights and privileges would be guaranteed under his rule. He then wisely set about constructing a fortress (now the core of the Tower of London) as much to intimidate the good burghers of the city and dissuade them from rebellion as to watch downriver for possible seaborne rivals for the English crown.

But until Victorian times, London was rarely a peaceful city. Where it was not bounded by the Thames, it was protected in the Middle Ages by high walls with gates which were bolted at curfew time each night and kept bolted until reveille. There was a night watch to ward off anyone who might try to penetrate the city for evil purposes before dawn's early light. But inside the city walls, mayhem was habitual. An observer reported that it was a common practice "that a hundred or more in a company, young and old, would make nightly invasions upon the houses of the wealthy, to the intent to rob them; and if they found any man stirring in the city within the night that were not of their crew, they would presently murder him."

In the seventeenth century, London was described as "a city of squalor and darkness. Most of the thoroughfares were without pavements of any kind and such as existed were so sunken and broken that they were a source of danger to those who stumbled along them; rubbish was shot out of upper windows into the street beneath and the public squares were used as receptacles for all the filth of the neighborhood. After nightfall the certainty of having to encounter drunken bullies and highway robbers confined to their houses those citizens whom urgent business did not compel to walk abroad; even in daylight there were districts where peace officers dared not venture."

Highwaymen were so bold that they stuck notices on the doors of rich people warning them for their safety not to travel about without carrying sufficient sums of money and watches of which they would be relieved. In his history of the police in England, Melville Lee wrote of street gangs whose "way is to meet people in the streets and stop them, and begin to banter them, and if they make any answer, they lay on them with sticks and toss them from one to another in a very rude manner." Sir Robert Walpole, the first prime minister of England, was mugged in Hyde Park in broad daylight in 1736.

Amidst this bedlam of lawlessness and squalor, a different kind of London emerged. During the late Middle Ages, craft guilds had emerged to dominate London's politics and economy and would do so for centuries to come. Those guilds were closed shops formed to protect their members from competition and generally to promote their interests. Vestiges of those organizations survive today in the eighty-nine ceremonial "livery companies" still active in The City, including the Apothecaries, Barbers, Distillers, Haberdashers, Saddlers, Weavers, Merchant Taylors, and Wax Chandlers. Some still have elaborate halls, including such notable London landmarks as the Ironmongers Hall, Goldsmiths' Hall, and Fishmongers Hall. Their present-day members, when not gainfully engaged in the much more modern money-making institutions of The City, find time to devote themselves to good works for charity, schools, and noble causes in general and strutting around in their traditional livery on ceremonial occasions.

The ordinary folk of London, periodically enraged by excessive taxes, lawlessness, and religious controvesy, from time to time frightened the city fathers into action to remedy their grievances. But usually the commercial interests of the guilds and other City institutions predominated. To this day, each autumn, a week after the new Lord Mayor of London is installed, the prime minister testifies to the continuing clout of The City by journeying to Guildhall, the venerable center of City of London government, to fill assembled City dignitaries in on the government's intentions for the year ahead.

The London Museum was opened a few years ago to provide Londoners and visitors from elsewhere with an elaborate guide to the history of the British capital. It is an excellent showplace, one of the city's most diverting spectacles. In one sense, however, the museum is redundant. London is itself a museum. It is dotted with bits and pieces retrieved from ancient times, salvaged from the mists of medieval obscurity or retained from the days of British imperial splendor.

A remnant of original wall which encircled Roman Londinium

can be seen through a picture window of the museum on a street appropriately called London Wall. Most of Westminster Abbey dates back to the brooding Gothic intensity of seven centuries ago. A hundred years before that, King Henry I, an early critic of traffic congestion, decreed that London streets be broad enough for sixteen knights to ride abreast along them, or for one loaded cart to be able to pass another without damage to either. The narrow lanes that wind through some parts of what remains of medieval city planning reveal how little effect the good king's decree had.

Many of London's streets bear names identifying the trade or craft that predominated in the area—Bread Street, Woolgate, Milk Street, Poultry, Apothecary Street. Pudding Lane was where butchers once dumped their "puddings"—the inedible entrails of animals. The Great Fire of London which practically obliterated the city in 1666 began in Pudding Lane and was finally brought under control at Pie Corner, prompting a local moralist to suggest at the time that the blaze had been God's punishment for the sin of gluttony exhibited by his fellow Londoners.

Pall Mall, lined today with wall-to-wall gentlemen's club palaces and office blocks, had previously been an expanse of grass where the forerunner of croquet, a game called "paille maille," was played. Piccadilly, London's most famous street, leading into Piccadilly Circus, was named after "piccadillies" which were stiff, frilled collars, the height of fashion for both men and women in Elizabethan times and sold in the vicinity. The Strand, a bustling artery feeding traffic into Trafalgar Square (which is named after a British naval victory), was in fact really a *strand* (shore) of the River Thames. Land was reclaimed from the river and built upon where cars and buses now get bottled up in traffic congestion. The famous Savoy Hotel on the Strand stands on what once was several feet of water. Mayfair, the London district noted for its luxury hotels, smart restaurants, and fashionable offices and apartments, was open countryside where the May Fair was held to welcome the coming of spring each year centuries ago. It was also considered a notoriously lewd place, a hangout for libertines and others of questionable character. Again today, London police are concerned about the number of ladies of the night who ply their trade on the now fashionable streets of Mayfair.

Few vestiges remain today of London high-society life for which the British capital was once renowned. Very rarely does a member of the royal family or a senior blueblood put in an appearance at Annabel's, Wedgies, or other fashionable nightclubs. It's not really their cup of tea (though there are indications that Queen Elizabeth's second son, Prince Andrew, may turn out to be a man about town).

Now that the British movie industry has practically collapsed because of financial pressures, union trouble, and resulting inability to compete with Hollywood, screen stars are also no longer much in evidence on the London scene, except when passing through for location shots, to make television appearances, or en route somewhere else. A handful of would-be exclusive nightspots succeed each other in vogue among what's left of the British end of the international set. But for the most part, the gossip columnists of the *Daily Mail* and *Daily Express* have no easy task titillating their readers with a steady supply of tidbits about the rich and famous.

The days of the debutantes is gone for good. Until about thirty years ago, an upper-class girl reaching the age of eighteen "came out." That was her only purpose in life at that age. She plunged into the social whirl of the London "season," a hectic romp with a ball or two, or a party or two every night. She was "presented" to the queen at Buckingham Palace, an assembly-line event for many dozens of debs, each of whom had spent weeks practicing how to avoid being clumsy getting out of the car in their gowns, walking in a dignified fashion up stairs, curtseying and backing out of the queen's presence without bumping or tripping over things. Queen Elizabeth put an end to that charade in 1956 by which time it had begun to seem foolish even to those who participated.

The main function of the season was to provide debutantes with an opportunity to encounter suitable, eligible young men. It was an undisguised marriage market as well as a long-established ritual of the patrician class. No self-respecting person who valued his or her position in society could afford to miss it.

Shortly before the first of May, when the season began, high-society families would abandon their stately country homes and converge on their less grand but equally well appointed dwellings in London's Mayfair or Belgravia districts, having sent the appropriate servants on ahead to revive those town houses from their undisturbed winter slumber.

The season was punctuated by a series of events, occasions, and diversions which everyone-who-was-anyone felt obliged to attend or participate in and which most of them enjoyed largely because of the social distinction and class identity conferred or confirmed. One was with one's own kind. There was the season-opening private view of the art exhibition at the Royal Academy on Piccadilly, opera at Covent Garden, morning horseback rides or promenades along Hyde Park's Rotten Row, the annual Eton-Harrow cricket match, the regatta at Henley, horse racing at Royal Ascot. Social climbers couldn't consider themselves successes unless they were at all of those, as well as at the right balls and parties—and accepted by others who were casually in the swim by right and tradition.

During the season, there would be much leaving of calling cards and making of the appropriate contacts in order to guarantee invitations to all important society dos, though only those who could reciprocate at their own London town houses, and had the proper social credentials, could be certain of climbing onto the May-to-July merry-go-round. This was a very closed society of perhaps 3,000 families. Only at the beginning of this century were the rules relaxed to permit the invitation of a few of the most distinguished individuals from outside the patrician class. Not until after the Second World War were people whose only credentials were recently acquired wealth able to penetrate this upper-class frolic, by which times the girls themselves had grown weary of the marriage-market milieu and had begun doing peculiar things like going to universities (a practice which had previously been dismissed as "frightfully brainy") or getting jobs.

The season, like everything else about aristocratic living, depended enormously on servants. When the families descended on London, they sent ahead, or brought with them, their butlers, grooms, maids, coachmen, governesses, nannies, and all the rest of the help they required to make life comfortable. It has been estimated that early this century, 15 percent of London's work force were domestic servants. The world wars changed all that, sending men to the battlefields and women to the factories. The transformation of the servant situation made the demise of the London season inevitable. An elderly female blueblood, looking back on the old days, noted, "One was always served. There is no service today."

SIX

The Other Britons

IT IS NOT ALWAYS EASY for people looking on from afar—or for visitors passing through—to grasp the extent to which regional differences persist in Britain. Vestiges of the past cling tenaciously in quaint corners of the countryside: the official hornblower sounding off in the market square of the Yorkshire town of Ripon at nine each night to assure the townsfolk that all's well; midsummer night bonfires in Cornwall; morris dancing in Oxfordshire. But regional diversities are much more fundamental than that.

Many people do not fully grasp the significance of the fact that Britain consists of three distinct countries—England, Scotland, and Wales. (The United Kingdom, which is a larger entity, includes troubled Northern Ireland as well.) Though more than four-fifths of the population are English and though English ways predominate, Britain's other component parts have clearly defined, distinguishing traits and reputations. In some places, people strive desperately against the odds to retain those identifying marks and keep from being absorbed into the English melting pot.

The people of Scotland, for example, take great pride in being very different from the English. There are those among the Scots (usually only foreigners call them Scotch) who are convinced that the Act of Union between Scotland and England, signed almost three centuries ago after hundreds of years of conflict between the two countries, should never have happened. Scottish nationalists assert that by accepting that merger, Scotland surrendered its independent identity and, despite its rich heritage, gained little in return. By rights, they say, even though it has a population of only five million, about the same as greater Philadelphia, Scotland should be a separate nation today, master of its own fate, like Holland or Belgium. They nurture the sentiments contained in the fourteenth-century Declaration of Arbroath: "For so long as a hundred men survive, we will never in any way submit to the domination of the English." They point out with occasional bitterness that British North Sea oil comes mostly from the waters off Scotland and claim that it is, therefore, Scotland which is keeping the rest of Britain from going bankrupt.

Scottish members of Parliament generally belong to the Conservative or Labor parties or other all-British political movements. But from time to time, the Scottish nationalist movement arouses a surge of popular support and manages to send a representative or two to the House of Commons where they devote most of their energies to decrying English treatment of the Scottish nation which, despite everything, still exists as a unique and recognizable entity. Nor is its uniqueness dependent on such stereotyped Scottish trademarks as playing bagpipes, wearing kilts (which few Scots still do, many considering them frivolous and ostentatious garments), eating haggis (the ground innards of a sheep mixed with oatmeal and boiled in an extracted sheep's stomach—an acquired taste, if you're lucky), and drinking the local hard liquor (which, unlike the people, may be called Scotch instead of Scottish but which people in Britain generally refer to simply as "whiskey"—an abbreviation of a Gaelic expression meaning "water of life").

There are still much more significant distinctive Scottish institutions: a legal system which is different from that of the English; a Scottish currency (though English money is equally acceptable); an established Church of Scotland (Presbyterian, though its head is Queen Elizabeth, who is also head of the Episcopalian Church of England); a Scottish language (Gaelic) which, however, is spoken only by a small fraction of the Scottish people. Scottish children, beneficiaries of an educational system superior to that of England, know all about the fourteenth-century battle of Bannockburn in which their king, Robert the Bruce, decisively vanquished the English and, for a time, guaranteed Scottish independence. They also know all about Flodden and Culloden, subsequent battles in which the outnumbered Scots were slaughtered by the English. If they forget, the English, who tend to nurse their guilt feelings about past transgressions, remind them with superb television reenactments and graphic literary reconstructions.

Nevertheless, the history of hostility between the English and the Scots has left a residue of antagonism. "Once there was a Scotsman," begins a joke told south of the border, "and now there are millions of the bastards." The most common impression English people have about Scots is that they are misers. According to a cockney quip, a Scotsman is a person who "keeps the Sabbath and everything else he can lay his hands on." But though the church—the *kirk*—has played an important role in the development of Scottish life and character, to picture the Scots as parsimonious humbugs and mean-minded people is not only unjust and untrue, it blinds people to what they really are like.

Many Scots do indeed tend to be solemn, dour, and taciturn. The Scottish writer Albert Mackie has noted that while most people think of the English as cold and remote, "to the Scots, the English appear gushing and sentimental." This Scottish severity has too often been misinterpreted as stinginess. A person miserly with his feelings is thought unlikely to be generous with anything else.

However, Scottish frugality has an altogether different origin and dimension. As a people with a history of sustained poverty, the Scots nourish tribal memories of thrift, extracting value for what little money and other resources were available. In that respect, they are distinctly canny. But if value is there, a Scotsman is as likely as anyone to be willing to pay for it, and to do so ungrudgingly. Perhaps because they are not squeamish in dealing with money matters, the Scots are more capable than most people of distinguishing between good and better, between bad and worse when things are bought and sold. What upsets the English is that they are not subtle about it, that they see no moral defect in openly showing their inclinations when such embarrassing matters crop up.

The Scots exhibit a firm, uninhibited sense of proportion on questions of monetary value. It contributes to making a visit among them a sometimes curious and always interesting experience. A butcher shop in Perth is the only such establishment I've ever seen where the butcher advised a woman shopper that a cheaper beef he had on display was just as good and possibly better than the more expensive cut she had asked for. Edinburgh is the only city in which the owner of a store (a fruit store) ever strongly advised me not to buy something he was selling (a pineapple) because he felt it wasn't worth what he was obliged to charge for it.

Such discriminating judgment is not confined exclusively to value for money. Scottish slowness of speech is commonly matched by quickness of mind and strength of conviction. The shortfall of small talk among the Scots usually means that whatever they do say is, if not necessarily interesting, at least to the point. They find sophistication, convoluted logic, or grandiloquence deeply suspicious. They equate such frippery with fancy packaging for goods of little worth. Their brisk nature often conceals an unwitting dry humor. A Scotsman giving no-nonsense, insistent, "do-as-I-say!" directions to a driver who has gone lost in the Highlands can put on a hilarious show (unless the recipient intimidates easily) though the man would be deeply offended if the beneficiary of those directions presumed even to smile. Levity is a moral failing. The Scots don't take things lightly. It was altogether appropriate for "Scotty" to be chosen chief engineer of the "Star Trek" space ship Enterprise.

While Scots may nurse a disdain for the "soft" English, the English reciprocate in a strange way. Aside from libeling them as skinflints and being vexed by their bluntness, they have developed a grudging regard for Scots and particularly for self-possessed, self-respecting Scottish mannerisms. A great many Scots have distinguished themselves in English society. The English medical profession and business world have always numbered strayed Scotsmen among their most accomplished practitioners. Among their many illustrious compatriots were James Watt, inventor of the steam engine; John MacAdam, pioneer in road surfacing techniques; John Napier, inventor of logarithms; Kirkpatrick MacMillan, inventor of the bicycle; Sir William Ramsay, who discovered helium; Adam Smith, who founded the science of political economy; Sir Alexander Fleming, who discovered penicillin; and Alexander Graham Bell, who had something of an idea of what the telephone was all about before he emigrated to America to invent it there.

One of every three British prime ministers in this century has been of Scottish origin. British military men greatly value the spirit and fighting skills of such elite Scottish regiments as the Argyll and Sutherland Highlanders, the Black Watch, and the Scots Guards.

Though the Scottish contribution has been impressive in so many professions and endeavors, there is another Scottish stereotype, the butt of many a joke and one which which arouses considerably less admiration. When the hard-drinking, belligerent, shabbily attired "Jock" descends on London for major soccer matches involving Scottish teams, pubs near playing fields and in the center of London bolt their doors and board up their windows. Drunkenness—a pathological fondness for drink—is particularly rampant in Scottish industrial centers. The story is told of the man from Glasgow who, while carrying a bottle of whiskey, the contents of which he and a friend had liberally been knocking back, slipped, fell to the ground and felt a spreading wetness around the pocket where the bottle was. "Och, Jimmie!" he cried in despair to his friend, "I hope it's blood."

The ugly and tragic consequences of drunkenness and abstemious religious traditions have collaborated to turn Glasgow into a center for a dynamic temperance movement as well. Arriving parched at a small Glasgow hotel at midnight one day, I was refused a room until I convinced the desk clerk that though I had asked if there was something to drink, I was perfectly happy to settle for a glass of water. Breakfast the next morning came with friendly but firm warnings about the perils of boozing.

Glasgow, with its half million population, is Scotland's biggest city. It is also its toughest and most outrageous place, Britain's crime capital, and a city where religious animosities have for many people turned into a way of life. About half the population is Catholic, mostly Irish immigrants or their Glasgow-born descendants. (Ireland is just a few hours away by ferry.) Almost all of the others are Protestants of Scottish origin. Most Glaswegians are easy-going people. They boast of the contrast between their own warmth and openness and the gloomy aloofness of other Scots and English people. But there are enough of the more bellicose sort on both sides of the religious divide to sustain perpetual hostility, the mindlessness of which was once immortalized by the Glaswegian who declared "There are two things I can't stand—religious intolerance and Catholics." Religious hatred is most forcefully expressed in the bitter rivalry of the fans of the city's two major professional soccer teams—Celtics (backed by Catholic fans) and Rangers (Protestant). Charges have been made on television and elsewhere that the Rangers management believes that the religious antagonism promotes attendance at the games and has, therefore, not done as much as it could to try to tone down the often bloody clashes in the stands or outside the stadium. Each contest between the two teams is as much a religious war as a sporting event, with the ever-present threat of violence among the fans. Glaswegian writer Clifford Hanley has commented wryly, "The truly dedicated fan is throwing his bottle or removing his neighbor's incisors not merely in sport but to the greater glory of God. We don't go in for religious apathy like some people."

Glaswegians—of both a violent and peaceful disposition—do not think much of their fellow Scots in Edinburgh, the Scottish capital two hours away by car. They consider Edinburghers miserly cold fish, despicably would-be English with their superior airs and unsociability. The people of Edinburgh are, in turn, contemptuous of Glasgow, considering it a home of boorish, unbridled, and embarrassing vandals who, through some tragic error, also happen to be Scots. While parts of inner Glasgow are distinguished by magnificent Victorian architecture and tasteful parks, the city is far better known for its crime-ridden slums. Edinburgh, on the other hand, is, aside from being a beautiful city, a place of great dignity, exuding solidity, orderliness, and purpose. This is the city of John Knox whose zeal, stern ethical codes, and oratorical skills were the centerpiece of the puritanical Protestant reformation in Scotland in the sixteenth century. It is also the city where native son Robert Louis Stevenson set his tale about *Dr. Jekyll and Mr. Hyde*, the pre-Freudian study of how good and evil can reside in a single individual, a hint of the dark secrets that might lie lurking even in a place as proper as Edinburgh.

Whatever secrets once may have lurked in the back streets of Scotland's third largest city are now irrelevant. It is impossible to predict what will finally become of Aberdeen, Scotland's (and Europe's) oil capital. In the decade or so since North Sea oil riches were confirmed, tens of thousands of new Aberdonians have helped transform this serene, granite port city of the far north into a thriving community, replete with steel-and-glass edifices, dormitory suburbs, and a general boom atmosphere. Some old Aberdonians are not happy with the drift of things but it's hard these days for anyone seriously to speak slightingly of prosperity when there's so little of it around anywhere else in the country.

Though more elevated and undulating than most of the rest of Britain, the southern half of Scotland, including Edinburgh,

Glasgow, some fine stretches of farmland and picturesque touring country, is called the Lowlands. The northern Highlands are a land within a land—one of the last easily accessible great wildernesses in the world. This is a place of wild, craggy landscapes, deep brooding lochs, haunting glens, and primeval wooded gorges. The Highlands are lonely, remote, and magnificent, the mountains there mesmerizingly folding behind one another, backdrop behind backdrop, on and on into the horizon. The sight can be breathtaking.

This is the home of red deer, shaggy Highland cattle, the elusive wildcat, the soaring eagle, and mighty salmon plunging through clear, rapidly flowing streams. Out of tourist season, snow permitting, you can drive for hours along Highland roads without passing another car. In season, the Highlands are a magnet for people seeking the mysteries of raw nature but the region is big enough to make congestion rare. Over much of northernmost Scotland there are no roads at all and, if you're so inclined, you can walk forever across its bracing expanses without encountering another person.

This is a realm once inhabited by mountain clans and ruled by clan chieftains who exercised the power of life and death over all within their remote domains. For centuries, Lowlanders were as fearful of these rugged, fierce Highlanders as people south of the border once were of Scots in general. The ancient Romans, who had managed to push their way deep into the Lowlands during their occupation of Britain, finally gave up trying to rule the untamable Highlanders, pulled back and built Hadrian's Wall clear across the country—fifteen feet high, at least eight feet thick, with garrisoned fortresses every mile—to keep them at bay. Its remains can be seen today near the English-Scottish border.

Clan chieftains once were lords in the service of the Scottish king in Edinburgh. But no Lowland monarch could hope to retain control of the Highlands for long. Local chieftains grasped absolute power for themselves and defied all outsiders to do something about it.

Each Highland clan occupied a reasonably well-defined turf but regularly skirmished with neighboring clans. Quarrels were even more enduring than hillbilly family feuds in the mountains of Kentucky a while back. (Daniel Boone's origins were Scotch-Irish.) Loyalty to the clan and to the "laird" were the key obligations of these tough mountain folk. But the battlefield defeat of united clans by the English in 1745 heralded the end of their way of life. Wearing kilts and speaking Gaelic were forbidden by English overlords. Though these prohibitions were later lifted, fundamental and long-lasting changes were in the making—or already made. The Scots were a defeated people and many of their lairds followed up on that military disaster on Culloden Moor (the last pitched battle between armies on British soil) by perpetrating an even greater defeat on their own followers. They recruited gangs of strong-arm thugs to expel Highland folk from their ancestral lands. They realized that if they depopulated this vast region, they could amass fortunes by letting sheep graze freely over the countryside. It has euphemistically been called "the clearances."

Financial pressures have since induced Scottish aristocrats to sell off parts of their huge estates. But they still own vast underpopulated expanses of the country. The clearances and hard times drove large numbers of Scots off in search of more tolerable circumstances elsewhere. People of Scottish descent in the United States, Canada, Australia, and New Zealand have long outnumbered those living in Scotland itself—by five-to-one, according to a recent estimate.

It is said that if you stand on a street corner in a city in Wales and for no particular reason shout, "Yes!," at least ten people you've never seen before, much less spoken to, will shout back, "No!" The rules of reserve which apply for most other parts of Britain have no place among the Welsh. They are spontaneous, defiant, articulate, and eternally willing to expres firm convictions. It is not that they are reflexively argumentative, though many an Englishman will contend that they are. It is more their profound reluctance to squelch either the fact of their presence or their compulsion to sound off. Dylan Thomas, the best known of modern Welsh poets, expertly displayed their extraordinary fondness for and skill with the music of words:

> I was born in a large Welsh town . . . an ugly, lovely town, or so it was and is to me; crawling, sprawling by a long and splendid curving shore where truant boys and old men from nowhere beachcombed, idled, and paddled, watched the dock-bound ships or the ships steaming away into wonder and India, magic and China, countries bright with oranges and loud with lions. . . .

There are few more stirring sounds in all the British Isles than that of a Welsh choir, voices raised in effortless harmony, singing the Welsh anthem, *Land of My Fathers*:

> *The land of my fathers is dear unto me,*
> *Old land where minstrels are honored and free;*
> *Its valiant defenders so gallant and brave,*
> *For freedom their life's blood they gave.*

Neither the words (which I'm told lose far too much in translation from Welsh) nor the quality of the singing tells the whole story. The pride and patriotism carry a strong burden of sorrow and regret because, unlike Scotland where national identity is defiantly flourished despite the preponderance of the English and English influence in all of Britain, the grandeur of Welsh culture seems increasingly to be a thing of the past, a recollection, a relic.

Not that all distinctive Welsh traits are disappearing. The people of Wales remain more open, more accessible, more prone to let off steam than other Britons. They will speak or sing, laugh or fulminate at the slightest provocation. Their celebrated music and poetry *eisteddfods* (the word means "sessions") are highly competitive festivals. They begin as local events, with winners going on to regional competitions. The winners there meet at a annual national eisteddfod, one of the major events on the Welsh calendar, which combines high-caliber talent with substantial doses of exhibitionism. (An impromptu sing-song of local men in a pub I popped into in Llangollen one night outshone the high quality of choirs participating in the national eisteddfod then in progress in that delightful Welsh city.)

Unlike the English, who prefer their most popular spectator sports, soccer and cricket, to be without body contact and with little possibility of injury, the Welsh are famous for their passion for the rough, punishing game of rugby in which players can get seriously hurt, though dirty play involving deliberate efforts to disable other players is considered despicable. Aside from specific penalties for such behavior, it can earn a perpetrator the cold shoulder even from his own teammates.

Unlike the Scots who are precise and mechanically minded, the Welsh are people of soaring imagination, outlandish perceptions, and extravagant behavior. Their best known sons tend to be models of some or all of those traits, such men as Dylan Thomas, Lawrence of Arabia, spellbinding orator Lloyd George who was British prime minister during the dark days of World War I, composer Vaughan Williams, Nye Bevan, who formulated the British National Health Service, and flamboyant actor Richard Burton.

There aren't very many Welsh people. Fewer than three million of them inhabit an area half as big as Switzerland, poking out into the Irish Sea west of England. Other than a few signposts, there is no visible border between England and Wales. As a traveler ventures deeper into the Welsh countryside, however, distinctive features become apparent. The country's pretty towns, gentle landscapes, verdant valleys, and craggy risings radiate a gentle comeliness, accentuated and enlivened by the audacious friendliness of the people and musical lilt of their accents (which can, however, grow abrasive when points are pressed too hard. A leading British trade union official, a man whose particularly strong Welsh twang is frequently heard on radio and television, is sometimes referred to as "Mr. Shrill.").

In southern Wales, there's a grim, uninviting belt of heavy industry—coal mines, steel works, oil refineries—and of people with deeply lined faces who have seen bad times too often. When the British economy is on the rocks, this area is invariably in the vanguard of those who suffer. There have also been other dismal consequences for the industrial landscape of this part of Wales. In 1966, 116 school children and 28 others died when a towering coal tip collapsed on the mining village of Aberfan. Since then, prodigious efforts have been made to eliminate such ugly and hazardous blights and reclaim the land which they disfigured.

The most attractive and inviting part of Wales is far away from the mines and plants. It's in northern Wales, particularly in Snowdonia National Park with its scraggy terrain and deep blue lakes, wild horned goats and polecats. It's an area of great scenic beauty and would rival Switzerland as a tourist attraction if it didn't rain there so much. This is the part of the country where a good portion of the people still speak Welsh, "the language of heaven," thereby guarding what remains of the Welsh heritage.

Among the many militant and sometimes violent nationalistic movements in the world, the Welsh Language Society is hardly a contender for international headline coverage. But though small and comparatively unknown, it is an active, far from timid organization which uses its well-publicized strivings to save the ancient Welsh language from extinction as its main weapon for arousing the sagging national feelings of the people of Wales. It is not an easy job. Only a small fraction of the Welsh—one-fifth perhaps—still speak Welsh. The Welsh National Party, *Plaid Cymru*, has had very limited success in its campaign to elect members of Parliament. (As in Scotland, most Welsh parliamentarians belong to all-British political parties. In Wales, because of its history of economic woes, they're mostly Labor Party men.) Violent acts, such as burning down English-owned holiday homes in remote corners of the Welsh countryside, draws some attention but generates no panic. Most Welsh deplore such vandalism and, when they bother at all, confine expressions of their national feelings to less dramatic actions, like pasting stickers on their car bumpers saying, "Keep Wales Tidy. Dump Your Rubbish in England."

But the predominance of English culture has been a fact in Wales for a long time. Most people there appear content to speak English rather than Welsh, to read English rather than Welsh newspapers and books, and to watch English rather than Welsh television programs. A hunger-strike victory for a leading Welsh nationalist who had demanded more time for Welsh language TV could serve ultimately to undermine his noble cause. If, despite that victory, viewer ratings for Welsh-language programs remain low (a distinct possibility), indifference from most of his compatriots to the cause of a Welsh revival would be undeniable.

The feelings of the English and the Welsh toward each other are not as heavily burdened by a history of conflict and confrontation as English-Scottish feelings. As long ago as 1486, the descendant of a Welshman sat on the English throne and established the Tudor dynasty which included such formidable English rulers as Henry VIII and Elizabeth I. Unlike those in Scotland, the Welsh upper classes have been totally Anglicized for centuries, sending their sons to English boarding schools and heartily displaying their loyalty to the crown.

While Welsh nationalists are bitter about the English cultural incursions into their countries, they are not like the Scots in

resenting English mannerisms. Too many Welshmen—both prominent and humble—display those mannerisms for such a resentment
to be tenable. As for the English, though they tend to consider the
non-Anglicized Welsh to be long-winded, overly emotional, and
presumptuous, they have stopped teaching their children that Taffy
(an old English nickname for a Welshman) is a crook, as expressed
in a once popular nursery rhyme:

> Taffy was a Welshman;
> Taffy was a thief.
> Taffy came to my house,
> And stole a leg of beef.

The Welsh are descendants of tribes of Celts, the first identifiable
people to inhabit the British Isles. They were merged into a nation
by the efforts of Saxon invaders to conquer them and occupy their
land. Their stubborn resistance to the Saxons finally led King Offa,
a Saxon chieftain, to have a deep ditch dug to isolate the irascible
Celtic tribesmen on the far side of it. Remains of Offa's Dyke can
still be seen. It served as a national boundary behind which the
Welsh nation and language evolved, untarnished by the Anglicizing
impact felt elsewhere in Britain.

But the Norman conquerors of England were less timid than their
Saxon predecessors. Despite determined resistance, they fought
their way deep into Wales to begin the destruction of Welsh
independence. Not long after Norman overlords had themselves
been absorbed into the English nation, the beginnings of Welsh
absorption was formalized by the practice of naming the heir to the
English crown the Prince of Wales. (That's still done today. Prince
Charles injected new life into that tradition by spending part of his
college career at a Welsh university and learning to speak some
Welsh.)

A formal Act of Union with England in 1536 accelerated the
process of attrition which had nibbled away at separate Welsh
identity since Norman times. The process has lately been accelerated by the wonders of television. An English soap opera regularly
boasts the highest viewer rating in both Wales and England.

England—the largest and most densely populated of the three
countries of Britain—is divided into a series of counties which are

in turn divided into districts and parishes. But the most striking geographic and cultural division in England is between north and south. It is not an official boundary, nor is it marked by a chain of mountains or any other natural barrier, so it's not always easy to tell where one ends and the other begins. Each person has his own ideas about that, particularly since account should also be taken of a sizable chunk of "midlands"—an industrial heartland—in between.

But so deeply rooted is the north-south divide that prejudice can plunk the barrier line down just about anywhere on the map above London. Many a southerner is convinced that once you've strayed north of the capital city, you aren't really heading anywhere worth going, unless it's to natural beauty spots like the Lake District which are granted special dispensation. At the same time, many a northerner, lured to the capital by its glitter and rewards, considers himself a renegade and doesn't feel cleansed and redeemed until he's back in Rochdale or Bradford telling friends and family about the posh perversities of southern folk.

The north-south cleavage is part of British history. The ancient Romans divided occupied England into two major provinces: the south was under civil administration; the north was under military command. A Roman soldier or official assigned to duty in Britannia preferred to be based in the south where life was civilized and under control rather than in the north where conditions were rugged and you could never tell when even tame locals might turn nasty.

Southerners continue to think of northerners as provincial, uncultured, and boorish. They amuse each other with stories of northern dynamos (the North is a fertile breeding ground for plucky, hard-nosed, self-made entrepreneurs) who amass considerable riches but have only grotesque ideas of what to do with their wealth, like the Oldham businessman who built a countryside mansion for himself and his wife but eats his meals in his shirtsleeves in the kitchen.

Northerners see nothing wrong or comical about a man choosing to take his tea in the kitchen rather than making a show of dining rooms and such stuff when there's no one around to impress. They abhor snobbishness and consider themselves essentially just plain folks. Their politicians make a point of cheering on local soccer teams and popping into local pubs for drinks with the boys in a way that their southern counterparts would consider clownish and beneath their dignity. Northerners see southern derision as typical of the snootiness down South where they hold the people to be false, effete, and devious while they see themselves as straightforward, honest, hard-working (when there's work to be had), and tough. The North is a region of plain, less dandified clothes, stronger beer, and plumper women.

Even Britons who consider themselves immune to prejudice tend to expect a southerner or northerner to behave according to prevailing uncharitable stereotypes, though they are gratified when this does not happen. When asked for his reflexive impressions of the north of England, a Londoner spoke of the charms and beauty of the Yorkshire Dales and other pleasing wonderlands of virtually untouched nature up there. He confessed that he preferred not to think at all about the places where almost all northerners live, the northern cities, most of which are grim, dreary, and uninviting. British national newspapers, which are all London-based, have more reporters covering New York than they have covering all of the North. Mr. Justice Melford Stevenson, a distinguished High Court judge not normally given to irrelevant interjections, said of a defendant in a case he was hearing: "He chose to live in Manchester, a wholly incomprehensible choice for any free human to make."

It was not altogether fair. Manchester has much to commend it. It has two excellent theaters, a deservedly world-famous orchestra, a lively university community (particularly strong on science and technology), some dynamic business leaders and imaginative local government officials. Nevertheless, it is not an interesting city to live in or even walk through. Nor is Leeds, or Newcastle, or Sheffield. Nor are any of the other northern cities which festered into congested activity in the eighteenth and nineteenth centuries when British inventiveness transformed the face and fate of the country and the world by devising the steam engine, the Bessemer converter for steel production, the spinning jenny, and other contrivances and methods for stoking the Industrial Revolution into existence. Despite the vast wealth created in times past, the cities of the North were fated to stagger from recession to depression to austerity the better part of this century as younger, more spirited industrial nations overtook and bypassed Britain.

Hard times have taken their toll in morale and atmosphere.

Despite their shiny new shopping streets (each with rows of identical branches of the same chain stores), their new housing developments and their imposing town halls and civic centers, many of them built when the going was good, they exhude a mood of pointlessness like that which dominated the rows of dreary back-to-back dormitory hovels built for wretchedly paid workers a century ago, some of which are still inhabited.

In some of those cities, public transportation closes down well before midnight. In most it would be impossible to find a restaurant meal worth remembering. In many, passable Indian and Chinese restaurants provide the best the city has to offer. When the North produces gifted writers, actors, and entertainers, they tend to scoot southward where the action is as soon as their talents are recognized. A handful of acclaimed writers and painters who have stubbornly clung to their northern roots are unjustly branded as "professional northerners," a throwback to a few years ago when a northern accent was briefly fashionable in chic London circles and was cultivated even by some born-and-bred southerners.

Northerners grudgingly concede the attractions of the South. But they deride what they consider the phony, frantic aspects of London life. Though only the elderly among them have firm personal recollections of it, grindingly hard work and even more grinding poverty are crucial to their concept of their own history. It adds a fiery, righteous touch when they speak scathingly of degenerate frills and shameful conspicuous consumption in the South. "There's not much fun in the North," a Salford man conceded. But he insisted life there was more genuine, less pretentious, more in contact with the facts of life. In his study of *The North Country*, Graham Turner noted, "To some people who live in the North coming South feels like entering a foreign country."

Until the eighteenth century, northern England was sparsely populated. It was virtually all countryside with few of its cities boasting populations of more than 20,000 people. But within decades of the coming of the Machine Age, country towns were transformed into booming industrial zones, magnets for the folk who abandoned the surrounding countryside where survival had grown increasingly difficult.

New agricultural methods and machinery required the services of far fewer farm laborers. Those who were squeezed out took their families and trudged off to sign on in the "dark, satanic mills," as William Blake called them, and plants of Bradford, Darlington, Wigan, and Jarrow. That's where the only available work was. People turned their backs on the rustic timelessness of their forebears to clock in on time at the shipyards of Liverpool and Newcastle, to go down the mines of Durham and Yorkshire, to keep furnaces roaring full blast in Barnsley and Wolverhampton. Halifax's smoking chimneys earned it the name of "Hell's Cauldron." A clergyman fell asleep while traveling in a carriage at night, awoke while passing a blast furnace shooting out flames and fell to his knees crying, "Not yet, dear God! Please, not yet!"

In this part of the world migrating birds were said to fly backwards to keep the dirt out of their eyes. It was where George Orwell later observed, "You lose yourself in labyrinths of little brick houses blacked by smoke, festering in planless chaos round miry alleys and little cindered yards." The northern cities sold their souls. The factories, mills, and mines which spewed forth the dirt, grime, and fumes became the meaning of life for them. When they were booming things were good. When they were not, people were in trouble.

But even the reassuring stench of hellfire from the thundering furnaces did not ease the presure on northern workingmen. The pool of labor was huge and growing all the time. Wages were low and work conditions were horrendous. A spinner in a cotton mill where interior temperatures soared could be fired for opening a window. Weavers were sometimes required to take part of their pay in contaminated, inedible grain. Managers and foremen kept close watch on all stages of work to see that employees did not relax their labors. Efficiency, as it was then conceived, ruled. "Flaggers" were employed to whip children awake if they fell asleep during their fifteen-hour shifts.

In many places, piecework was the standard system. But when enterprising workers produced more in order to earn more, the rate for the job was slashed. Initiative was thus discouraged. A reflexive distrust, bordering on hatred of employers, managers, and foremen was implanted, becoming a tenacious tribal memory. That's where people should have looked for the causes of seemingly pointless strikes in the North in recent years, mass walkouts tying up whole industries because, for example, a foreman swore at a worker. Efficiency became a dirty word. The boss became the nemesis.

As a trading center since Roman times, London was the money end of northern industriousness. London bankers and businessmen handled the commercial side of the industrial explosion while the people up North produced the goods. Inevitably, northerners resented their southern compatriots. They considered them parasites who, while not getting their own hands dirty or their own thoughts smothered by the soot of factories and mines, lived comfortably off the sweat of those who did. Ignoring the growth of industry in the South as well, they saw southerners as idle and pompous. They saw them engaging in frivolous pursuits grandly called culture and indulging in absurd charades of manners and fashions for which northerners were far too busy creating the wealth of the land and anyway far too genuine to stomach. Northerners knew life was a struggle.

Nevertheless, the North had to rely on the South and the commercial services it could provide. When the North suffered economic setbacks, people there found they were even more dependent than they had imagined. Commercial decisions were reached in the South where the banks and the government had decisive influence when it came to which business or plant would survive in bad times, which areas would suffer the worst unemployment, in which direction government aid or encouragement would be channelled.

During the great depression between the world wars, hunger marches and long parades of the unemployed made their way down to the South—the men advancing in anger, in reproach, in supplication, exhibiting all their wounds and feeling profoundly humiliated in the process. More recently, the unemployed and those threatened by imminent joblessness chartered trains and buses to carry them southward to make their feelings known in London—at Parliament, at 10 Downing Street, at the national headquarters of their employers and of their unions, and to any other southern toff who cared to listen.

The general impression a Londoner had of the North remained no less disparaging. The annals of London theater were overstocked with hilarious comedies about country bumpkins from that part of the world making asses of themselves in London Town. The current equivalent is the southern image of northern workers as lazy good-for-nothings who want to be paid for doing nothing now that their great days of heavy industry have been preempted by the Japanese, Koreans, Americans, and everybody else who makes things the British once made. While waiting for an economic turnaround, the North has been reduced to trying to salvage some share of the industries it once pioneered and in which, in some isolated cases, it still excels. Like a runner who permits himself so strong a spurt at the beginning of the race that he is soon burnt out, northerners who led the way for the industrialized world are now paying the price for having been first and fastest. Only the post-industrial revolution can bring new life and flair to their grim cities—if it takes hold.

While it is true that an outsider visiting the North might be excused for momentarily forgetting whether he is in Darlington or Doncaster or any of a dozen other cities, Liverpool is special. Liverpool is unmistakably Liverpool and nothing else. In defiant contrast to the defensive posturing of many other northerners, Liverpudlians flaunt their municipal identity with a genuine pride bordering on conceit.

There are those who question whether such vainglory is deserved, or even rational. Despite its impressive "twin" cathedrals (Anglican and Catholic), Liverpool is by no means still worthy of Charles Dickens' description of it as "that rich and beautiful port." Many of its slums have been cleared away, but many remain and most of the new housing is boxlike, insipid, and unimaginative, much of it squatting in soulless new suburban dormitory communities which have found little favor or sympathy in the eyes of their transplanted inhabitants. Vandalism is rife.

Liverpool is a rough city where, according to one Liverpudlian, a person can lose all his teeth before he is sixteen years old while minding his own business. Once the most vibrant port in all of Europe, it flourished with the slave trade and then grew even richer on less despicable commerce. But it has declined glaringly, with the active collaboration of the men who earn their living on the docks.

The Liverpool stevedores have always had a reputation for being a bloody-minded lot. They emerged from the ugly tradition of casual labor in which dockers showed up each morning never knowing whether they'd have jobs for the day. Not being able to rely on work, they made certain work could not rely on them. They made work last as long as possible and compensated for irregular, low pay by pilferage from "broken" shipping crates on the docks. The introduction of containerization made both go-slow practices and pilferage difficult where not impossible. But the dockers refused to adapt to the cost-saving methods, so cargo ships began passing their city by and moving on to less cantankerous British ports like Felixstowe or over to more adaptable Holland.

Liverpool's once prominent shipbuilding industry also declined sharply. This was partly because competition from Japan was horrendous. But much of the blame can also be fixed on desperate union efforts to stretch available work and protect jobs. Demarcation disputes between unions, often over trivial matters, regularly brought work at the Liverpool shipyards to an expensive standstill until it reached a stage where the British government felt compelled to pay a good part of the price to induce Poland to order a ship for a Liverpool yard.

There is, however, little in the surface attitudes of the people of Liverpool to indicate they are demoralized or subdued by developments. They are cocky and confident, irreverent and ribald. Mostly of Welsh and Irish stock, Liverpudlians are not much given to reserve, understatement, or other British traits. Neither Wales nor Ireland is far away (Dublin is closer than London) and many Scouse (Liverpudlian) attitudes are derived from a blending of the characteristics of those two very un-English folk. (Scouse originally meant a stew of cheap, tough meat.)

As musicians, the famous Beatles might have sprung up anywhere. But as irreverent, boyishly charming, sharp-witted young men, the Beatles individually were Liverpool through and through. Their quickness in off-the-cuff response was proof of that (like the line later incorporated into one of their movies but emerging from an interview with a newspaper columnist who asked what their early, distinctive browline hairstyle was called and was told it was called "Arthur"). Liverpudlian fast-talk, speech mannerisms, and accents can be distinctive enough to prove an impenetrable code to most other English people and even small Scouse children seem prepared to cross verbal swords with their elders when circumstances require. Being street-smart is as much a part of Liverpool as it is of Harlem.

Some years ago, Liverpudlians Frank Shaw and Fritz Spiegl tried to help outsiders understand the language of their city by compiling a phrase book with translations called *Lern Yerself Scouse—How to Talk Proper in Liverpool*. It included such listings as:

GISALITE   Could you oblige me with a match, please?
BOOGAROFF   Please depart.
YER WHA?   Do I hear you all right?
MUCK IN, YER AT YER GRANNY'S   Hearty appetite!
MIND ME URDU   Do not ruffle my coiffure.
DESE ARE ME BEZZIES   These are my best clothes.

But phrase books, while they can be informative and amusing, cannot fully capture the feeling of a vernacular shot out with the speed of machine-gun bullets and subject to all sorts of inventive, musical nuances as Frank Shaw illustrated in his book, *My Liverpool*.

> *I useter be left-handed but now I'm ambiguous*
> *Me daughter's quite uninhabited.*
> *I always try to be unscrupulously fair.*
> *Two negatives make an infirmary.*
> *It wuz enough to make your head stand on end.*

There is clearly much more to Liverpool than meets the eye—or the ear. Nor can anyone deny that several northern towns are charming, inviting, picturesque, and unburdened by a weighty residue of past nightmares.

The quaint flavor of York's old town and the majesty of its Gothic cathedral make it an enchanting city. With its galleried streets, the pleasant ancient walled city of Chester has also managed to avoid serious desecration. The medieval heart of the city of Durham is one of England's most attractive urban patches.

But the true charm of northern England is its countryside—the Yorkshire moors and dales; the majestic forests of Northumberland; the Lake District; the finely chiseled rocky crags of the Peak District and the expanses of grassland and heather they overlook;

the hauntingly bleak Cheviot Hills with their wild goats; the Pennine Way, a high footpath meandering 250 miles through wild backbone country of England. Exhilarating, pretty countryside rolls teasingly practically to the doorsteps of all the colorless northern mill towns. Those who work in those towns, and can manage it, live amidst greenery outside the urban blight.

Much of the region is dotted with castle fortresses, ghosts of the past. With the ferocious Scots not far off, this was fighting country once upon a time. Like the rest of Britain, this region also is dotted with pleasant villages, most of them dating back many hundreds of years.

The British village is an institution in itself. But it is an institution under serious threat. There is talk of a decline and fall of British village life and, alas, it's not just talk. Villages were once primarily agricultural communities. But now, with increased mechanization in the countryside, only a tiny fraction of the British population (about three percent) is engaged in farming.

Craftwork, which was a village cottage industry, has virtually been eradicated by the introduction of mass-produced craftsy things, a lot of them imported from Hong Kong, Korea and other low-wage areas, and by the surge of inflation which has made remaining village-made products too expensive for most people. Coming across a village carpenter asking £550 for a sturdy oak table for which he was able to charge less than half that sum two years earlier explains a lot. Many industrial villages which sprang up around quarries and mines have been transformed into ghost towns because those quarries and mines have been played out and will never be worked again.

With work opportunities sharply limited in the villages, people there have been drifting steadily into the towns and cities over the last two decades. Government spending cuts have trimmed bus and train services to remote areas and reduced the number of local post offices, contributing to the further isolation of many small communities. The exodus of village families with children has led to a reduction in the number of village schools and that has led, in turn, to still more families shifting townward. Each village once had its own church and its own vicar. Now in many places, one church has to serve several villages in the same neighborhood. Nevertheless, an estimated 10,000 villages survive in Britain and a movement has been launched to glorify and perpetuate that attractive and worthy portion of the national heritage at a time when people are increasingly aware of the shortcomings of big city life.

A village is a community in a rural setting made up "not of fine mansions finely peopled but of cottages and cottage-like houses." There are different kinds of villages. Among the most attractive are clusters of at most 4,000 people. Some have populations of just a few hundred. They have evolved over the centuries around pretty bits of what is now the village green, where once sheep or cattle grazed and sometimes still do. They consist of modest dwellings, sometimes thatched, half-timbered, or stone, reflecting local styles, a general store, a candy/stationary store, a butcher shop, a small church (old enough to attract archaeologists from far away as well as local worshippers), and a venerable tavern. Many of Britain's traditions survive in such timeless settings: maypole dancing on May Day, cheese rolling on Whit Monday, sword dancing and such obscure pastimes as Shrovetide football as it is played (perpetrated is a better description) in the village of Sedgefield where it is a no-holds-barred scramble with as many participants as care to risk kicked shins, sprained ankles, or skinned knees.

Some villages are picturesque coastal communities, like Clovelly in Devon and Mousehole (pronounced *mau-zil*) in Cornwall where fishing was the heart of the community existence and sometimes still is. Other villages grew at important road junctions where passing traffic or a weekly market might be expected to provide a livelihood for villagers. Some villages, like Castle Combe and Bourton-on-the-Water, are of such spectacular beauty that they have become major tourist attractions and have had their charm threatened by tourist congestion and an unseemly explosion of tasteless shops and restaurants trying to cash in on their popularity.

In addition to guarding the charms of rural life, British villages have been custodians of some fine, quaint, and curious place names, like Giggleswick, Great Tew, Sutton-under-Brailes, Crayke, Temple Sowerby, Upper Slaughter, Lower Slaughter, Frampton-on-Severn, and Widecombe-in-the-Moor.

These are fairy tale names for real places, but pretty names are not enough to save a village from ruin. A new element has, however, been introduced which might guarantee that they will not be obliterated wholesale. Good roads permit remaining villagers to commute daily by car (and even bicycle) to work and schools in towns and cities not far away. In many places it's only a car ride of twenty minutes.

Many city-dwelling Britons have second homes in the villages a little further out to which they retreat every weekend. Some of these second-home-in-a-village people exhibit so desperate a longing to escape the cities in which they live and work that not even storms can keep them from squeezing into their cars Friday evenings to spend time in their small, wholesome other worlds, usually less than two hours away.

Some villages have been helped to survive by a new development in domestic tourist habits. Even some which are off the normal tourist track have become countryside attractions, a bit of the old world to be explored while they last. More and more people are whizzing out along motorways, then onto local thoroughfares, and finally out onto country roads to see what picturesque village life, from which Britain originally sprang, is like today.

The man was the manager of a large hotel in Belfast—and a Protestant. He was a pleasant, friendly man and was obligingly anxious to solve my nuisance of a room problem. His hotel, in which I was staying, was full but I needed a different room than the one I had been given. I needed one of the few in the hotel which still had an old-style telephone, the kind from which I could unscrew the mouthpiece and to which I could affix my tape recorder with alligator clips and a lead so that I might transmit a recorded news interview from Northern Ireland to a radio broadcasting studio in New York.

An ugly confrontation between British troops and a crowd of Catholic kids the night before had been widely reported—one in which the kids had heaved barrages of bricks and bottles at the troops. "What's the answer to all this?" I asked the hotel manager after he had succeeded with great effort and persistence in getting me switched to a suitable room. "There's no problem," he replied. "If those soldiers stopped using only *rubber* bullets against those hooligans and began using real ammo, everything would soon quiet down."

He was mistaken. The troops had used real ammunition; sometimes they had no choice. Counterviolence was only intensified.

What was most unnerving was to hear a view like that so casually offered by a man who otherwise seemed so gentle and obliging. It was equally depressing to hear a Catholic Belfast taxi driver insist with a snarl later that day that he could spot "a bloody Prod" a hundred yards off just by the way he looked.

The question practically asked itself—was everyone in Ulster, Protestant and Catholic, vicious and full of hate? They are not. Most are decent folk, sympathetic to the problems of others and desperately wishing to live together in peace. But a determined corps of them are bitter, reckless, and cruel people and it is they who will keep that unhappy region bubbling with hatred and terror for the foreseeable future.

Ulster, by which name Northern Ireland is commonly known, is officially part of the United Kingdom rather than Britain. As such, it could be considered beyond the scope of this book. It would, however be impossible to ignore the Ulster "troubles" in a study of the British when it would be hard to find people more determined than the Protestants of Northern Ireland to be British subjects, to express loyalty to the British crown and to fly the British flag at every opportunity. It would also be impossible to ignore the fact that the British army has been patrolling the streets and rural regions of Northern Ireland for more than a decade and has lost a lot of men in the process. The serene setting of English, Scottish, and Welsh countryside churchyards is repeatedly intruded upon by pallbearers carrying the flag-draped coffins of soldiers cut down in Belfast backstreets or along country roads elsewhere in Ulster.

The history of the Ulster dispute is complex but the pertinent facts are brutally straightforward. A large majority of the people of Ulster are Protestants. They fiercely oppose proposals by the Catholic minority that the region be incorporated into the adjoining Irish Republic whose large population is virtually entirely Catholic. Aside from their desire to remain in the United Kingdom, most Protestants fear their religious identities would be submerged in a predominantly-Catholic united Ireland.

These religious antagonisms have a long history. Protestant militants invoke triumphs over the Catholics in Ulster centuries ago in their frequent parades and rallies. Catholics, in turn, invoke stories of past British tyranny and oppression in Ireland. These invocations and the emotions they arouse show how deeply rooted the bitter feelings are and how difficult it will be to eradicate them.

Northern Irish Catholics are unshakably suspicious of Ulster's Protestant leaders—and with good reason. Though there has been some improvement in recent years, they have long been victims of discrimination in jobs, housing, and education. They are convinced the Protestant leadership will never willingly surrender a share of control of the administration of the region. Bad feeling would be trouble enough but the pot is kept boiling furiously by the activities of the Catholic Irish Republican Army and the Protestant Ulster Defense Association and various smaller but no less militant armed units on both sides of the religious divide, bent on assassination as a means of expressing their grievances.

Britain and Ulster have strong ties. Many distinguished Britons have been of Ulster stock. Ulster men have fought in many wars on behalf of the British crown. Their fighting talents and spirits have always been highly prized. In the Second World War, Northern Ireland provided a sizable chunk of the top British military command, including Field Marshals Montgomery, Alexander, and Alanbrooke. Many Britons consider Belfast as much a British city as Leicester or Bristol.

But most people in Britain have grown weary of the seemingly endless Ulster turmoil; the ceaseless bombast of the antagonists; bombings and shootings; the recurring television clips of young soldiers being hauled back from Northern Ireland for burial. Most Britons probably would not be averse to a withdrawal of British peace-keeping forces (who, ironically, were sent in to protect Catholic communities from assaults by mobs of Protestant toughs in 1969 but who soon became the primary target of the Catholic IRA). However, the British government says there will be no troop withdrawal and no merger between Ulster and Ireland unless a majority of people in Ulster agree.

The Protestant majority will not agree. Nor will the Catholic militants call a halt to their terror campaigns. There is no solution to the Ulster dispute, not even a suggested "independence" for the region to let tempers cool while a long-term answer is sought. If war weariness does finally drive the British troops out, leaving the Ulster police force to cope, Protestant militants will, as they have threatened, be likely to embark on a campaign of violence to block even the suggestion of a merger with Ireland. They are known to have the weapons and the obstinancy. If Irish troops were then dispatched across the border to protect Ulster's Catholic communities, they would be unlikely to be any more successful in coping with Protestant terror than the British have been in coping with the IRA. There was once a hope that a new generation of Ulster youngsters would grow up without the hatreds and suspicions of so many of their forebears. But it appears that more youngsters have gravitated toward the hard-line organizations than toward the let's-live-together-in-peace activists.

There are likely to be temporary truces, pauses, and interregnums in the conflict from time to time. But for the foreseeable future the region, which despite a dismal climate has areas of great natural beauty, is doomed to unrelenting insecurity and strife unless the British can come up with sufficiently advanced and effective electronic devices for helping their troops monitor and control terrorist activity. They've made some advances along those lines but not yet nearly enough to do the job effectively, much less conclusively.

It seems the only real answer would be an unfamiliar exposure of economic prosperity in the region. All things considered, it is a remote prospect. But if it ever happened, there might be enough jobs, suitable housing, and decent education for all. The antagonisms nurtured for centuries might finally fade away. Until that happens, the gentle-mannered, tough-minded hotel manager and the hard-slogging, embittered taxi driver will have to put up with each other and the British probably will have to put up with them both.

The Royal Image

SHORTLY AFTER he was deposed and exiled to face the rigors of life on the French Riviera, the late King Farouk of Egypt moaned that one day there would be only five kings left in the world—four in a deck of cards and the king of England. It was no peevish exaggeration. Though a handful of other monarchs still cling to their crowns, and occasionally serve a useful purpose, only in Britain is there still a monarch on a grand scale with an active sovereign fulfilling a necessary function and popular royal occasions brimming with pomp and pageantry. Only in Britain has the crown worn well enough for "The Palace" to continue to play a notable role in domestic and international affairs.

The reigning British monarch, Elizabeth II, is an intelligent, dignified woman. Born in 1926, she is, by Grace of God, Queen of the United Kingdom of Great Britain and Northern Ireland and Her Other Realms and Territories, Head of the Commonwealth and Defender of the Faith. Through some fancy genealogical footwork, her ancestry can be traced back through fifty-nine previous monarchs to a Saxon king of England 1,200 years ago. By pedigree and calling, she is as royal as royal can be.

Only the most mulish of anti-royalists would deny that Elizabeth Alexandra Mary Windsor has been a worthy queen. If she has not brought glamour or flair to the throne, it might be noted that such qualities are no longer appropriate for the sovereign of a democratic country where upstaging elected representatives of the people would not only be in bad taste but politically questionable as well. Elizabeth has certainly pursued her royal duties with devotion and diligence. Appearances to the contrary, however, and despite the undeniable significance of the monarchy, she wields only a shadow of authority and virtually no political influence worth talking about.

Officially, the queen has the power to conclude treaties with foreign countries, declare war, make peace, dissolve Parliament, pardon criminals, and decide what becomes the law of the land. In fact, she can do none of those. Officially, the queen is commander-in-chief of Britain's armed forces and head of the British civil service. But it has been a long time since the last British monarch could order the army into battle or instruct government officials how to go about their business. If she tried to do so today, a political earthquake of colossal proportions would ensue and, before the dust had settled, the Royal House of Windsor would have been, at best, badly shaken.

The queen still appoints the prime minister. In practice, however, she is required to appoint whoever commands a working majority in Parliament (traditionally the leader of the dominant political party) no matter what she personally thinks of that person. Everything she does related to governing Britain is done at the "advice" of her various government ministers whom she also appoints, after being given their names by the prime minister. Queen Victoria, more than a century ago, was the last monarch to block the appointment of a minister of whom she disapproved. For a monarch to do so today would be unthinkable.

No bill passed by Parliament becomes law before it receives the Royal Assent. But it is no longer conceivable for a British monarch to withhold such consent once Parliament has made up its mind. The necessary royal approval is, in effect, automatic. As head of the Church of England, the queen appoints bishops of the Anglican Communion but, again, only at the advice of the prime minister who is expected first to consult leading Anglican clergymen.

There are, of course, genuine fringe benefits to the job of wearing the British crown, aside from the personal prestige and glory attached to whoever sits on the throne and whatever satisfaction might be derived from devoting a life to performing an important service for the British nation and people. The substantial expenses incurred while living a royal existence are borne by the taxpayer. The queen herself is exempt from taxes on her substantial personal fortune. She cannot be sued. Nevertheless, the queen does not rule. She does not govern. In many ways it is a spectacular pretense.

Each autumn, the queen, traveling in the resplendent Irish State Coach drawn by matched horses and escorted by troops of the Household Cavalry in their glittering uniforms, rides in stately procession to the House of Lords to deliver The Speech from the Throne. (No monarch has been permitted to enter the House of Commons since the seventeenth century when King Charles I rushed there too late to arrest five parliamentarians he considered treasonable.) The Speech from the Throne is composed by whoever happens to be prime minister at the time and the queen might personally detest the policies it contains as, indeed, she has more than once since her coronation in 1953. A cartoon in the irreverent London magazine *Private Eye* showed the queen reading the speech while thinking, "I hope you realize I didn't write this crap." We've come a long way since the imperious days of the first Queen Elizabeth four centuries ago. If Parliament today passed a law banishing the monarch to the storm-swept Outer Hebrides, the Virgin Queen's present day namesake would be obliged to sign it.

That won't happen. Despite all the play-acting and make-believe, the British monarchy contributes meaningfully to the country's political life and self-regard. It gives the government in London vital continuity which Britain's endlessly feuding political parties (they keep alternating in power and reversing each other's policies) could never produce. It permits a change of government to take place in the course of a single afternoon if the voters opt for such a change, while the American hand-over period lasts two fidgety months. It is HMG—Her Majesty's Government—whether conservative or socialist, Labor or Tory, or anything else. Nor should anyone underrate the fact that the existence of the monarchy kindles an enduring romantic imagery. It lends Britain an enviable splendor even superpowers cannot generate.

Queen Elizabeth is greatly esteemed by her subjects. She is undoubtedly the most popular single individual in Britain. When the twenty-fifth anniversary of her coronation was celebrated a few years ago, the block parties, the flood of congratulatory messages, the sprightly sense of occasion were testimony to the enormous affection in which the queen is held by her people. It is an extraordinary phenomenon because, aside from being British monarch, a competent royal administrator, a nice woman, and very knowledgeable about horses, horse racing, and show jumping, there is little that is remarkable about the queen. Had she not been born into the royal family, she probably would have remained an obscure, pleasant lady, never given a chance to display her executive talents. The grandeur is in the office rather than the woman—though another woman might easily have made a mess of the job.

Elizabeth is even-tempered and self-disciplined. She has shielded herself with great success from any memorable act of controversy. While other members of the royal family, feeding the gossip columns of London's sensational press, step out of character or commit gaffes of one kind or another in public from time to time, the queen's unfailing discretion and sense of propriety are second nature to her and sometimes make her seem colorless.

Journalist Lord Altrincham (who gave up his title to settle for his original name, John Grigg) was once criticized in the press and had his face slapped by a stranger in public for contending that the queen has a manner of public speaking that is "a pain in the neck" and the voice "of a priggish schoolgirl." It was an exaggeration—the queen deliberately adopts a discreet, neutral monotone when speaking in public. It is not unpleasant but it can get tedious. The substance of her public speeches, except the Speech from the Throne prepared for her by the prime minister, is invariably uncontroversial and uncomplicated, like a recent royal Christmas message when she reminded her subjects "that the world we would like to see can only come from the goodness of the heart." The queen's taste in clothes has on occasion been criticized by sticklers who suggest she looked as if she were still dressed by a nannie. But impeccable good manners and unshakable self-control are her trademarks. She offers no public displays of personal opinion, no public eruptions of private emotion, no public flashes of wit—though she is known to be capable of all three.

Elizabeth has handled her difficult and complicated job with selfless dedication but if, at this stage, the second Elizabethan era were to be assessed, it would not be judged to have been a time of glory. It has been notable primarily for economic doldrums, the winding-up of the British Empire, and Britain's general decline as a major power.

Nevertheless, the queen and the monarchy remain the center of satisfied public attention. Not only is she held in high regard among her own people but, as monarch after monarch elsewhere has been banished, dispossessed, or belittled, the British monarchy and the queen herself have grown in international stature and reputation. Unlike the situation prevailing in other places, in Britain the crown is still a potent symbol of patriotism, national unity, and pride, even for those Britons who do not consider themselves excessively patriotic or overly concerned with the state of the country. Historian Philip Howard has called the crown "the validating symbol of British nationhood." The queen who wears that crown is its personification.

Deprived of authority or power, she cannot be held responsible for Britain's economic or political difficulties. But she can be credited with being the unruffled custodian and preserver of timeless, elegant ritual, of real-life fantasy replete with costumes, courtiers, and processions. It is true that such things appeal particularly to people who are partial to fairy tales. But they appeal also to those who prize traditional, graceful, ceremonial spectacle and who see in such spectacle a wholesome defiance of the disagreeable demands of modern reality.

A reflection of those romantic values is the reverence accorded to honors awarded by the queen. These are several grades of honors. A very distinguished subject, like Winston Churchill, or a foreign king with particularly close ties might be made a member of the Most Noble Order of the Garter, an honor dating back to the fourteenth century. A devoted senior civil servant like Foreign Office Permanent Under-Secretary Michael Palliser, a gifted scientist like astronomer Bernard Lovell, an accomplished writer like novelist C.P. Snow, a television personality like newsman Robin Day, or a sports celebrity like soccer star Bobby Charlton might be dubbed a knight, thereby becoming a "Sir," or to be made a Commander of the British Empire and have the letters "CBE" placed grandly after his name from that moment on, or to be graced with any of a variety of greater or lesser honors.

Some of the honors originated as a device for conferring social distinction on men who were rich or powerful enough to extract from the crown, often for a price, an award of higher status than their birth had bestowed on them. It was a royal payoff and in a certain sense it still is, though now most recipients are nominated by the prime minister rather than the crown.

At least one prime minister earlier this century (David Lloyd

George) was cynical enough about the system to have the monarch distribute honors in exchange for financial contributions to his political party. More recently, honors have been awarded to some individuals whose service to the nation has been less than noteworthy—cronies, the trainer of the queen's racing horses, the milkman at 10 Downing Street. A raincoat manufacturer, a personal friend of Prime Minister Harold Wilson, was made a member of the House of Lords a few years ago and was later imprisoned for theft and falsifying business accounts after having fled the country and having been tracked down by Scotland Yard.

There are other paradoxes. The Order of the Garter was originally awarded for skill at jousting. But the only meaning "lance" might have to some of those inducted into that exclusive order these days is what you do to troublesome boils if a salve doesn't get rid of them.

Overdue recognition of the status of women in the honors system has raised questions. When a man called Thomas Jones becomes Sir Thomas after having been dubbed a knight by the queen because of his services to the nation, his wife automatically becomes Lady Jones. But if she, for equally valued service, becomes Dame Jane, her husband remains just plain Mr. Jones.

Some people eligible for honors turn them down, believing the system to be artificial and arbitrary, seeming to imply that some people are better than others. Others reject the nominations because they feel the honor offered them is of a lower grade than they deserve or because they feel the whole system has been debased by the indiscriminate distribution of honors. But most find their qualms and objections evaporate when they receive the letter from the prime minister's office asking if the proposed "mark of Her Majesty's favor" would be acceptable to them. Regardless of the paradoxes and arbitrariness of the system, royal honors— prominently reported in the press—confer honorable national recognition on those who receive them. They remain part of the magic of the monarchy.

Despite its overwhelming popularity, there is a stubborn group of Britons who don't care much for the monarchy. Its ranks include those who appreciate its useful political role but who consider royal pageantry and the whole shebang irrelevant and absurdly expensive folderol. The monarchy costs the British taxpayer about forty-five million dollars a year. More than eight million dollars are earmarked for paying the expenses of members of the royal family as they go about their full-time duties. These include making official visits, attending opening ceremonies, attending receptions and meetings, and giving banquets.

The queen gets most of that expense money and most of her share goes to paying the wages of her administrative, ceremonial, and domestic staff. Devout monarchists are incensed when people choose to speak of the royal allowance as a salary, as if the queen were just another civil servant. They insist it is the best possible investment the people of Britain can make.

Most of the remainder of the allocation for the queen and the rest of the royal family is for transport expenses associated with official travel. Use and maintenance of royal planes, ships, and limousines don't come cheap. Also included is the upkeep of the three royal palaces—Buckingham Palace, Windsor Castle, and the Palace of Holyroodhouse in Edinburgh—as well as other royal buildings. The mansions and estates of Balmoral in Scotland and Sandringham in Norfolk are privately owned and maintained by the queen though expenses are claimed for when she is in residence there.

There is much pressure, particularly in times of economic uncertainty, on the royal family to join everybody else in cutting costs and expenditures. It is an embarrassing matter because royals are not supposed to pinch pennies or to haggle about whether they're doing all they can to economize. But the subject is recurringly aired by a small group of staunch anti-monarchists in Parliament which has the power to trim, and even abolish, royal expense allowances. Royalty-bashers are wont to contrast comfortable royal lifestyles with the way most other people live. Monarchists consider the comparison irrelevant and few people really take it seriously. But when the queen's husband, Prince Philip, said that the monarchy was slipping into deficit and suggested jokingly that financial difficulties might force the queen to move into a smaller residence, it aroused neither smiles nor sympathy.

But the royal lifestyle is not all that it is usually imagined to be. While the queen is not yet reduced to having to pop out for fish-and-chips for dinner, luxury and fripperies have been trimmed. Though far from having trouble making ends meet, the queen engages in a determined effort at economies. It would not be dignified for the Palace to boast about such savings but word slips out now and again. For example, it is known that the queen no longer follows the demands of fashion that she wear her expensive state occasion dresses and outfits once and once only. It is a game among those who keep close watch on her activities to try to recognize on which foreign visit or domestic occasion the queen last wore the dress she has again donned. The long-sleeved, high-necked dresses specially made for a visit to Saudi Arabia were cut down for subsequent wear in the less puritanical atmosphere of appearances in Britain. In exchanging gifts during that visit to oil-rich Arab countries, she presented her hosts with comaratively modest silver salvers while they gave her wildly expensive gold-and-diamond-studded ornaments. Though not themselves having to count their pennies, they understood.

The same sort of understanding is not forthcoming from anti-monarchists at home, of whom Britain has long had a fair share. It should be remembered that Tom Paine, the determined vilifier of kings, was an Englishman who had arrived in the American colonies from London less than two years before signing the Declaration of Independence.

The same sort of castigation of royals has been administered of late by Willie Hamilton. Hamilton, an outspoken, public-spirited member of Parliament, is fundamentally opposed to the existence of the monarchy. He says the crown "thrives in our deferential, class-conscious, irrational society—a society laden with snobbery, humbug, and hypocrisy." He and a few like-minded parliamentarians have accused the royal family of being irresponsible in its claims on public funds. Hamilton called one request for an increased allowance for the royal family "the most brazen pay claim in the last two hundred years." He saw the headline-grabbing announcement of the engagement of Prince Charles as a device for diverting public attention from soaring unemployment levels in the country.

Some anti-monarchists want the monarchy abolished. Others grant that it should be retained as a useful institution but say the cost of maintaining it should be sharply cut back. The queen, they say, should be paid "the rate of the job" and required, like everyone else, to pay taxes on her income. It isn't likely to happen. Britons generally believe they are getting their money's worth. It is hard not to agree that they are.

As to the size of the queen's personal fortune, it is a secret which has inevitably produced a welter of guesses and estimates, up to two hundred million dollars and growing substantially all the time because of tax exemptions. Palace spokesmen repeatedly declare that such astronomical suggestions about the queen's wealth are exaggerated and that Her Majesty consistently dips into her own coffers to cover deficits in her parliamentary expense allowance and to meet the expenses of other royals whose allowances don't always suffice. But no one denies that the queen is very rich indeed.

Contrary to storybook ideas about royal lifestyles, the queen of England works very hard. Though she has no power to make or change government policy, she is British Head of State and has the right and duty to be continuously informed and consulted on government affairs. As Head of the Commonwealth—which is the residue of the old British Empire transformed into an association of independent nations—Elizabeth is also kept informed of developments in its forty-four member countries around the world. She is queen of fifteen of those countries, including Canada, Australia, Jamaica, and Barbados.

Elizabeth is required to spend a lot of her time appearing and performing in public—opening schools and bridges; laying foundation stones; visiting factories, agricultural shows, and hospitals; calling in on local government bodies and the headquarters of various charities; and attending luncheons, dinners, major sporting events, and all sorts of receptions. As head of Britain's armed forces and colonel-in-chief of several British regiments, she regularly visits military installations. Aside from state banquets, she regularly gives small luncheons at Buckingham Palace for politicians, business leaders, union officials, clergymen, and other prominent or interesting Britons she and her husband would otherwise be unlikely to have a chance to meet personally. She considers it a duty as well as a pleasure. Each year she personally bestows more than two thousand awards, decorations, and medals. Speeches and small talk with hosts and guests at the various functions she attends are part of her daily life.

She has been carefully raised to be prepared to cope with those

chores, but being British monarch is a demanding calling nevertheless. The queen's father, George VI, who stuttered and was very
shy, was appalled and frightened when his brother, Edward VIII,
who had been trained for royal duties, unexpectedly abdicated the
throne in his favor in 1936 to marry a divorced woman and live out
his life in exile as the Duke of Windsor. Neither King George, who
grew enormously in stature despite his unpreparedness and speech
defect to become a major national asset during the Second World
War, nor Elizabeth ever forgave Edward for that. (He never fully
understood why. After he had abdicated, he had to be discreetly
advised not to keep trying to tell the new king how to go about his
business.)

Edward's abdication may have been influenced also by the fact
that he didn't really enjoy being king. He found the job irksome,
full of drudgery, and extremely tedious. But Elizabeth either enjoys
her exhaustive duties or lets her profound devotion to duty override
the temptation to work less hard or perform less thoroughly. In
addition to her previously mentioned activities, she receives a
steady flow of dispatch boxes containing official government
documents for her examination, and digests the bulk of them. She
sees all cabinet papers and the minutes of cabinet meetings, copies
of all important Foreign Office cables and dispatches, and a daily
summary of parliamentary proceedings when Parliament is in
session. In addition, she receives more than one hundred letters
each day, most of which she at least scans and some of which are
answered personally. Her secretaries deal with the others.

The prime minister visits Buckingham Palace at least once a
week when Parliament is in session—usually on Tuesday evenings—to brief and consult with the queen. Other ministers also
consult with her from time to time. Former Prime Minister Harold
MacMillan called Elizabeth "incredibly well informed" and former
Prime Minister Harold Wilson said that if he didn't come fully
prepared for his briefing session with her, he felt like a schoolboy
who hadn't done his homework.

As head of state, the queen is required to extend lavish hospitality to distinguished visitors from abroad. Many of them consider
a visit to London a particularly attractive prospect because of the
regal razzmatazz associated with such trips—the rides through
crowd-lined London streets in stately carriages accompanied by the

queen and escorted by mounted dragoons, and the glittering receptions at the Palace. Since such visits are essentially diplomatic events, the queen is often required to make return visits to the countries of her distinguished visitors. It is not necessarily an onerous chore but it is one which restricts the queen's choice of where she would like to spend her time. There are, however, occasional ironic murmurings about how Her Majesty often appears to call in on nations in the sun-washed Caribbean, the South Pacific, or Africa when less than agreeable winter weather stalks London.

To cope with the formidable duties of the British monarchy, the queen is assisted by a small troop of aides, advisors, and retainers. Her chief assistant is her private secretary who is both personal advisor and royal handyman. Among his duties is keeping the queen aware of political moods and trends in the country. This is something the prime minister is not always prepared to do adequately, being too politically partisan to satisfy the queen's appetite for unbiased political gossip which, though discreetly displayed, is said to be hearty. The task of filling Her Majesty in on who is doing what to whom in Britain's political arena has therefore fallen to the private secretary. But most important, with his staff, he keeps the queen informed on public reaction to her own activities, writes many of her speeches, and monitors preparations for royal activities and jaunts with an eye to sorting out potential difficulties before they cause embarrassment or complications. Private secretary to the monarch is clearly a job of considerable consequence and responsibility. It has generally been filled by men who have previously distinguished themselves in other pursuits, often as senior civil servants or military officers.

The Lord Chamberlain is officially senior member of the royal household. He oversees the ceremonial occasions of the British monarchy—royal weddings, state visits, state banquets, palace garden parties, etc. He also superintends the upkeep of the royal palaces, the priceless royal art collection and the appointment of such figures as royal chaplains and royal physicians. In the seventeenth century, King Charles II, who ironically objected not at all to hanky-panky at the royal court, gave the Lord Chamberlain the authority to censor unsuitable theater plays, a power he continued to exercise until 1968 when theater censorship was abolished in Britain. But the Lord Chamberlain still dispenses the much-prized royal warrants which testify that the queen or another member of the royal family uses a particular product—jam or shoe polish, light bulbs or shotguns. The warrants are granted free of charge after a member of the royal family has contentedly used the product in question for at least three years. Notice of "By Appointment to Her Majesty, Queen Elizabeth" or "By Appointment to His Royal Highness, the Prince of Wales" can be discreetly deployed in packaging and advertising by the lucky manufacturers or retailers. Excessive or tasteless use of the warrant would result in its withdrawal.

Day-to-day housekeeping affairs of the queen are the responsibility of the Master of the Household. His staff sees to the performance and maintenance of the royal domestic staff and the provision of food and drink for the royal homes which have to be maintained by staff even when the queen is not in residence.

The queen's senior personal attendant, traditionally a duchess, is called Mistress of the Robes, though she no longer concerns herself with the queen's wardrobe, a task which falls to three "dressers" (in effect, lady's maids). Women who served as Mistress of the Robes in the past were always considered influential because of their regular direct contact with the queen, a matter of less significance now that royal clout is much reduced. In addition to accompanying the queen on more important state occasions, the Mistress of the Robes oversees the Ladies-in-Waiting, the small contingent of female aristocrats who take turns attending the queen during her public appearances.

A number of royal retainers hold ancient ranks, some of which have limited current significance and some of which are unpaid or which receive only token recompense. These include the Keeper of the Royal Racing Pigeons, the Keeper of the Royal Philatelic Collection, the Royal Bargemaster, the Keeper of the Queen's Swans, Gold Sticks (ceremonial bodyguards, usually distinguished men of advanced age), the Master of the Queen's Music, and the Poet Laureate, who is expected to dash off appropriate verse to mark notable occasions. The Master of the Queen's Horse often attends the queen in public. Not only does he look after the royal stables at Buckingham Palace but he is by tradition ceremonially responsible for the queen's safety whenever she is on horseback or in a horsedrawn carriage (though the queen's less conspicuously attired detectives are never far from her side.)

There are about 350 members of the royal staff at Buckingham Palace. The chief housekeeper and the housing administrator at the Palace have small apartments and some unmarried domestic staff have rooms there but most are there only during the day. They arrive in the morning and leave in the evening, except for the small number who have later shifts and those required for state receptions or other special Palace functions. There are about fifty cooks and other members of the Palace catering staff, about sixty maids and about fifty pages, footmen, and porters. Most of the day workers are members of unions and their salaries are comparable to those of others in similar, non-Palace London jobs.

Nary a tourist passes through London without joining the crowds watching the Changing of the Guard at Buckingham Palace. But unlike paying visitors to many of the stately homes of England, only invited guests can penetrate the gates of the Palace, though the busbied guards standing ramrod straight outside serve only a decorative purpose. Police are nearby in case they're needed.

Buckingham Palace—sometimes known familiarly as Buck House—is the main residence of the British monarch. It was built by the Duke of Buckingham at the turn of the eighteenth century on the site of what had been a mulberry grove. It was bought by King George III, from whom the American colonies won their independence, for his wife. But it didn't officially become a royal residence until Queen Victoria ascended the throne in 1837. The white marble, wedding-cakey Victoria Memorial—a thirteen-foot statue of Victoria on a pedestal, attended by images representing, among other things, Truth, Justice, and Motherhood—is planted in the square in front of the Palace. The Palace has been *the* home of the British monarch ever since Victoria's reign.

It is a massive edifice, squat rather than elegant. None of the kings and queens who have lived in it seem to have had anything nice to say about it. The queen's great grandfather, Edward VII, called it a "sepulcher" and the comments of others have rarely been more flattering. Prince Philip has described residing there as "living over the shop."

The Palace is said to contain some 600 rooms, though that is a technical count, including corridors, cupboards, etc. The true figure is closer to 300 though only a comparatively few of those rooms are used by the royal family. Some are not used at all. There are apartments for members of the royal family (though the queen's married children, Prince Charles and Princess Anne, live elsewhere) and suites for distinguished guests. The furnishings are far from shabby and some of the furniture is priceless but much of it is undistinguished or in need of repair—a point repeatedly made by those fighting charges of extravagance leveled against the royal family.

In his book, *Majesty*, Robert Lacey reports, "You go into the office of the Queen's principal private secretary expecting the habitat of a successful company director or your own bank manager at least and discover instead the faded study of a minor public school headmaster, the genteel decrepitude of a gentleman's club that has known better days." The Throne Room, the state dining room, the ballroom, and other rooms used for royal ceremonial occasions are, however, magnificent chambers, exquisitely furnished and maintained.

The Palace is situated at the head of The Mall, that broad, tree-lined boulevard reaching down toward Trafalgar Square. It comes equipped with a post office of its own, a fire station, and a gas station. It also has a sick bay with a resident nurse and a doctor on duty each morning, workshops for repair and maintenance of Palace equipment and property, hothouses, and a royal art gallery which, with the Royal Mews, is the only part of the palace open to uninvited visitors. There are special dining rooms for senior staff and a self-service canteen for others in the Palace basement.

The queen's apartment of twelve rooms includes her bedroom (outside of which a uniformed police officer is on duty each night through when the queen is sleeping there), the bedroom of her husband, a "tea room" where the royal couple occasionally have their meals alone, and a royal living room ("sitting room") where they read, relax, and watch television. The royal apartment looks out on the sprawling Palace gardens (forty acres with wooded areas, tennis courts, and a lake). It cannot be seen by passersby beyond the Palace walls, most of which border on heavily trafficked London streets. When the high-rise Hilton Hotel was being built several years ago within binocular-viewing distance of the Palace, it was feared that prying guests in the hotel's upper floors would be able to violate the royal privacy from afar, but that fear proved groundless.

It is said that it was love at first sight when Queen Elizabeth met her third cousin and future husband. She was a thirteen-year-old princess at the time and Prince Philip was a dashing eighteen-year-old naval cadet. They were married six years later in 1947 after Philip had served in the Royal Navy during the Second World War.

That wartime duty was important because his name at christening was Philippos Schleswig-Holstein-Sonderburg-Gluecksburg, an unlikely handle for the suitor of the heiress to the British throne. (The fact that the family name of the queen's grandfather, George V, had been anglicized from Saxe-Coburg-Gotha to Windsor at the time of the First World War had been long forgotten.) Philip was also the grandson of the King of Greece and, to this day, irreverant Londoners have been known to call him "Phil the Greek." But by serving Britain—with his name changed to Mountbatten—when it was threatened by enemies from abroad, the future consort of the future queen dispelled any disquiet about his foreign origins which could have had an adverse effect upon royal popularity once Elizabeth ascended the throne.

Philip's main job as prince consort is to escort his wife on her travels, to relieve her of some of the burdens of office (he regularly represents the queen on official visits and at official ceremonies), and generally to support her as she fulfills her regal role. An attractive, forceful man with a lively sense of humor, he has done all of this reasonably well, contributing a distinctive personal touch to his performance. He is, of course, identified with the queen but unlike her, Philip tends to be publicly outspoken, impatient and though often surprisingly informal in public, is subject to occasional, unbecoming flashes of arrogance.

The press has also been able to count on him for an eye-catching headline, like HOT SHOT PRINCE DEFENDS HIS FIELD SPORT SLAUGHTER or PHILIP BLASTS CANADIANS. Fed up some time ago with rough treatment at the hands of some of London's popular newspapers, he dared to call one of them, the *Daily Express*, which has a readership of millions, "a bloody awful newspaper." It was a luxury the queen could never have permitted herself. But everyone—except the people at the *Daily Express*—seemed amused by this undiplomatic show of temper. Philip was, after all, invoking an Englishman's right to speak his mind. The Canadians were not nearly as amused when, during a royal visit, after some of them had taken exception to being reigned over by a distant monarch, the prince declared, "We don't come here for our health. We can think of better ways of enjoying ourselves." And he has never really been able satisfactorily to explain away the contradiction between his presidency of the World Wildlife Fund and his sportsmen's love for shooting at wild birds.

Some years ago, a few sensational magazines in Europe—ceaselessly panting after royal scandal—printed suggestions that the prince was something of a philanderer. But their stories seemed based more on bids to boost their newsstand sales than on fact. There has never been any indication that the royal marriage has ever been anything but happy and untroubled.

The future king of England, the queen's eldest son, Prince Charles, is an unlikely candidate for the throne he is destined to ascend. He is modest, shy, unassuming, undemanding, and seemingly surprised to be seen by others as someone worthy of reverence and acclaim. Charles was born in Buckingham Palace in 1948 and from the start was treated in a way that sharply contrasted with the traditional coddling of royal offspring. It was during the postwar austerity period and his mother's decision to have him issued the same kind of ration book for orange juice and cod liver oil that other British babies were given reflected the queen's determination that the heir to the throne should not be insulated from the real world.

Charles was the first British royal child to receive anything like a thorough education. Though the social mix was limited at the prep schools he attended, many of his school mates fell far short of boasting the exalted social credentials previously required for associating with princes. One of those schools was famous for the cold showers and marathon hikes to which Charles as well as the other boys were subjected. At another of his schools, in Australia, the emphasis was on self-reliance and country craft.

In college, at Cambridge University, Charles concentrated his studies on the past, majoring first in archaeology and anthropology and then history. While at college, he played both the cello and polo (a sport at which he excels) and performed in college plays, in one of which he appeared as a singing garbageman. He was then, as he is now, likable and unpretentious. He has called his upbringing a happy one and has attributed this to his "sensible parents who . . . created a marvellous, secure, happy home." It may have been the first time anyone had publicly called Buckingham Palace a home, though Charles probably was referring to the atmosphere of his family life rather than to any geographical location.

After college, Charles entered on a brief but thorough military career, training first with the Royal Air Force, in which he flew jets. He then joined the Royal Navy, serving for five years and ending his formal navy career by captaining a ship, a coastal mine hunter. By that time, he had learned to fly helicopters and had trained as a frogman. He also trained with Britain's Parachute Regiment, of which he is colonel-in-chief. As he matured, the prince was called upon by his mother ("commanded" according to traditional usage) to undertake duties which fall to members of the royal family. He started traveling around the country and abroad to appear at functions and ceremonies, enhancing them with his princely presence. He gradually developed a reputation as a competent and entertaining after-dinner speaker, with a dry wit as well as a genuine interest in serious matters.

For a royal who was supposed to be insulated from controversy, he was known to be deeply concerned about matters of some delicacy—the extent of racial prejudice in Britain and the dangers involved in wire-tapping by the security services. Despite a touch of somberness that seemed to have crept into his character as he matured, he has retained the image of being a very decent bloke— not a quality normally associated with run-of-the-mill majesty.

By the time Charles becomes king of England, he will be better trained for his job than any monarch has ever been before. That may not be for a long time. Suggestions that the queen might abdicate are pooh-poohed by those familiar with the queen's feelings about her duties. To step down from the throne would signify that to be queen is merely a job like any other, from which a person gets pensioned off at a certain age. Elizabeth is said to believe it would dilute the magic and mystery that keeps the British monarchy alive and vibrant. The queen's mother, grand-mother, great-grandmother, and great-great-grandmother (Queen

Victoria) all lived to be more than eighty years old. Charles may well be in his sixties before he finally inherits the crown. Queen Victoria's eldest son, Edward VII, was fifty-nine years old and a grandfather before he succeeded his mother on the throne. The possibility of a similar fate doesn't seem to worry Charles though, displaying a contemplative turn of mind, he has expressed concern about what his role in life may turn out to be.

Some of the queen's subjects used to express concern about something else as the prince passed his thirtieth birthday, still unmarried. Great fuss about a royal romance was made in the popular press whenever he was spotted socializing with a young woman and he confessed to having been in love (with whom was of course not revealed). But as time passed, it became clear that attractive, unmarried females of Charles's age who had not had affairs with others which would tarnish their suitability were hard to find.

It was beginning to look as though he might be heading toward confirmed bachelorhood, leaving the future king without a consort or the opportunity to produce an heir of his own. (If there is no such heir, next in line for the throne are his brothers Andrew, born in 1960, and Edward, born in 1964, of whom, no doubt much more will be heard in the years to come.) When, in 1981, when he was thirty-two, the Palace cut short a frenzy of press speculation to announce that Charles had become engaged to nineteen-year-old Lady Diana Spencer (the engagement photographs and television interviews showed them to be an attractive, modest couple). The news was received with satisfaction by the people of Britain generally, and with relief by true-blue monarchists who tend to prefer succession by royal offspring rather by royal siblings.

The woman Prince Charles chose to be the next queen of England, Diana Spencer, has a pedigree almost as long as his own, though not as exalted. She is the daughter of an earl and the prince's eleventh cousin, both of them being descended from a seventeenth-century king. She is a shy, pretty, unsophisticated young woman with a pleasant girlish giggle and an informal manner. She handled herself with remarkable charm, control, and dignity when mercilessly hounded by armies of reporters and photographers from around the world after word of her romance with Charles leaked out prematurely.

To escape the attentions of the press during the early days of that romance, she and the prince had to make intricate arrangements for secret meetings at the homes of friends and at other places, though the Palace, with uncharacteristic anger, denied a suggestive newspaper report that she had spent time with Charles one night aboard the royal train on a deserted siding.

Diana had a typical patrician education—prep school, followed by a few years at an exclusive private high school, followed by a brief bash at finishing school in Switzerland. She did not shine academically and did not go on to university.

By the time she came of age, it was no longer fashionable for debutantes to "come out." That was fortunate because the indications are that she would not have relished a compulsory round of parties and balls which once were an automatic part of the coming out process for young ladies of her background. Instead, she moved into an expensive apartment which her father bought for her in central London. She shared it with three other girls who paid her a small rent and who became her close friends.

She found a job as an assistant teacher at a kindergarten where she was liked both by the staff and the children. She often bicycled around town and drove through London in a compact "mini-metro" car. She is a good swimmer and an outdoor girl but, unlike other members of the royal family, does not have an almost pathological fondness for horses and does not ride.

Her engagement to the prince meant an immediate transformation in her lifestyle. She gave up her apartment and moved into the royal residence at Clarence House in London with Charles' grandmother, Queen Elizabeth the Queen Mother. She had to give up her job at the kindergarten and her freewheeling movements around town as she prepared to assume the role she now has, princess and future queen.

It is, however, too early to tell what changes she may make in the habits of the royal family. It has long been believed that while it's all right for the king of Sweden to wheel about on a bicycle through the streets of his capital city and for the queen of Holland to pop out to a supermarket now and again, such behavior is not really suitable for British royalty. The people of Britain, it is said, don't really expect that sort of behavior from their royals. With both Charles and Diana standing far less on protocol and ceremony than their regal forebears, things might well be different in the future.

The wedding of Prince Charles and Diana Spencer on July 29, 1981, was undeniably a memorable event. There were those who were dazzled by the grandeur of the occasion into making obsure extravagant comments about its significance, like the London *Times* which noted that "a princely marriage is the brilliant edition of a universal fact and, as such, it rivets mankind." There was also a small group of Britons who were offended by the public expense and unrestrained idolatry involved and who refused either to partake or to watch.

But most Britons, and a good part of the rest of the world, were deeply impressed and even moved by the occasion. In Britain, the wedding eve was marked by the lighting of a chain of fire beacons clear across the country to signal the imminent advent of the great day. The day of the marriage itself was commemorated with the jubilant pealing of church bells throughout the land. There were block parties and house parties and a general mood of celebration.

On the wedding morning, more than half a million people converged on the flanks of the route of the marriage procession through central London, along the Mall, the Strand, Fleet Street, and Ludgate Hill. Some had settled into place as much as three days before the event—and had bedded down there—to make certain of a good vantage point from which to watch Charles and "Di," the queen and invited dignitaries, elegant horse-drawn state carriages, and the brilliantly uniformed mounted escort guardsmen go by.

Around the world, an estimated three-quarters of a billion people watched the royal nuptials, the ritual and regalia on television. That included many, like those in America, who because of international time differences had to rise with the dawn not to miss the extravaganza. A group of anti-monarchist Britons took an excursion ferry over to France for the day to escape the all-pervasive ballyhoo at home but found that the non-royalist French were spending a good part of the day glued to their television sets in order not to miss the pomp and elegance from which their visitors had fled.

If not an historic event, the wedding will certainly turn out to have been one of the most enchanting spectacles of the century, bathed in pageantry, rich in ceremony, graced with an agreeable, charming, unpretentious royal couple. From the moment they set off for St. Paul's Cathedral (he from Buckingham Palace, she from

Clarence House nearby) till the moment they boarded the train at Waterloo Station to begin their honeymoon (mostly on board a royal yacht cruising through the Mediterranean), all of Britain glowed with a special glory.

The Mall in London and the rest of the route to the Cathedral was so crammed with people wanting personally to be part of the occasion that hours before the proceedings were to begin, it was virtually impossible to move any distance along its sides. An ocean of Union Jacks bobbed over the heads of the crowd. When the wedding was over and the wedding party returned to the Palace, tens of thousands of well-wishers—a veritable sea of Britons— massed in front of the Palace, beneath its balcony, calling repeatedly on their next king and queen to come out and accept their cheers and congratulations. Out Charles and Diana came, again and again, finally even responding to the crowd's call for them to kiss, a true lovers' embrace, not unworthy of Hollywood.

It was suggested that day that royal weddings, as elaborate exhibitions of regal continuity and panache, are something the British do exceedingly well. Indeed they do.

If Prince Charles is unique in the thoroughness of his training and the gentleness of his manner, his aunt, Princess Margaret, four years younger than the queen, is unique in a different way. Rarely in recent times have the personal tribulations of a member of the royal family been so doleful, so soap-opera-ish, and so thoroughly publicized as hers: family disapproval, blighted love affair, unhappy marriage, overweight problems, gossip column derision. If reports that one stage she was seeing a psychiatrist are true, it would be understandable.

A lighthearted, playful girl, Margaret grew up in the shadow of a sister who was destined to be monarch and who was virtually from the start somberly mindful of her duties. The young future queen repeatedly admonished the princess to be less girlishly mischievous and more aware of her obligations as daughter of the king to behave in a dignified fashion. Much less dedicated than Elizabeth to being a public figure, the princess was still a young woman when her royal identity first blighted her life. Having fallen in love with Peter Townsend, a World War Two flying ace and a royal equerry, a handsome and worthy man, she was forbidden by the queen and the

Anglican Church, of which Elizabeth had only shortly before become supreme governor, to marry him because he was divorced. Royals are not permitted to be as cavalier as others in their attitude toward marriage vows.

Some time later, Margaret married socially prominent photographer Anthony Armstrong-Jones. By the time that marriage proved untenable—their incompatibility and public squabbles long having been common gossip—the attitude toward divorce had eased sufficiently to permit that union to be dissolved without protests or pontifications from others. As is the case with less well-placed divorcées, she got custody of the two children and he got visiting rights.

Margaret's personal woes did nothing to diminish the merciless attention paid to her by the popular press. Unflattering photographs of the princess overweight, sometimes accompanied by unflattering comments, appeared with brutal regularity, alternating with reports of crash-diet programs on which she was said to have embarked. Similar scrutiny was given to her romance with a socially well-placed would-be singer seventeen years her junior with whom she visited a farming commune in Wales (later raided by the police because of drugs consumed there). The trips she took with him to a Caribbean island playground also attracted much publicity. On one such journey, they were defiantly booked on the flight out of London, where they were bound to be recognized, as "Mr. and Mrs. Brown."

Criticism of her behavior and attitudes appeared frequently in the newspapers. There was, for example, talk of her habit of often being agreeably informal with social inferiors and then suddenly turning frigidly haughty when they responded similarly.

Less public attention was paid to the fact that of all the British royals, Margaret has been the most interested in the arts, probably the most intelligent and the wittiest. She is known to be an amusing mimic and to have a lively command of repartee. But she has been repeatedly charged with not earning the allowance granted her by Parliament, of welshing on the time and energy she is expected to expend performing royal duties, attending functions, etc. Willie Hamilton was particularly biting, declaring, "She makes no attempt to conceal her expensive, extravagant irrelevance and it is impossible to make any honest case for her being much use to anybody." It was a cruel comment, but no crueller than the circumstances which transformed a bright, playful, happy girl into a moody public figure.

Whatever criticisms can be made of Princess Margaret, she is undoubtedly an interesting woman. The same is not generally thought to be true of her niece, the queen's daughter, Princess Anne. Anne, who was born in 1950, has been called the country's strongest anti-royalist argument. She led a sheltered life as a girl. She was not as exposed as her older brother, Charles, to situations and people where social distinctions had limited significance.

Though assigned various royal duties by her mother as she emerged into young womanhood, and while she took on various honorary titles—president of the Save the Children Fund, president of the Society for Film and Television Arts—her undisguised primary passion, aside from her immediate family, was and is horses. She is an excellent horsewoman, having competed for Britain in equestrian Olympics. Efforts by the Palace to expand her image to embrace a catalogue of worthwhile causes and interests have, however, failed to shake the prevailing public idea of what the princess is like. Aware of this, she once commented bitterly, "When I appear in public people expect me to neigh, grind my teeth, paw the ground, and swish my tail." As far as the British newspapers go, if it's Anne, it's almost always horses. It makes her seem a reluctant royal, someone who would much rather have been a simple rich girl with no public obligations and no need to justify her existence or preferences to the press or anyone else.

Kidnap victims are invariably exciting personalities, at least temporarily, and when a psychopath bungled an attempt to kidnap Anne a few years ago, it momentarily enhanced her public image. But irrepressible haughtiness and intermittent public displays of pointless arrogance—so unlike the graciousness of her mother and brother and the chumminess of her father—have done her reputation no good. In Australia once, a photographer presuming to call her "love"—a common, inoffensive, casual lower-class form of address to friends and strangers alike—prompted her stern rebuke, "I am not your love. I am your Royal Highness!" (When union leader Joe Gormley called Prince Charles "Charlie," the prince responded by calling him "Joey.")

Though the royal family is careful to keep strains in family relations out of the public eye, it is known that Charles and Anne, as they grew up, often rubbed each other the wrong way and often still do—much like siblings in many ordinary families. It is believed that the queen also has at times been unhappy with her daughter's behavior. Once, on a royal train approaching a station, an official, forgetting to knock first, opened the door of the sitting room compartment to tell the queen it was five minutes from arrival time and found himself looking at Anne, in a fury, angrily informing her mother, "I did not say that!" What it was that she didn't say remains a mystery because when the official—having backed quietly out—knocked and opened the door again thirty seconds later, the family was all smiles, having put on its public face.

Like her aunt, Anne is continually accused of not being worth the money the taxpayer spends on her upkeep. When her husband, the previously obscure but socially acceptable Captain Mark Phillips—also a dedicated horseperson—accepted a substantial sum for doing advertising work for the British Leyland car company, it was seen as unseemly cashing in on his royal marriage. Nor was there much sympathy when Captain Phillips suggested that he and Anne were just like another young couple paying off a mortgage, when their home is a million-dollar farm in Gloucestershire, a wedding present from the queen.

An index of criticisms of some members of the royal family might lead some people to suspect that the monarchy might be wearing thin. It might seem logical to conclude that when individual royals are commonly considered less than majestic, when they are judged by the same yardstick as ordinary mortals, when they are said to be unacceptably temperamental, when pounds-and-pence matters are repeatedly raised concerning royal expenses, then the whole idea is in danger of being brought down to earth and exposed to all sorts of pertinent, trivial considerations which make a mockery of the pageantry which is an essential element of monarchical survival.

An anti-royalist in Parliament is convinced that before this century is out "the monarchy and all its prostituted entourage [will be] dumped in the garbage can of history." Presidents and prime

ministers can be made to pass continually in review before the
critical eyes of the popular press of today and no great damage need
necessarily be done. But can the British monarchy maintain its
mystery and its following when it is exposed to the same pedestrian
treatment?

The answer is that it can, and without special effort. Britain is
fortunate to have an intelligent, dedicated monarch at the moment.
But even in times past, when the kings who sat on the same throne
were less admirable, when they were murderers, philanderers,
gluttons, and mentally unbalanced, there seemed to be little danger
to the monarchy itself, though individual kings and dynasties were
at times less than secure. For many centuries, kings of England
were under continual threat from rival claimants to the throne,
many of whom succeeded bloodily in their intrigues. Shakespeare
knew it well:

> . . . let us sit upon the ground
> and tell sad stories of the death of kings,
> How some have been deposed; some slain in war;
> Some haunted by the ghosts they have deposed;
> Some poison'd by their wives; some sleeping kill'd;
> All murder'd: for within the hollow crown
> That rounds the mortal temples of a king
> Keeps Death his court. . . .

Only little more than half the kings who have sat on the throne
of England survived to the age of fifty (though its two most
noteworthy queens—Elizabeth I and Victoria—survived to ripe old
age clinging effortlessly to the crown). When William II was
accidentally dispatched by an arrow while hunting in a forest, it
was considered perhaps no coincidence that his younger brother,
who then inherited the throne, was hunting in that forest at the
same time. Edward II aroused contempt for showering greater
affection on a handsome French knight than on his queen who
recruited an army to overthrow the king and whose lover arranged
for His Majesty to be dispatched for good.

Richard II was imprisoned and executed by his successor. Six
hundred years after the fact, arguments still rage among historians
over whether Richard III, who later was cut down in battle by forces

of another claimant, really had his two young nephews smothered in the Tower of London because they were a threat to his right to the throne. Elizabeth I agonized long and hard before deciding but she ultimately had Mary, queen of Scots and would-be queen of England, beheaded for plotting against her. George III wandered blind and insane through the corridors of his palace during the last years of his life. George IV was worn out early by his extravagant appetite for both food and women.

The first Briton to bear a royal title and make an impact on history was a woman who burnt down London. That was in 61 A.D. when the future capital of Britain was an outpost of the Roman invaders, against whom Queen Boadicea led her people in a bloody uprising. Ultimately defeated by veteran Roman legionnaires, Boadicea took poison. A statue of her—triumphantly astride a war chariot—stands at the foot of Westminster Bridge in London.

Despite her grand title, Boadicea was only one of several regional chieftains upon whom a rank befitting a monarch was arbitrarily conferred by early storytellers. It's likely that the type of soldier-hero about whom the legend of King Arthur was embroidered was a local warlord, like Boadicea, locked in combat with Saxon invaders who colonized Britain after the Roman withdrawal from the off-shore island to superintend the decline and fall of their disintegrating empire. They had occupied Britain for 403 years but left nothing more than bits of wall, remains of roads, and an assortment of other archaeological curiosities, mostly now found in museums. The coming of the Saxons marks the real beginning of English history.

The Saxon word *cyning*, referring to clan leader, is the root word of *king*. The seeds of what was to become a national monarchy were planted in Britain by the Saxons and other migrating tribes from northern Germany, including the Angles from whom the name England derives. These tribes established seven miniature "kingdoms" on English soil (wisely staying mostly clear of the warlike Scots and Welsh).

The emergence of full-fledged kings, in the commonly accepted sense of the word, was accelerated by the conversion of England from Saxon paganism to Christianity. Though pockets of heathenism persisted long afterwards, it was a remarkably rapid process, taking little more than sixty years following the arrival in

England of St. Augustine and the small bands of monks dispatched by the pope to undertake this enormous missionary task. During and after the conversion of the English, the bishops and other clergy sought and received the protection of local "kings" who had been won over to their faith. They, in turn, legitimized and nourished the regal pretensions of their secular protectors, offering them what would later become the divine right of kings to rule over their subjects, provided they did not challenge the spiritual authority of the Church.

But not until Alfred the Great, the soldier-scholar ruler of the Saxon kingdom of Wessex in southern England, did a single king become conceivable as overlord of the entire country. Alfred welded together alliances among the clannish communities of the sparsely populated land to take on the ferocious Vikings who had settled down to occupy large parts of England and who were bent on extending their domain. He formulated a code of laws around which a centralized monarchy might one day function. It was, however, a little premature.

The British monarchy as an effective institution had to wait another century before becoming a reality with the arrival of William the Conqueror, Duke of Normandy, who crossed over from France to claim the English crown. William quickly swept away the regional legacies and peculiarities of Saxon chieftains. The country was parceled out to Norman knights and dignitaries who pledged allegiance to the king in their new land. A shrewd and suspicious man, William sought to make certain none of these new feudal lords would be strong enough to challenge his authority or be in a position to band together with others against him or his heirs. No doubt justified (the Norman knights were a greedy and grasping bunch), his caution marked the beginning of an enduring rivalry between kings and nobles which ironically would produce the Magna Carta, the first exposition of the fundamental rights of individual Britons, Americans, and all other people influenced by British traditions.

That "Great Charter" which the barons forced King John to sign in 1215 was not designed as the ringing declaration of freedom it has sometimes been described as being. It was meant to narrow down the king's power to keep the nobles in line, to tax and punish them as he saw fit. Those nobles would have been appalled had they been able to foresee what would become its democratic significance:

> No free man shall be arrested or imprisoned or stripped of his rights or possessions or outlawed or exiled or deprived of his standing in any other way . . . except by the lawful judgment of his equals or by the law of the land.

It was was to be a long time before the full meaning of that and other historic declarations contained in the Magna Carta were realized. Kings did not lightly surrender their prerogatives.

The parliament came into being later in the thirteenth century to use tax-raising pressures to influence the king's decisions and actions. By the seventeenth century, it was able finally to challenge the king's right to rule, by which time there had already been a sequence of revolts, rebellions, and insurrections against royal authority. These didn't endanger the monarchy. But they symbolized the exposed positions in which individual monarchs could find themselves—the Peasants' Rebellion in 1381 which the boy king, Richard II, squelched by offering to lead it; Cade's rebellion of 1450 against the corruption of the king's agents which failed because the rebels offended the burghers of London with their lawlessness; Wyatt's abortive rebellion against Queen Mary in 1554 because she intended to marry a Catholic king of Spain. Still, as recently as two centuries ago, it was widely believed in Britain that the monarch was so exalted that a royal touch was enough to cure certain diseases, particularly scrofula (glandular tuberculosis).

Though there was often "blood on the throne," only once in the long, eventful history of the British monarchy was that throne left vacant. That was when the Puritans, who had Charles I beheaded, ruled the country under the leadership of Oliver Cromwell, the Lord Protector. Puritan rule was, however, too rigid and demanding for the English and after just eleven austere, abstemious years, they welcomed back a king to reign over them—Charles II, son of the decapitated monarch.

But the days of the divine right of kings were drawing to a close. When Charles's successor, James II, persecuted Protestants and tried to reintroduce the Catholicism into Britain which Henry VIII had outlawed a century and a half earlier, he was driven from the throne and from the country and William of Orange was invited over from Holland to wear the British crown with the understanding that he and his heirs gained that right only by grace of Parliament.

It was the same anti-Catholic prejudice which led Parliament to invite a Protestant German prince to wear the British crown when Queen Anne died twenty-six years later without a suitable heir and the next Englishman in line for the throne refused to renounce his Catholic faith. The transplanted German, King George I, hated England, spoke only German, and was delighted to leave the conduct of affairs of the country over which he was supposed to reign to his English ministers. The chief of those became the prime minister by title as well as function. Successive kings would attempt to regain some of the regal authority which had been confiscated by Parliament over the centuries and the monarchy continued to play an important role in the formalities of government and in the morale of the country. But no longer could anyone suggest, as James I once had, that "kings are justly called gods" because of their "resemblance to divine power on earth; they have power to exalt low things and abase high things and to make their subjects like men at chess."

Queen Victoria, who wore the crown for most of the nineteenth century, was the longest reigning British monarch. She ascended the throne in 1837 as a girl of eighteen and stayed there sixty-three years, until she died in 1901. The Victorian era was marked by an enormous expansion of the British Empire (Victoria was dubbed Empress of India) and by the emergence of Britain as the world's leading technological, industrial, and commercial country. Victoria's children and grandchildren were to ally the British throne with a half dozen other European royal families, producing some anomalies. Shortly before the outbreak of the First World War, Victoria's son and heir, Edward VII, could murmur casually that his nephew "Willy" (Kaiser Wilhelm of Germany) was contemplating war, a conflict that would end up costing both nations and the rest of Europe millions of dead.

Historical developments favor different nations at different times. During the Victorian era, Britain was most favored of all. None of Victoria's successors were able to match the grandeur of her reign nor the grandeur of Britain during her reign. Nor is it likely that any ever will in the future.

Can it be justifiable anywhere for there to be a hereditary king or

queen who may or may not be worthy of such rank and responsibility, whose forebears were more often than not of no special
quality, who is furnished by the public with luxuries and privileges,
and who is honored, loved, and respected simply for being the
monarch? The indefensibility of it all is why there are so few kings
and queens sitting on national thrones today.

However, it is unlikely that the British monarchy will soon fade
from the scene. Regardless of how anachronistic much of its
trappings may be, the British are far less fickle than most people.
The undiminished popularity of their monarchy, untarnished even
in hard times, sustains it. Where its popularity does not suffice, its
role in providing the necessary element of continuity in the
turbulent arena of politics serves to keep it meaningful and active,
though an alternative political device probably could be devised,
and probably would be demanded, if ever an out-and-out incompetent or villain mounted the throne.

It is extremely unlikely that the monarchy will ever regain the
authority or influence it once wielded. But it is not beyond the
realm of possibility. If the instruments of decision-making in the
government were ever paralyzed by economic disaster or political
stalemate, a strong, popular monarch could conceivably step in to
save the country from floundering. In the process, that monarch
could restore something of the monarchy's former glory to match
its enduring pageantry.

Looking past the bigotry it displayed, there is a lingering moral in
the insistence of Edward VII at his coronation that the obscure
visiting king of a cluster of Pacific islands be treated with the
proper respect and protocol due to his rank: "Either the brute is a
king or else he is an ordinary black nigger, and if he is not a king,
why is he here?" Either the monarch is a monarch or else why the
fuss and bother?

Ruling the Roost

A BIG SURPRISE awaiting many a visitor to Britain is the remarkable shenanigans perpetrated from time to time on the floor of the House of Commons. A few hours in the visitors galley of that august chamber can sometimes be enough to demolish whatever image of the dignity of "the mother of parliaments" or the sanctity of "the birthplace of democracy" the visitor might have brought with him.

Raucous unparliamentary practice is not at all unusual in the place where parliamentary procedure was invented. Members of Parliament jeer and taunt opponents like enraged yahoos and frenzied schoolboys. They regularly shout each other down, or try to, only reluctantly obeying the Speaker's repeated pleas for "Order! Order!" If a parliamentarian, lacking confidence in either his memory or his powers of impromptu oratory, presumes in a debate to read his argument from a prepared paper, opponents will jeer "Reading!" at him like malicious adolescents until he stops. If, during formal "question time" for ministers, a parliamentarian makes a statement, opponents will screech "Question! Question!" until he rewords that same statement in the form of a question ("Does the minister realize that. . . ?") as if the form were important and not the substance. It is often astoundingly fatuous.

Most of the oratory in Parliament is more concerned with political in-fighting than with governing the country. Regardless of how well or poorly they are doing their jobs, in the House of Commons government ministers are primarily intent on finding suitably meaningless words to evade answering questions from the opposition on matters of policy. Opposition spokesmen who were

179

government ministers before their party was voted out of power indulge in ringing, outraged declamations, demanding solutions from their successors for current problems which were problems they themselves could not resolve when they were in office. The main objective of practically everybody is to score points, which is why many Britons derisively refer to Parliament as a "talking shop." It often seems merely a place for clever politicians to try to show just how clever they are.

There has been violence on the floor of the Commons. Angered by a Conservative government move to end debate on a controversial measure, Labor Party parliamentarians physically blocked the exit until they got their way. Conservative Michael Heseltine, outraged by the behavior of Labor members who had burst into song to celebrate a minor victory, seized the ceremonial rod of the House and flourished it over his head like a club (he has been called Tarzan ever since). One afternoon, Bernadette Devlin, a young woman representing a Northern Irish Catholic constituency, marched across the central aisle of the House to slap the Home Secretary across the face (thus waking him up, according to some observers).

Such incidents are not common but the sound and fury is an expression of relentless antagonism that exists between Britain's political parties. The Conservatives (commonly called Tory) and Labor (socialist) are the main parties. There are also a smaller Liberal Party and a newly formed Social Democratic Party which is striving energetically to capture and hold the middle ground in British politics and thus be able to form a government before too much longer, perhaps in coalition with the Liberals.

Though much of the noise that accompanies the unrelenting hostility between the parties is vain nonsense, it has ironically been important for the maintenance of democracy in the country. Without it, with harmony reigning supreme in the House of Commons, the British political system might be a set-up for the imposition of tyranny.

The way the British govern themselves is deceptive and, despite all the exuberance, it is subtle. Their political system is like a well-preserved antique automobile which is elegant despite the very inelegant sounds it sometimes makes. It doesn't always work exactly as it should but it has proved sturdier than many newfangled models. People keep expecting it to break down as it goes through its paces, and there are things about it which are less than admirable, but it has proved tenaciously durable through thick and thin.

The most intriguing component of the British political system is the British constitution—there is none! At least there is no comprehensive written document to define and thereby limit the authority of the government and prevent it from assuming dictatorial powers. What the British call their constitution is a body of individual laws and practices which have been handed down over the centuries. Theoretically, they can all be reversed, revised, or overruled without too much complication or strain. The British do have a Bill of Rights. It dates from 1689 but was drawn up primarily to prevent the king from pushing Parliament around and to make certain, at a time of profound religious hatreds, that a Catholic never mounted the throne. There is no absolute legal guarantee of the civil rights of the individual as there is in that British offspring, the United States.

Officially—and here's where the major peril seems to lurk—the law of the land is ultimately only what Parliament says it is. If Parliament in its wisdom decreed that elections and freedom of speech should be abolished, that newspapers should be censored and opponents of the government clapped in irons, no legal authority in the country would have the power to countermand instructions for those decisions to be implemented by the appropriate authorities. Parliament is supreme. Lord Denning, one of the country's most eminent modern jurists, urged not long ago that its judges be given authority like that enjoyed by the American Supreme Court to determine whether laws passed by Parliament are an abuse of government power. But that proposal has aroused little interest among working politicians or the general public. The only power Parliament is still said to lack is the power to turn a man into a woman, though medical science seems to be in the process of eliminating that restriction.

But the threat of a totalitarian coup by the theoretically almighty Parliament cannot really be taken seriously. Too many differing and conflicting opinions and philosophies are continually, energetically, and furiously at play there. In practice, dictatorship in Britain would seem to an outsider a great possibility from another built-in source. As things stand, absolute power could conceivably be assumed by a single individual, the prime minister.

The British political system is geared to giving the prime minister the kind of authority an American president can only envy—to decide what legislation should and should not be initiated in the omnipotent Parliament as well as the power to push desired laws through Parliament, after which all the instruments of government, and the courts, could be mobilized to enforce those laws regardless of how tyrannical or unprecedented they might be.

Despite these apparent dangers, the specter of dictatorship does *not* cast a shadow over Britain. And it's not simply good taste that keeps it at bay. In order to control Parliament, the prime minister must control a working majority in the House of Commons, and the British people have recurringly elected governments with majorities small enough to discourage delusions of grandeur in any individual. More important, even when the prime minister's majority is solid and supportive, there is an intricate interplay of customs, procedures, attitudes, and expectations that would effectively frustrate a would-be "unconstitutional" dictator. There are parliamentary committees, not nearly as influential as congressional committees in the United States but influential enough to be a serious nuisance to the government in crunch situations. There is the House of Lords, no longer able to veto legislation but capable of delaying its passage. Though the prime minister appoints and can sack cabinet members, they are usually important figures within the prime minister's party. Serious disapproval of prime ministerial policies within the cabinet would carry much weight, as would a thumping outburst of criticism within party ranks. That sort of criticism had to be taken into account by Prime Minister Thatcher when her economic policies showed few signs of working. And though the policies of the major parties are in fundamental conflict, there is a measure of self-restraint each exercises in wielding governmental authority when in power. Each realizes that respective power positions might be reversed at the next election and is thereby encouraged to play the game of politics by rules established through tradition. Such practices as stacking parliamentary committees and making inappropriate, biased civil service appointments are thus generally unthinkable.

However, the most important element in the peculiar British system which has guaranteed liberty and justice longer than any other system in the world was pinpointed by the British judge who said, "The safeguard of British liberty is in the good sense of the people." Former government minister Michael Stewart noted that, "The sovereignty of Parliament is limited by the fact that everyone expects Parliament to be periodically dissolved and reelected, so that the last word shall rest with the people." By law (which Parliament can but won't change) the prime minister must call new elections at least every five years.

The rule of law is central to the British political process. Nothing can be done by government officials unless Parliament passes specific legislation to authorize it. When the government is granted emergency powers, to cope, for example, with crippling strikes affecting essential services, Parliament (with the prime minister's approval) invariably tacks on a proviso requiring those powers to be regularly reviewed so that arbitrary privileges do not become addictive to government officials as they have, for example, in France where the rule of law is not fundamental to the workings of society.

Even ministers who have engaged in widely acclaimed activities are sometimes held to account. When, in 1980, elite Strategic Air Service (SAS) commandoes were sent in, guns blazing, to quickly and efficiently end a takeover of the Iranian embassy in London by gunmen who had seized hostages there—an event televised and admired throughout the world—a member of Parliament rose in the House of Commons to warn that "it would be a deplorable precedent if (the SAS) were given immunity from prosecution for carrying out summary executions of terrorists."

There is considerable efficiency in the British parliamentary system. With a few comparatively minor exceptions, the power to introduce and pass laws is confined exclusively to the government. The opposition cannot introduce legislation—it can only try, usually in vain, to block or alter government proposals. Thus the party chosen by the voters to form the government generally has enough leeway to implement at least the core of the program with which it campaigns for election.

Whether it does so depends on circumstances. When, for example, Mrs. Thatcher was elected prime minister with a comfortable parliamentary majority in 1979, Britain's economic problems were so frightening that, as she later regretted, she felt constrained by the possibility of doing further damage from fully ramming through all the drastic changes she favored, particularly in slashing government spending. Her predecessor, Labor Prime Minister James Callaghan, had so slender a majority in the House of Commons that he too refrained from doing all he would have liked to have done. The machinery is there—*even for dictatorship.* Circumstances and tradition circumscribe its use.

Nevertheless, executive authority to make quick, surgical alterations in government policies and performance is recurringly invoked and whatever advantages in efficiency it contains are often counterbalanced by the damage such authority can wreak. With the policies and ideologies of the major parties clashing so fundamentally, each party continually sounds off about its intention to change key laws passed by the other. When elected, it can have the power to do so. The result is that important issues, like those related to education and health care, defense and control of industry, become political footballs. Government decisions on them are implemented, altered, and altered again. The British steel industry was nationalized by a Labor government in 1950, denationalized by the Conservatives three years later, renationalized by Labor in 1967, and "restructured" by the Conservatives in 1979. It's a confusing, wasteful, and expensive process. What's more, promises by an opposition party to reverse things when it's voted back into power can induce cynicism among civil servants whose job it is to put government policies into practice.

As governments come and go, it is the function of British civil servants to maintain the continuity of government performance. Sometimes cabinet ministers play musical chairs, staying in their ministries only a few months—barely enough time to learn what the job is—before being shunted to another ministry in a government reshuffle. In the meantime, taxes must be collected, public expenditure must be channeled out (or reigned in), foreign policy must be implemented, social services must be maintained—the work of the ministries must go on.

If senior civil servants relied only on the instructions of the ministers who head their departments, the processes of government would soon break down. Over the course of time, they have therefore assumed powers that are not officially theirs in order to keep their departments functioning efficiently according to their own experience and standards. Sometimes those standards conflict with those of their ministers, the elected masters they are expected to obey. More than one former cabinet minister has claimed that his wishes were repeatedly ignored or downplayed by officials who supposedly were in their jobs only to follow his instructions.

Saddled with a minister who is determined to make major department changes, and is thus intent on rocking what they consider a smoothly sailing boat, civil servants are not adverse to engaging in a discreet form of sabotage to have their own way. They might conceal vital information from the minister or hide the fact that his instructions are being ignored, or secretly promote policies contrary to his own in such a way that he ultimately has no choice but to accept them. Former minister Gerald Kaufman, in his book *How to Be a Minister*, said civil servants operate on the principle that their minister is an imbecile. He warned future ministers that rejecting the advice of civil servants can lead to "rearguard action so skilled as to leave you breathless with admiration and fury."

Politicians are elected by the people and may therefore be understandably frustrated and enraged by such behavior from men and women exceeding their authority. But the British civil service is for the most part a dedicated and efficient group of people who play a vital and usually constructive role in the British system. A minister bent on a major change in department policy can always make that change if he is persistent, determined, and shrewd enough, as he should be if he is worthy of office. But aside from providing essential continuity for the processes of government, the British civil service exercises a meaningful braking effect, restraining precipitate action by ministers new to their jobs and unaware of possible ramifications and consequences of hasty action.

Civil servants are held in much higher regard in Britain than they are in many other countries. Theirs is generally considered a reputable if colorless profession and they are deemed so reliable that they are offered advantageous automobile insurance rates. A long bout of selective strikes against government activities called by the civil service union in pursuit of a pay raise not long ago chipped away a little at their reputation for reliability. But it also underscored their importance. Among other things, with the inflow of collected taxes reduced to a dribble by the strikes, the government was forced to borrow money to pay its bills.

But even before that, concern could justifiably have been expressed about some aspects of civil service influence on the democratic processes. Civil servants are so much in control of the government's day-to-day activities that ordinary citizens have very little opportunity of successfully challenging government procedures or decisions. Individuals can complain to their representatives in Parliament who might take their grievances up with the appropriate ministries or with the Parliamentary Commissioner for Administration who is empowered to investigate charges of maladministration. Out-and-out maladministration by ministries is not habitual in Britain but cases do exist, as in the inefficient, wasteful running of the National Health Service. Yet the complaints arrangement has produced few dramatic revelations or changes and rarely has resulted in civil servants being called upon by their ministers to explain what in hell is going on and to do something about it.

This is frequently true as well in local government councils which concentrate exclusively on community matters—schools, housing, zoning, real estate taxes, garbage collection. Local government officials tend to be public-spirited and competent. But individuals with grievances don't always find it easy to get satisfaction from them. Cash shortages are often responsible but there have been, for example, countless cases of people in public housing being frustrated when trying to get their local councils to make essential repairs to their roofs, walls, or plumbing.

Britons are reluctant to join pressure groups to press their complaints against officialdom (it's not their style). As individuals, they are more often than not also reluctant to fight City Hall. When they do, they generally receive a fair hearing though too often they're too late, the pertinent decisions on project design, cash expenditure, or work loads already having been made. The paucity of effective public pressure groups means necessary information about controversial local government action is rarely adequately disseminated in the community. That's convenient for civil servants. It means less public protest, particularly at times when public money is in short supply when they have to indulge in unpopular trimmings of public services and even less popular real estate tax increases.

To be outspokenly critical of the government is a time-honored British custom. But the press in Britain, which might be expected to be the vanguard of such irreverence, can be surprisingly timid. British newspapers (the London morning papers are national papers read throughout the country) are informative, lively, and generally a pleasure to read. The best of them—the London *Times, Guardian, Daily Telegraph, Sunday Times, Observer*—are agreeably literate and impressively perceptive. Others—like the *Daily Mail, Daily Mirror* and *Standard* (London's evening newspaper)—are provocative and entertaining. But though they are not censored and regularly take vigorous exception to government policies, they are all roped in by legal constraints and restrictive habits which blunt their reporting flair and keep them from tenaciously pursuing public causes.

Legal restrictions on the press are sharply defined. Laws of libel are strict and penalties for violations can be inflicted by the courts on printers and newspaper distributors as well as on publishers, editors, and reporters. An accepted definition of libel shows how careful the newspapers have to be: "A libel is a defamatory statement reflecting upon a person's character or reputation which tends to lower him in the estimation of right thinking members of society; or which tends to bring him into hatred, ridicule, contempt, fear, dislike or disesteem with society in general; or which causes him to be shunned or cut off from society generally." Subject to a libel law like that, lawyers for newspapers in America would be spending practically all their time in court.

Matters before the court in Britain are formally described as under judicial consideration *(sub judice)* and may not be reported in any detail unless reporting restrictions are specifically lifted by the court. Violations of this restriction is contempt of court which can be severely punished. There is also a system of "D" (for defense) notices under which newspapers and other reporting organizations are advised not to use certain stories if the authorities say they affect national security. Though it's only advice, virtually all the media automatically respect "D" notices.

Occasional leaks from government or ministerial sources make good stories but the Official Secrets Act is a potent threat which keeps such disclosures to a minimum. Any civil servant who, without proper authorization, reveals to unauthorized persons information which might be "prejudicial to the safety or interests of the state" is committing a crime, can be brought to trial, and might be sent to jail.

These formal constraints on press initiative are reinforced by self-imposed curbs, primarily those affecting the elite of British political journalists, the "lobby" correspondents. The "lobby" is the antechamber of the House of Commons to which a selected group of about one hundred leading political reporters and commentators may gain access to mix and mingle with parliamentarians and ministers and "chat them up." They also have early access to government papers and special briefings with government officials. It is understood, however, that lobby correspondents will not violate confidences which come their way by virtue of their privileged status unless permitted by their sources.

The result is stultifying. The journalists involved are spoon-fed information. Their inclination to go out and dig up stories on their own is blunted. As a consequence, scoops are extremely rare. It is unusual for one newspaper or news broadcast outfit to produce a story its rivals don't also have.

There are signs, however, that British newsmen are growing restless and are more inclined these days to bridle at legal and traditional constraints. Investigatory journalism, particularly as practiced with such dramatic consequences in the United States, has proved infectious. A new breed of British journalist is springing up, less prone to be content with occasional rations of handouts when worthy stories could be lurking beneath the surface waiting to be dug out.

That development could have far-reaching implications. If the Fourth Estate, with its insatiable hunger for new, exciting stories and its propensity for thriving on scandal and disaster, did genuinely become as influential a force in Britain as it is in the United States, British society would be in for a considerable shock. Prevailing British values would become vulnerable to fundamental alteration. Whatever the benefits (and politically they could be substantial), many Britons would deeply regret the resulting excitement and controversy. A variety of British habits and customs which survive well enough outside the limelight might face extinction if the media in the country began throbbing with competitive investigatory and puritanical impulses of the kind which now propel their American counterparts on to exposé after exposé.

Probably among the first to go (and not to be sorely missed) under the searing scrutiny of an inflamed press is the significance attached to excessive, often irresponsible political loyalties in Britain. Rarely will a Tory politician back a Labor Party proposal, nationally or locally, and vice versa, no matter how reasonable that proposal might be. To do so, except in the most extreme situations, would be considered betrayal of political principles.

It is accepted as gospel in British politics that the overriding duty of an opposition party is "to oppose." In this land of eccentrics, a politician learns early in his career to stick up for his own side, and to take issue with the other side, no matter what. When the elected Labor Party chairman of a local government council in northern England announced no Tory supporters would from then on be hired to fill vacancies at Town Hall, some disapproval was voiced here and there but the matter was soon forgotten. It might or might not happen but was not deemed so extraordinary a thing for a council chairman to say.

The Labor Party is particularly inflexible when it comes to party loyalties. When, as happens, individual Laborites change their political allegiances, leave the Labor Party to form a new political grouping or—horror of horrors!—to join the hated Conservatives, they are savagely denounced and methodically ostracized, their crimes being considered a few shades worse than murder. (Recent efforts by doctrinaire leftists to seize control of the Labor Party have, however, made moderate Laborites distinctly uncomfortable and have, in many cases, diluted the intensity of their traditionally reflexive political loyalties.)

The Conservatives are not immune from such narrowness. When a Conservative member of Parliament quit the party to join the Social Democrats, he considered it wise to resign as well from a London gentlemen's club much frequented by Conservatives to avoid possible unpleasantries there. That a person has changed his political philosophy or has been disillusioned by the leaders of the political movement to which he belonged is considered a limp excuse for that kind of fickleness. Ignoring the great problems of choice most of us have to confront in life, a Conservative politician declared, "To break ranks with one's party and vote against one's own government is the most disagreeable decision any member of Parliament has to take."

The stodginess of British political loyalties has a serious inhibiting effect, compounding the average Briton's reluctance to get involved in the political process that intrudes upon his life. An occasional collective protest against government intentions has proved effective in, for example, blocking the construction of a disputed highway through an attractive residential area or preventing the destruction of an historic landmark. But when things go wrong, supporters of the party in power feel obliged to defend the authorities while its opponents feel obliged to exaggerate the problem. Questions which should have very little to do with political loyalties—whether certain streets should be closed to traffic, whether the gates of a local park should be locked at night, whether public money should subsidize a local theater—persistently take on political coloring. It dilutes whatever urgency those questions might have and tends to discourage even usually dauntless individuals from getting implicated in the political wrangling that ensues.

The consequences are evident in more serious matters. Britons regularly accept huge periodic increases in telephone, postal, gas, and electricity charges with nary a murmur other than to mention how expensive things are getting. Though there are all sorts of legal advice centers and legal advice manuals, Britons have generally digested such assaults on their living standards without seeking ways to reverse or stem the tide.

They don't want to appear to be troublemakers. Although theirs is a system based on the rule of law, "going to law" is not something the British do readily. One reason is the expense involved. Poorer people are adequately protected by free legal aid. But there is no American-style system of contingency fees for lawyers to cushion expenses for individuals seeking legal redress. Furthermore the British two-tier lawyer system can be intimidating.

People turn to solicitors when they have legal problems. But if the case goes to court, those solicitors must call in barristers who are the only ones who can plead a case before a judge and jury. The client rarely has much to do with the barrister and sometimes doesn't even see him privately. Barristers are "briefed" by the solicitors who are supposed to gather all the necessary information from the client. It means that a person taking a case to court (or being taken to court without the benefit of legal aid) must pay two lawyers right through the trial, one of whom he might have very little to do with directly, and the services of experienced barristers can be very expensive. A leading British judge noted, "In this country, justice is open to all—like the Ritz Hotel."

The drawbacks of such a system are obvious but so is its main advantage. Unlike the United States where people seem inclined to rush off to lawyers with the intention of suing others at the slightest provocation, the British pride themselves in not having a "litigious society" with all the anxieties, hostilities, anguish, and uncertainties that go with it. (The case of an American woman suing a weather forecaster for getting things wrong was reported with amusement in Britain. Word of incidents in America in which people were taking their clergymen to court for giving faulty spiritual advice was received with incredulity.)

Resident foreigners and visiting businessmen complain that British lawyers spend most of their time telling them what they cannot do rather than how they might be able to do it. Court procedures often seem archaic and embellished with charming ritual which result in needless delays and increased legal costs. Reforms would clearly be in order. But, despite the survival of a few doddering judicial personages, the dedication to justice, intelligence, and reasonableness of the typical British judge is impressive. So is his determination to make certain that all concerned in a case know exactly what is happening at all times. His careful, sometimes seemingly dull-witted interrogation of people giving testimony is often designed to make certain that members of the jury who might be less sophisticated than others understand exactly what has been said. ("You say you met the defendant in a McDonald's. What, pray, is a McDonald's?") Nevertheless, legal costs are such that the only people guaranteed adequate access to and representation in British courts are those poor enough to receive legal aid or rich enough not to worry about legal expenses— only about twenty-five percent of the population.

British magistrate courts, where all criminal charges are first heard and from which more serious cases are sent on to the higher courts, also provide an admirably efficient and equitable means for dealing with minor infringements of the law. There is a small number of professional magistrates. But most magistrates are not professionals. They are senior members of the community, including teachers, businessmen, and doctors, often retired. They are unpaid and rarely have any legal training. They use their good sense and rely on their law clerks for interpretations of fine legal points. They deal with misdemeanors in an eminently fair and unbiased fashion. (This is said *not* only because a magistrate once ruled that although I had broken the law by making a forbidden turn out of congested London traffic, the circumstances which led me to break the law were such that the act was not unreasonable or dangerous and that I, therefore, should not be penalized.) The magistrates court is so much a reflection of the common acceptance of the rule of law in Britain that during a strike which was roundly condemned by the government and the newspapers as irresponsibly damaging to the British economy, the union leader who led the strike was eligible to sit as a magistrate in his community, where he had a reputation for passing wise and appropriate judgment on those caught drunk-and-disorderly, breaking-and-entering, and committing other offenses.

British respect for human rights and the rule of law goes back a long way. The existence of only a comparatively small population in the formative years of the country played an important role in establishing respect for the dignity of the individual. In more densely populated parts of the world, transgressors who broke the rules of the community or disobeyed the orders of lords and masters could be executed or beaten without a second thought. In Britain, the supply of labor was limited. To wantonly kill, maim, or incapacitate someone who was needed to bring in the harvest was self-defeating. A high regard for human life and for the well-being of the individual was thus developed. Though there have been moments in British history when life has been considered cheap and brutality has been rampant, this regard was translated into law and morality and remains central to British law and morality today. The proper and admirable functioning of British justice and government depends to a great extent on the skills and sense of duty of its elected and appointed officials. But respect for the individual is a potent obstacle to any conceivable imposition of tyranny in the country.

Some years ago, a Scotland Yard spokesman told me that "the Yard" was delighted that, unlike policemen elsewhere, the British cop did not tote a gun. It meant, he said, that British criminals were unlikely to carry firearms either. There was, therefore, less chance that anybody would get hurt.

Now the pace of events has transformed the working habits of the British police. While the possession of handguns is still illegal without hard-to-get licenses, the threat of gunfire in the streets was introduced a few years ago by foreign political terrorists fighting foreign battles on British soil. Special police squads had to be armed against them. Not long afterward, homegrown British criminals began using guns, posing an unprecedented threat to public order.

The "bobby" on the beat—often a fresh-faced youngster barely out of his teens—is still unarmed and incidents recur in which he (or she) nevertheless bravely takes on a criminal wielding a knife or other weapon. But now one out of every ten policemen has been trained in the use of firearms. A substantial number of them (notably among the elite Diplomatic Protection Group) are armed at all times and just about every police station has its own armory to draw upon in case of emergency. Though probably inevitable, it is a regrettable development.

Perhaps even worse, the once incorruptible British policeman has been tainted by scandal. Several policemen have been arrested, expelled from the force, or suspended after being accused of taking bribes to overlook crimes or engaging in crimes themselves. Others have been accused of seriously mistreating prisoners in police custody.

Claims that police systematically harass innocent black youngsters are widespread. Street riots in British cities, mostly directed against the police, revealed the extent of resentment against "the men in blue" in non-white and some poor neighborhoods. It is apparent that policemen, particularly young ones, have been unprepared to cope with the strains which have developed in multiracial districts of British cities.

However, there is no reason to believe that most British police officers are anything but honest, dedicated, and fair. Visiting foreigners, of course, often tend to see things differently than locals, but those who have some reason to deal with the British police almost invariably find them to be pleasant, courteous, and helpful, unlike their counterparts in, say, France or Spain. Generally speaking, a person driving a car in Britain and spotting a police car behind him is not automatically gripped by the uncomfortable gut feeling he often has in America that he may be doing something for which he can be penalized.

Nevertheless, the picture of the British policeman as a firm but gentle pillar of rectitude, a true-blue, straight-as-a-die lawman, has suffered distinct erosion of late and may suffer more as the British press grows less timid than it has been up to now. Charges that police improprieties are not as forcefully dealt with by the police authorities as they should be are commonly heard these days.

The effectiveness of the bobby on the beat as a law enforcer has also been noticeably diminished. John Alderson, chief constable of Devon and Cornwall, noted recently, "When I joined the force just after the war, the sight of a blue uniform walking down the street was enough to restore order." Now the British police in city centers feel the need to have sophisticated protective gear ready to be donned if needed, as well as heavy back-up equipment, including armored vehicles and water cannons.

Incidentally, Hollywood and television may have mistakenly led some people to imagine British detectives to be dapper, excruciatingly polite, quietly shrewd, upper-class-accented sleuths with computer-like brains, pigskin gloves, and snazzy walking sticks. In fact, the average British detective is a tough, hard-working policeman who has usually graduated from beat duty. His origins, as displayed by his accent, are usually working-class. He is too busy out on the street pursuing villains to indulge in leisurely contemplations of the kind which helped Sherlock Holmes to crack so many cases. It is a pity that his reputation has been muddied by disclosures about the improper behavior of a comparative handful of his colleagues.

As anyone who has used it can testify, the British National Health Service is an extraordinary phenomenon. Its workings make it possible for Britons never to have to worry about being able to afford essential medical treatment. The benefits accrue not only to ordinary, everyday people. An Englishman explained, "If I wanted to, I could kiss my job goodbye, trot off to live in a hut in darkest Wales and never have to worry about what might happen if I broke my leg jogging down a mountainside."

Everyone, except a small number of rich Britons who choose not to use the service, has a neighborhood family doctor to whom he can go free of charge for advice, prescriptions, or referral to specialists. Specialist care and hospitalization are also free under "the National Health." No Briton is forced to calcuate how much his health or that of his family might cost. If he has to be rushed to the emergency ward of a hospital, no questions are asked about payment and no charge is made for treatment. Compared to money-conscious medical care elsewhere, it is a great, civilized mercy.

But, alas, the system is not the medical paradise its planners thought it would become. No one imagined how expensive it would be for the taxpayer to finance a free health service. Charges for medicines prescribed by the family doctor, though usually still far below the market price, have risen. There is talk of leveling a token charge for hospital patients. Some hospitals have had to be closed and the facilities of others reduced. New forms of financing—perhaps through a national insurance scheme—are being considered. But the money problem remains unresolved.

Anyone needing emergency care is seen to immediately by National Health doctors without question—another merciful and civilized aspect of the system. But one percent of the population of the country who require non-emergency operations (for hernias, hip replacement, etc.) are waiting to be called in for surgery. Facilities are simply not adequate to deal with everyone's problems as they crop up. Some people have been waiting for their operations for years. Some will die before their turn comes.

A lottery was held at a Liverpool hospital not long ago to determine which nine of fourteen women would be admitted for the non-acute gynecological surgery they all needed. The losers kept returning for the lottery to take their chances with new patients until their numbers came up. The doctor who decided which of the eligible candidates for free heart transplants under the National Health Service would be chosen for the operation, and which would not, resigned the job because it had become "too worrying." There weren't enough funds for all and playing God was not his cup of tea.

These shortcomings explain the growing success of private health insurance schemes and private hospitals in Britain. Despite the free National Health Service, an increasing number of Britons have decided to pay health insurance premiums to be certain of getting the treatment they want when they want it. Most people who subscribe to those insurance programs also use the National Health Service—paid for out of their taxes. Which they choose to use depends on which system is more suitable and convenient for their particular medical problems as they arise. For difficult, acute surgery, treatment at one of the big well-equipped, well-staffed National Health hospitals is considered advisable. For most other things, aside from relatively minor consultations with their family doctors, private medical care is more accessible.

The result is not what the architects of the National Health Service had in mind when they dreamed of a system under which every Briton would have the same access to superior standards of medical care. But though those able and willing to pay can get privileged treatment, it remains true that no one in the country has to dread being wiped out financially by poor health.

NINE

Foreigners and Their Peculiar Ways

HAVING DECIDED long ago that God is British, the people of Britain sometimes have trouble accounting for the existence of so many people who are not. "I'm not a foreigner; I'm a bloody Englishman!" protested an outraged Liverpudlian, setting straight a German traffic cop who had presumed to suggest he was from foreign parts after stopping him for speeding on a road outside Frankfurt.

The problem is that so many foreign parts seem both attractive and accessible. Not unlike their forebears who took along their dinner jackets on safari in the wilds of Tanganyika in the old days, the British today form cricket clubs in California, open pubs dispensing best bitter in Paris, crowd transplanted fish-and-chips emporiums in Torremolinos ("better than that foreign muck!"), and converge on British Council libraries in Kuala Lumpur and Lusaka for a regular fix of Agatha Christie and Graham Greene.

As for foreigners on their home ground, the British approach was neatly summed up by V.S. Pritchett: "The attitudes to foreigners is like the attiude to dogs: dogs are neither human nor British, but so long as you keep them under control, give them their exercise, feed them, pat them, you will find their wild emotions are amusing, and their characters interesting. . . . The [London] landlady gazes at her spaniel and says with proud complacency, 'He's trying to say something.' So is the foreigner. After a year or two of resentment, the foreigner recognizes that London is a place where we are all mongrels together, mainly on leash, but let out for short, mad daily scampers in the park."

The British concede that their country has slipped considerably down the scale of influence among the nations of the world—that the Americans make better movies, the Germans have better union-management relations, and the Japanese display a knack for too many things. The Union Jack hasn't been waving as proudly as they would like of late. Too many Britons have to subsist on unemployment insurance and other social welfare payments. But with the television license paid up, an occasional flutter on a nag at the turf accountant (bookie) down the High Street, a candy bar for "elevenses" each morning, the landlord of the pub at the corner keeping the tone of the place about right, and a couple of weeks by the seaside each summer, most Britons are, despite everything, well enough pleased, thank you, not to be numbered among the foreigners. Only the fact that the vocabulary of racial prejudice has become distinctly uncouth keeps them from voicing their long-held belief that "the wogs [worthy Oriental gentlemen] begin at Calais," Calais across the English Channel in France being the nearest port of call outside the British Isles.

The British understand perfectly why so many foreign political refugees have chosen over the ages to scamper for sanctuary to their homeland, including in this century such notables as Lenin, Freud, DeGaulle, Nureyev, the Sultan of Zanzibar, and the last president of South Vietnam. Two centuries ago, they provided asylum for thousands of loyalists who chose to flee back from the American colonies to the mother land when George Washington's ragtag army succeeded in the revolt against the crown.

The British have been befuddled about the United States ever since. It's not simply a matter of whether individual Britons are pro-American or anti-American. Many who have been most vitriolic in their criticism of American policies identify more strongly wih native American heretics who share their views than they do with anyone else anywhere. They visit the United States often and feel perfectly at home there. A prominent spokesman for a campaign for ending Britain's alignment with American foreign policy, a man who insisted American attitudes were malicious and dangerous, took time out from that campaign to teach at an American university where he was received hospitably. There are complex links between the people of the two countries which transcend day-to-day differences.

The British attitude to America has been a potpourri of wonder and disdain, amusement and despair, admiration and disapproval— sometimes all at the same time. Arnold Toynbee saw America as "a large, friendly dog in a very small room. Every time it wags its tail, it knocks over a chair."

Admiration wasn't much in evidence before 1776 when sophisticated Englishmen tended to consider compatriots who had settled in the American colonies to be brash bumpkins, bereft of wit, polish, and an appreciation of the good things in life. As the first stirrings of the American independence movement were felt, it was not hard for them to picture Americans as bumbling, stumbling Yankee Doodles, backwoods hicks with lunatic pretensions. When an independent, dynamic United States pushed out past the smallish patch of east coast, where most of the disloyal colonials had clustered, and expanded across the North American continent, visiting Englishwoman Frances Trollope wrote in her *Domestic Manners in America*, "I do not like them. I do not like their principles. I do not like their manners. I do not like their opinions." Sometime later, poet and critic Matthew Arnold updated this scornful view by decrying what he saw as terribly un-English American traits—"hardness and materialism, exaggeration and boastfulness, a false smartness, a false audacity, a want of soul and delicacy."

It has always been chic in London to be cleverly dismissive about America (and about every place else as well). Oscar Wilde, though generally much wittier in his abuse, called America "one long expectoration." Somerset Maugham said Americans had "invented so wide a range of pithy and hackneyed phrases that they can carry on an amusing and animated conversation without giving a moment's reflection to what they are saying and so leave their minds free to consider the more important matters of big business and fornication." Such words can still be heard in smart London circles. But the impressions they foster are misleading and have been for a long time.

Even before the California Gold Rush, the Oregon Trail, and the opening of the West to all comers, the attractions of the New World tended to outweigh its shortcomings and crudities, both for those who couldn't resist those attractions and those who merely contemplated the possibilities. America was commonly thought of as a place:

Where a man is a man even though he must toil,
And the poorest may gather the fruits of the soil.

An early British guidebook for settlers in America said, "In no part of the world is good neighborship in greater perfection than in America." Closer than other immigrants in language, customs, and religion, the three million Britons who planted roots in America between 1820 and 1920 blended easily into their new homeland (and were, thereby, denied the ethnic distinctions which many other groups cherished and perpetuated). In one of his stories, Arthur Conan Doyle had Sherlock Holmes express the hope that one day the two nations would be united under one flag—half Union Jack, half Stars and Stripes.

America was the land of the future, the land of prosperity and promise, an impression that was to be confirmed when the United States entered the First World War to help bring that horrifying slaughter to an end in little more than a year. An arsenal of freedom and supplier of badly needed fighting men in the Second World War, America sustained that impression (arousing both affection and disdain among ordinary folk through the generous, innocent distribution of chewing gum, cigarettes, candy, and other scarce goodies by individual American servicemen on British soil). When World War Two was over, America was the only country with the wherewithal (and vision) to provide all its allies (and other countries) with the capital and food required to revive after the cataclysm. A British minister called the Marshall Plan which performed that task "the most unsordid act in history."

The British developed a new image of America. It was a land of culture, a new Athens. Distinguished British poets and writers, including W.H. Auden and Christopher Isherwood, emigrated across the Atlantic, as had such celebrated actors as Ronald Colman and Charles Laughton. Engineers, doctors, businessmen, advertising men, singers and musicians, specialists of all sorts rushed to the place where things were happening and dreams came true.

And then the dream suddenly went sour. Racial tensions, the murder of John F. Kennedy, the travail of the Vietnam War, Watergate, the seeming inability to cope with Soviet expansionism succeeded each other with confounding rapidity. Britons began to wonder whether it was true that America had produced the only civilization in history which had gone from promising adolescence to depressing senility without passing through satisfying and enriching maturity.

There was talk of a "psychological collapse" of America. British writer Christopher Booker wrote, "We no longer see her bestriding the world like a brash, generous colossus. We see her faltering, unsure, losing her way and sense of purpose. . . . her people even more trivialized than our own."

Appalled by the rate of violent crimes and murders in the United States, the London *Times* said it suggested "some kind of inner failure" for the country. Though some Britons felt reassured by the attempt by President Ronald Reagan to reassert leadership of the West, there was a noticeable anxiety—reflected in London newspaper editorials—that American tough talking on international affairs was reflexive rather than carefully thought out and potentially very dangerous.

Nevertheless, the British remain dazzled by their American offspring. They know that what happens in the States is about to happen in Britain as well—supermarkets or skateboards, waffle irons or Weight Watchers. A large portion of British daily television schedules consists of programs from America. Virtually all the films shown in British movie houses are Hollywood-made. Best-selling American books are eagerly awaited in London and often do very well in Britain, too. Vacations in America have become hugely popular.

The "special relationship" in international affairs is comfortably sustained between the two countries. Former British ambassador to Washington Peter Jay described that relationship as "a long-standing extramarital affair. It arises entirely from natural affection." In fact, it arises most of all from a fundamental identity of interests between the two countries, though the deeply-rooted sentimental links play their part as well.

American politics have never ceased to fascinate the British. They see it as one long jamboree, both outrageous and fabulous, both trivial and reflecting the deeper democracy of their American cousins. British humorist Frank Johnson, who went to cover an election campaign in smalltown America, came back to say it was "astonishing to find so many apparently incongruous offices which are elective in America and are not in other democracies. . . . How does someone campaign for coroner? . . . What issues are debated between rivals for office? Do they promise fewer deaths? Do they accuse each other of necrophilia?"

Another British observer encapsulated the ambivalent attraction

America holds for his countrymen by paraphrasing the Declaration of Independence from Britain: "When in the course of human events, otherwise rational men say they hold certain truths to be self-evident, and that the first of these truths is that all men are created equal—which is rot—then you can be sure that a powerful idea is at work and there's going to be trouble."

The future of British-American intimacy will be strongly affected by the consequence of recent developments in Europe. Throughout its history, Britain's tenaciously guarded insularity has primarily meant resisting influences from its neighbors in Europe and, as far as national interests allowed, avoiding being dragged into entanglements with them. But that insularity was subjected to powerful pressures after the Second World War as the European Economic Community (EEC) took shape. The EEC linked the major countries of western Europe for the purpose of promoting peace, stability, and prosperity for all of them.

Membership in the EEC—in which the prime movers were West Germany and France—implied a loss of some sovereignty by member nations. Arranging common tariffs, coping with budgetary problems, dealing in common with agriculture, and other crucial matters could not mean anything if each country insisted on maintaining absolute independence and sovereignty. But clinging to absolute independence was the reflexive reaction of the British to this ambitious new alignment. They stayed aloof, fearing they might be dragged willy-nilly into all sorts of awkward and unacceptable international complications. They feared they would find themselves, and their Parliament in London, stripped of mastery over the fate of their country. British representatives did flirt around the edges of European integration—Winston Churchill was one of the first to speak of a prospective "United States of Europe." But they carefully refrained from making commitments to it. The European Community evolved without them.

As the years passed, however, many British leaders grew apprehensive about the way the world's economy appeared to be developing. Western Europe was gradually emerging as a market bigger and potentially more prosperous than the United States. There was a growing danger that Britain, outside the European Community, could find itself in a cruelly exposed position. It could be denied the trading privileges which Community membership conferred and, at the same time, be vulnerable to trade restrictions in other parts of the world as well.

To many Britons, the prospect of going it alone as in times past, while their neighbors across the English Channel were happily and conspicuously hand-in-glove, seemed hazardous. This sense of vulnerability was magnified by the absence of effective American leadership of the West during the Vietnam War and Watergate periods. It was a time for scouting about for the possibility of forging links with other Western nations which were troubled by a similar concern, particularly in view of Soviet muscle flexing and confusion in the West about the Kremlin's intentions.

An energetic campaign was mounted—well oiled with funds from big British companies anxious to be locked (belatedly) into European markets—to convince Britons that their future was with Europe. This proposition was discreetly supported by the American government which likes the idea of a strong Western Europe capable of picking up a greater share of the increasingly exorbitant common defense burden.

Britain did finally join the EEC in 1973 but the task of persuading the British people that it should stay in the Community was not easy. Residual prejudices had to be overcome or at least played down. Some Britons were queasy about tying up with Germans against whom they had fought two devastating wars this century or with the French whom they had never trusted. Talk of the glory of pan-Europeanism was dismissed as starry-eyed gibberish. The frightening vision of strike-prone, low-output British companies trying, without the shield of import taxes, to outsell their highly efficient German competitors on the British domestic market once Britain joined the EEC made manufacturers and industry ministry officials shudder.

The stakes were high and sharp lines were drawn between pro- and anti-marketeers when the question of staying in or pulling out was put to the British voter in a special referendum in 1975. Motivated largely by worry about the economic consequences of withdrawing, the country decided by a convincing majority to remain part of the European Community. It has been an active member ever since.

It has, however, been an irascible member. By joining late after basic procedures and many basic problems had been ironed out, it was at a disadvantage. One serious consequence for Britain has been the EEC's agricultural policy. It seems to the British to have been designed mostly to enable French farmers to maintain their traditional, inefficient ways of farming by requiring other Community members to approve unduly high agricultural subsidies and accept artificially inflated food prices. With Britain importing almost half its food, the costs involved are particularly galling.

Agricultural overproduction in the EEC has been both expensive and grotesque, producing mountains of grain, lakes of excess milk and wine, and hoards of excess beef without bringing the price down for any of those commodities. There was widespread anger when it was discovered that so much butter was being stored uselessly away that large amounts of it were being sold to the Russians at a fraction of the price Britain and other European consumers were paying for it.

There have been other vexing consequences as well. The British fishing industry found its previously protected territorial waters opened to trawlers from other EEC countries and suffered a serious slump as a consequence. Britain was annoyingly required to adjust to a variety of foreign standards concerning, among other things, qualities of beer, sizes of trucks, and kinds of apples that could be sold. Many British apple orchards had to be bulldozed and the country was irritatingly subject to an invasion of EEC-approved French apples. Standards are being established for various professions throughout the Community—dentists, nurses, veterinarians, and some others—and grumblings can be heard that those standards may not jell with traditional British requirements.

It is unfortunate that a serious testing time for the EEC coincided with a worldwide recession. But the general impression that the EEC has been an expensive fiasco as far as Britain is concerned has stimulated widespread cynicism about the organization. There have been benefits for Britain—including free access to the European Community market and payouts to some troubled British industries. Those benefits have, however, not been enough to counteract the growth of a Get-Britain-Out campaign, which has particularly strong support in the Labor Party.

Those who have all along been opposed to Britain being "swallowed" by Europe have been joined by a contingent of formerly pro-

Europe converts. But the antis still face the strongly argued contention that, regardless of the rights or wrongs, a British withdrawal now that detailed links with Europe have become so intricate would be impossible, like unscrambling an omelet. It does look as though Britain can no longer extricate itself from Europe without doing itself drastic economic damage.

Obstinate pro-Europe Britons say it would be better to look forward to a time when Britain might be able to exercise more influence in the Community than it has up to now and thus remedy British grievances. They also look forward to a common European currency one day, a common European passport (already in the planning stage), a more effective European parliament (the one that now meets has very limited powers), a more integrated European defense system and, finally, as Churchill had suggested, a United States of Europe.

If all of this transpires, Britain's special links with America could not survive. Britain would be inextricably part of Europe and would not be able to enjoy a privileged relationship with the United States which its European partners did not share. Meantime, however, it has adopted a dual allegiance. At times its interests are best served by accentuating the special tie with America; at other times it flaunts its European identity to demonstrate it is part of a grouping powerful enough not to have to bow to American wishes. So long as European and American interests do not clash fundamentally, this presents no serious problems. But clashes in the long run are conceivable, and probably probable.

When they happen, the British—if they have resisted the temptation to extract themselves from the European Community no matter what the consequences—will have to decide which special relationship means more to them. Very likely they would opt for Europe for the same reason they joined the Community to begin with—that's where their economic future lies. The British-American special relationship may not be long for this world.

It takes a half hour to cross over by hovercraft from Dover to Calais, from England to France. That's about half the time it would take to drive across London from one end to the other if there were no traffic to slow you down. Yet the emotional difference between the two countries is immense. For most of the time since William the Conqueror and his Norman cohorts conquered Britain, hostile feelings between the two countries have simmered. William's heirs, kings of England but still claimants to French real estate, led their British subjects into sometimes glorious but ultimately futile campaigns to retain bits and pieces of Gallic countryside. Though English heroes were made on the fields of Agincourt, Poitiers, and Crecy long, long ago, much blood was spilled, much venom was generated, and the seeds of enduring enmity were firmly planted.

British attitudes towards France have been complicated and ambivalent for reasons far removed from ancient grievances. France is a conveniently reachable place to which Britons young and old regularly flit for an atmosphere completely different than their own—to Paris for its bohemian moods (though that's much less in evidence these days), to the Riviera for endless sunshine, to the Dordogne and the valley of the Loire for the delights of exotic rural life, to France generally for good eating, good wine, and a carefree approach which offers a welcome break from the confinements of British propriety. An Englishman who, at home, might walk into a room full of lovely women without so much as glancing at any of them might sit for hours at an outdoor cafe on Boulevard St. Germain, ogling the passing parade of Parisian beauties. An Englishwoman who is never completely sure of herself in anything as flimsy as a bikini on British beaches looks forward to a topless sunbath on seaside sands near St. Tropez. But knowing deep down that their own ways are better, more suitable, more civilized, the British indulge their whims in France and then return home to castigate the French for being flighty, temperamental, unreliable and perfidious.

This prejudice derives partly from the conviction that a place inhabited by people who are as publicly emotional as the French, who make scenes and cause commotions, who are so untidy, and where the police can be so rough and rude without fear of having to answer for it, must be hazardous terrain where anything might happen. But much of it is a result of a conviction that time and time again the French have proved themselves to be unreliable and contrary as allies and unprincipled as rivals in international affairs. Ramsay MacDonald, a British prime minister who had many dealings with the French between the two world wars (in which they had fought on the same side) had no doubt about their villainy.

He described them as "tricky, selfish and unscrupulous. . . . It is impossible to trust them, dangerous to make concessions to them and essential to keep up one's guard while negotiating with them." MacDonald maintained that "The idea of doing good for its own sake never enters the French mind."

The British were appalled and alarmed when the elaborate defenses the French had constructed to ward off a German military threat in the 1930s proved as leaky as overripe camembert, permitting enemy tanks to reach the English Channel within weeks of the outbreak of real hostilities in the Second World War. They were appalled again when, after the war, as the North Atlantic Treaty Organization planned its defenses against a possible Soviet threat, the French chose to withdraw from the military wing of the Western alliance, knowing full well that geographic and strategic considerations meant the alliance had no alternative but to defend France anyway.

The British were amused when high-ranking French officials, outraged by the spontaneous appearance of English words in the French vocabulary (le weekend, le sports car, etc.), officially sought to stem this franglais invasion as if it were an infectious plague which would undermine French culture if left unchecked. But they were humiliated when, having dragged their heels as the European Economic Community was being formed, the British found their first membership application vetoed by French President Charles de Gaulle who unilaterally decided they should be kept out because they were too closely associated with the Americans.

With a few exceptions (like the intelligentsia and the gastronomia), suspicion of the French, even dislike, filters through all levels of British society, though less so in Scotland. (The Scots have historic ties with the French dating back to times when they and the English were at each other's throats, making the Scots and the French natural allies.) Nevertheless, French is the foreign language most British youngsters learn in school and in which most university language students major. Countless ordinary British restaurants, trying to look chic, write their menus so that pig's feet (commonly referred to in British butcher shops as pig's trotters) come out as pieds de cochon.

French philosophical fashions, like existentialism and structuralism, are readily picked up and espoused by isolated groups of British intellectuals hungry for the convoluted logical expositions so natural to the French but rarely home bred on British soil. British women are captivated by French fashions (just as the French are smitten by the "English Look").

Weekends or longer in Paris remain extremely tempting propositions for Britons and come spring or summertime, they flock to Normandy, Brittany, and the French Mediterranean shore to savor delights and cluck over improprieties unfamiliar on home ground. It's not really a love-hate relationship—it's more as though the British are bewitched by something of which they fundamentally disapprove. For Britons, France is like a disagreeable mistress with all sorts of unpleasant habits but with a variety of exotic charms and attractions. The two countries make nervous neighbors and are fortunate to be separated by a channel of water, no matter how narrow.

Ironically, though the British have been allies with the French in two devastating conflagrations this century, they harbor fewer resentments against the common enemy in both those wars, the Germans. When memories and images of Nazi brutality were still very much alive immediately after the Second World War, contempt for Germany and things German was intense in Britain. But the passage of time has mostly cleansed and closed the wounds inflicted in those wretched days when London was set ablaze night after night by German bombers, when the heart of the city of Coventry was obliterated and other British towns suffered great numbers of casualties and extensive damage.

The differences between Britain and Germany have been exclusively geopolitical while the differences between Britain and France are profoundly cultural and emotional. Not only are the Germans generally an orderly people, in many ways even more dedicated to the concepts of propriety than the British, but there have long been close links between the two people. When Germany still had a royal family, its ties with the British monarchy were very close. But of greater significance, the Anglo-Saxons who founded the English nation were, after all, of Germanic stock.

It might be said that the Norman invaders who later conquered the Anglo-Saxons and planted their own stamp on Britain should have had a similar, or even greater, influence on British moods. But though the Normans came from France to make their mark on England, they were in fact descendants of Vikings who had conquered Normandy and had settled there before they grew sufficiently restless to do the same with England. Not much French blood flows through British veins.

The fine points of Britain's future international alignments will no doubt be strongly influenced by other factors, including East-West relations and economic developments. But if Britain does finally submerge itself in a greater Europe, it will have resolved the persisting conundrum pinpointed by former American Secretary of State Dean Acheson two decades back—that the British, having lost their empire, hadn't yet found another role to play in the world.

That other role has proved stubbornly elusive. Though unable to wield superpower influence, Britain has proudly declined to accept relegation to minor power status. It is one of the five permanent members of the United Nations Security Council, but that's a vestige of times past. No one, not even the British themselves, consider Britain one of the world's key countries.

The past begets the present and an understanding of what the British Empire was can offer insights into what the British are today. To be British in those glorious days meant to be a citizen of a nation whose writ ran beyond practically all horizons in the world. The British ruled over India and Australia, over much of North America, Africa, and the West Indies, over Ireland and islands and outposts across the globe.

The empire was built initially on commercial initiative and derring-do. Adventurers, with the backing of British mercantile interests and the crown, sailed off into the great unknown, or ventured into regions already claimed by such imperial rivals as the Dutch, Spanish, and French. Through enterprise, diligence, and sheer force, they wedged firm footholds in foreign parts. These were followed by more formal commercial enterprises. They took it upon themselves to establish far-reaching local political control, sometimes with company military forces, like those of the East India Company which fielded a formidable, disciplined army.

The primary object was to tap and exploit the natural resources of the colonial territories—sugar and molasses from the West Indies, fish from Newfoundland, furs and skins from the American colonies, tea, rice and silk from India, gold, diamonds, metals, rubber, an endless selection of valuable goods to which Britain made sure it had exclusive access. The imperial lifelines were guarded by the unchallengable Royal Navy which, during Victorian days, was at least as big as any two other navies.

The profits that accrued to Britain through its empire were incalculable. By British law, colonial overseas trading was confined to British merchant ships. Britain made itself sole market for imperial goods and the colonies were, in turn, kept as a captive market for British goods—whether the cotton products of the mills of Lancashire or, later, machinery and locomotives for the factories of Birmingham and Yorkshire.

British subjects were always more than welcome to settle in the colonial territories to help Anglicize them. Until very recently, few questions were asked of Britons emigrating to such underpopulated former colonies as Australia and Canada. In places like South Africa and India in the old days, Britons were immediately installed in positions of privilege over dark-skinned locals. Those who were highly placed had small armies of native retainers. All but the lowliest immigrants from Britain had servants to do their bidding in those lands. The attractions of the further reaches of the empire were clearly seductive.

This release valve for excess population was particularly meaningful when jobs were scarce in Britain and when injustice was rife. Much has been said and written about the wretched Britons who were "transported" to Australia as convicts and who worked on chain gangs there. But millions of their compatriots voluntarily sailed off as free men and women to the colonial territories to seek new lives.

It is impossible to overestimate the significance of such opportunities for the country. It siphoned off a lot of the discontented and restless elements in the community. The empire was a vast frontier, a place where dissatisfaction could be safely defused (or at least dispersed) before it could take root and blossom at home into something more dangerous, as it did in less fortunate countries. Who would want to join other down-and-outs on the barricades or storm the well-protected citadels of the London Establishment when the prospects appeared promising in Virginia, Cape Town, or Barbados, when a man might turn a fortune in the Australian outback or perhaps finally make something of himself in Saskatchewan or Salisbury?

The annals of the British Empire are divided into two major installments. The first was purely adventurous and acquisitive. The beginning of the second was signalled by the American Revolution against the crown. That revolt coincided with the emergence of changed attitudes toward worldwide possessions. Many Britons sympathized with the American revolutionaries who were, after all, of British stock. Colonial Philadelphia was, after London, the second most important British city. Many Britons would soon also sympathize with the French who revolted against tyranny, until the horror stories about the excesses of the terror which accompanied the French Revolution began circulating. It was an age of humane ideals and those ideals had a notable impact on the administration and fate of the empire.

Greater concern began to be felt for the well-being of colonial peoples. Development programs were introduced—bringing irrigation projects to parched colonial regions, exploring for methods to cope with tropical diseases, and extending the rule of law to the remotest of imperial corners. Missionaries penetrated jungles and traversed deserts to bring Christianity to the multi-religioned peoples of the empire. Rudyard Kipling, who had begun his professional life working on a British newspaper in India, spoke of the obligation to take up "the white man's burden" to civilize less fortunate races. It was an obligation which Britain obligingly shouldered. The vast profits and greater glory which accompanied that burden seemed a not undeserved by-product of devoted, altruistic duty to mankind.

Having done very well out of the slave trade, with which they introduced blacks from Africa into southern America and the West Indies to work the fertile plantations there, the British were converted to a recognition of the wickedness of slavery. They were among the first to abolish it and to ban the lucrative commerce in slaves (though some historians contend it had by then outlived its economic usefulness). Greater self-government was granted to colonies which seemed capable of benefiting from it. To British eyes at the time, that meant white or white-ruled colonies.

Not till the middle of this century did the spreading belief in the dignity of all peoples lead the non-white British colonies toward independence. Once the process started, with India in 1947, the empire was rapidly wound down. Within two decades, the institution which had turned a smallish island nation into the most powerful, most respected country on earth had become just a subject for historical research.

Despite recognition of the iniquities and shortcomings of imperial rule, the British were not the sole beneficiaries of their imperial adventure. Whatever arrogance and presumption might have been displayed and whatever injustices might have been perpetrated in the name of the British crown and nation, the British Empire was in many ways a constructive phenomenon. In several former colonies—including India, Nigeria, and Uganda—the lowering of the British flag was soon followed by political instability, insurrection, or civil war of horrifying proportions. Writing of India, *New York Times* correspondent Drew Middleton said, "British rule brought peace and justice to peoples hitherto sorely oppressed by irresponsible tyrants, many of whom were corrupt and decadent. The British . . . ended interminable little wars . . . and they labored to build highways, railroads and canals." It was, in fact, the Indians who did the actual laboring but there can be no doubt that British direction was responsible for what was accomplished. The historian A.L. Rowse claimed that during the British reign in Nigeria "an unarmed man could walk a couple of hundred miles in peace and security."

In times of turmoil, it is easy to be nostalgic about bygone eras and ignore such sources of current problems as the population explosion and its implications for adequate food supplies, crime, and overcrowded and underserviced cities. It is also easy to forget that in the good old days, communications were primitive. Horrors and outrages which now make headlines the world over simply were not reported—and certainly not on You-Are-There television.

But no matter how it is judged, the British Empire was artificial and contrived, an organism awaiting inevitable dismantling. The curtain fell when colonial peoples came to understand that British supremacy was not the natural order of things, when they tired of being underdogs in their own lands. The implications of that rejection for British national pride were obvious, especially when leaders of former colonies (which had not been obstructed in their moves toward independence) saw fit to say unpleasant things about Britain (like blaming it for their own horrific national problems) or to take sides with Britain's international adversaries.

More important has been the consequences for the British economy. As the empire slipped away, British companies could no longer be guaranteed preferential treatment when disposing of (or dumping) their products in colonial territory. No longer could Britain claim priority as a market for the goods of imperial regions nor could it derive the advantage of having its merchant fleet predominate in such trade. There hasn't been an extended era of economic stability in Britain since the imperial experience fizzled out like a punctured balloon.

In 1931, the British Commonwealth of Nations—dominated by the government in London—was formed by Britain and a handful of its white and white-ruled colonies and dominions. It was designed to provide a special link between them. Successive monarchs paid regular visits to Commonwealth lands, kept in touch with Commonwealth developments, and made flattering references to the Commonwealth in official addresses. Mutually advantageous, preferential economic agreements were evolved, and Commonwealth military forces distinguished themselves fighting for Britain in World War Two. Leading Commonwealth figures were respected and their advice was sought.

As non-white colonies gained their independence, they too became Commonwealth members. Former colonial territories in the West Indies, Africa, and other developing regions began to examine how the organization might be used for their own rather than Britain's purposes—to promote their own international policies and the development of their own economies. The end to white rule in Zimbabwe (formerly Rhodesia) dominated Commonwealth interest for many years though it was—as far as the British were concerned—essentially part of the wind-up of the British Empire.

The Commonwealth remains active today. Its headquarters remain in London. Britain continues to pay the lion's share of membership dues and ostensibly remains the senior member. The queen is still monarch of several Commonwealth countries. English is still the organization's operational language. British politicians maintain personal ties with many leaders of Commonwealth countries and can communicate with them informally and constructively on international problems. But usually the organization's central concern—the well-being of the poorer nations who make up a majority of its members—remain only peripheral to Britain's basic interests. It may have had its roots in the British Empire, but it is no longer the *British* Commonwealth. It happened very quickly. Britain is still adjusting.

What Next?

Each AUTUMN, as a series of special concerts draws to a close in London's Albert Hall, hundreds of college-age youngsters, crowded together on the vast ground floor level of the hall, join the orchestra in a proud, booming rendition of "Britannia Rules the Waves." It is a stirring moment, bursting with the surge of voices and drum rolls, youthful enthusiasm, unabashed patriotism, and the good fellowship of the occasion. Encore follows encore, each one belted out more exultantly than the last. It ends with an explosion of cheering and jubilant banner waving.

The event, which is televised, is great fun for participant and spectator alike. It is, however, all make-believe. It remains a fair guess that, as the anthem says, "Britons never, never, never will be slaves," but it has been a very long time since Britannia even pretended to rule the waves. Sporadic outbursts of joyous patriotism notwithstanding, the confidence of bygone times has fizzled out. Englishmen still paste *GB* stickers on the backs of their cars, but not even the *Encyclopedia Britannica* calls Britain Great anymore. Gone are the smug old days when thick mists which disrupted transportation to and from Britain could draw from the inhabitants of that proud island sympathetic regret that the rest of the world had thereby been isolated.

Chroniclers of gloom have been persistent and articulate in Britain of late. "We have neither the money nor the resources to do all the things we should like to do." "Britain suffers from a lack of purpose, a lack of faith." "The car wouldn't start this morning, just like the rest of the country."

Such judgments inspire an exaggerated image of hopelessness.

Despite its imperfections, Britain remains an agreeable place to live and a delightful place to visit. Nevertheless, the central reality of British life in recent years has been its inability to decipher devastating economic riddles. It is agonizing for so many people to be labeled "redundant" and thrown out of their jobs. It is ominous for so many businesses to go to the wall. It is distressing to travel around the country and see building projects dragging on or abandoned because the money has run out. It is bewildering for the completion of an imaginative project to protect London from potentially ravaging, possibly imminent floods delayed perilously *for years* by labor problems.

A few years ago, a British government promised a daring, dynamic technological revolution to restore British pride and economic might. But nothing spectacular happened and the country watched itself being relentlessly surpassed by other countries whose technological strivings proved more than talk.

It's not difficult to see why. Despite a skilled work force and reputable products at their disposal, British business managers have been staid, unimaginative, and often downright incompetent, bungling opportunities and failing to reap available benefits. Despite wielding enormous clout and having employers on a regular diet of humble pie, British trade unions have made largely paper triumphs. They failed to deliver fully on their promise to their members of a better life. The result: British businessmen, executives, and workers have comparatively the lowest standards of living in the non-Communist industrial world.

There have been times when a foreigner keeping an eye on developments might have been tempted to conclude that the British are ambling knowingly, inexorably, and sometimes unconcernedly toward oblivion. But anyone who has lived among them knows that can't be true. They have too much bloody-minded defiance to accept anything but a temporary setback. They have the ingenuity to slip back into the mainstream of advanced thought and accomplishment. They think too highly of themselves to accept subservience to foreigners. And they have too many ideas to let the world pass them by.

But the descendants of the managers who ran the empire with impressive efficiency forgot what management was all about. Deprived of profitable control of colonial territories and overtaken in technology by managers in other lands, they grew confused and lost their bearings. The country did the same, trapping its undeniable energies under a yoke of outdated class distinctions which developed into rampant class hostilities.

As the country slipped downhill, guarding or gaining special class privilege was the name of practically the only game in town that mattered—one in which the working class, through the unions, quickly learned the rough-and-ready rules. Tribal identification has provided much of the cement that has held British society together in a climate of decorum most other countries envied. But the price has been exorbitant. Energies that should have been devoted to exploiting British ingenuity for the good of the country have been squandered on paralytic and ruinous social posturing and group greed.

It was the British who invented nuclear power stations, commercial jet air travel, the hovercraft, vertical takeoff aircraft, terelyne, brain scanners and other modern wonders which, because of national atrophy, were taken up, commercially developed and made profitable elsewhere. It all happened at a time when London was (and it still is) one of the greatest financial centers the world has ever known, with expertise galore of the kind which could and should have been tapped to the country's much greater advantage.

London money men, bold and daring in international financial exploits, proved timid and coy when confronted with domestic opportunities. They didn't feel safe operating on home ground—domestic labor seemed too unreliable; foreign competition seemed too formidable. A new strain of the "English disease" evolved, the symptoms of which were self-destructive self-interest, developing into despondency and indifference.

However, there are hints that a new, revitalized Britain may soon try to emerge from the mesmerizing limbo in which it has been wandering. Surprisingly wide popular support has been attracted by the newly formed Social Democratic Party which declared one of its chief planks to be to break the mold of class antagonisms in the country.

New political movements have first flared and then foundered in the past in Britain, and the Social Democrats may stumble and go under as well as time passes. But it is noteworthy that a great many Britons—most of them probably themselves locked into class mannerisms—now recognize their tribal struggle to be a dangerous mistake.

It is hard for anyone familiar with the British to believe that they are about to shed their class mentalities. Most Britons have too many firm, distinctive, reassuring tribal commitments—to the jobs they do, the words they use, the clothes they wear. But there is growing realization among them that the antagonisms and cussedness their divisions have stoked up are responsible for Britain's costly inability so far to cope with today's world.

What is good and pleasing in the country still far outmatches what is disturbing and unsettling. But prospects for the future can be worrying. The time has come for a British renewal. The circumstances have never been more favorable. Oil gushing from its North Sea fields and hundreds of years worth of coal beneath the surface of its green and pleasant land (mostly reachable without environmental desecration) make Britain the only industrial country in the world without foreseeable energy problems.

It's time for muffled British skill, imagination, and flair to be reasserted. It's time for the us-against-them commitments that undermine British efficiency to subside. Some of the old British quaintness may be lost in the process but the gains would far exceed the losses. It will be a tragedy and a scandal if this chance is missed, if the country is permitted to continue winding slowly down like a fine old grandfather clock whose key is lost.

A
SELECTED BIBLIOGRAPHY

Batchelor, Denzil—*The English Inn*
Bence-Jones, Mark—*The British Aristocracy*
Burke, John—*English Villages*
Coveney, Dorothy and Medlicott, W.N.—*The Lion's Tail*
Doxat, John—*The Living Thames*
Glyn, Anthony—*The Blood of a Britishman*
Grosvenor, Peter—*The British Experience*
Hanley, Clifford—*The Scots*
Hibbert, Christopher—*The Court of St. James*
Howard, Philip—*The British Monarchy*
Hahn, Emily—*Meet the British*
Horne, Donald—*God is an Englishman*
Irving, Clive—*True Brit*
Jackson, Michael—*The English Pub*
Lacey, Robert—*Majesty*
Lee, Melville—*A History of the Police in England*
Lejeune, Anthony—*The Gentlemens Clubs of London*
Mackie, Albert—*Scottish Pageantry*
McElwee, William—*The Story of England*
McRae, H. and Cairncross, F.—*Capital City*
Marcus, Steven—*The Other Victorians*
Piper, David—*The Companion Guide to London*
Pritchett, V.S.—*London Perceived*
Renier, G.J.—*The English: Are They Human?*
Rose, Richard—*Politics in England Today*
Ross, A.S.C.—*U and Non-U*
Sampson, Anthony—*The New Anatomy of Britain*

Shaw, Frank—*My Liverpool*
Stewart, Michael—*The British Approach to Politics*
Thomas, David—*Wales*
Trevelyan, G.M.—*English Social History*
Ziegler, Philip—*Crown and People*

INDEX

A

Aberdeen, 128
Aberfan, 132
Accents, 55, 132
Act of Union, 123, 134
Agriculture, 137, 143, 204
Air pollution, 107
Alcoholism, 127
Alderson, John, 194
Alfred the Great, 175
Altrincham, Lord, 152
Amateurism, 33, 34
American Revolution, 211
Andrew (prince), 121, 166
Angles (people), 174
Anglesey, Marquess of, 29
Anglican Communion, 150
Angry Brigade, 35
Anne (queen), 177
Anne (princess), 55, 162, 171, 172
Anti-monarchists, 155
Apple orchards, 204
Archaeological sites, 16, 117, 119
Architecture, 23, 83, 104, 105, 111
Aristocracy, *see* Upper class
Armed forces, 62, 126
Armstrong-Jones, Anthony, 170
Art collections, 21, 57
Arthur (king), 97

Asians, 66
Australia, 61, 210

B

Balmoral, 155
Bangladeshis, 107
Bank of England, 113
Banks, 113
Bannockburn battle, 124
Barristers, 190
Bars, *see* Pubs
BBC, 89
Beatles, 141
Beer, 77, 83, 84, 94
    see also Pubs
Beer, Museum of, 106
Ben Lomand, 36
Benn, Anthony Wedgwood, 44
Bethell, Lord, 62
Bill of Rights, 181
Blacks, 66, 107, 193
    see also Racism
Blenheim Palace, 57
Blunt, Anthony, 40
Boadicea (queen), 174
Boarding schools, 44
Bonuses, 22
Breweries, 84

223

British Commonwealth of
   Nations, 213
British Empire, 209
British Movement, 67
British Museum, 106
Britons (people), 11, 33
Brothels, 96, 98, 100, 102
   see also Prostitutes
Buccleuch, Duke of, 57
Buckingham, Duke of, 161
Buckingham Palace, 106, 110,
   121, 155, 161
Business and business practices,
   39, 216
   aristocracy in, 62
   of British Empire, 209
   clubs and, 89
   EEC and, 203
   foreign trade, 202, 210
   in London, 113, 114
   of non-whites, 68
   and social classes, 43, 47
   unethical transactions, 116
   see also Economy, national;
      Industry
Butlers, 58
Butter, 204

                  C
Cabinet (government), 62, 182,
   184
Cade's rebellion, 176
Caesar, Julius, 18, 33
Callaghan, James, 184
Campaign for Real Ale, 84
Campbell clan, 16
Catholics and Catholic Church,
   91, 127, 145, 176
Celts (people), 134
Censorship, 187
Charles I (king), 100, 151,
   176

Charles II (king), 86, 100, 159,
   176
Charles (prince), 52, 85, 134, 162,
   164, 171
Cheese, 49
Chichester, Sir Francis, 29
Children, 28, 31, 45
Chinese, 107
Churches, 108, 143
   see also Religion; Religious
      intolerance
Church of England, 91, 150
Church of Scotland, 124
Cities, 81, 104, 136–138
City of London, 39, 106, 113
Civil rights, 181
Clans, 129
Class structure, see Social classes
Clean-air laws, 36
Clearances, the, 130
Climate, 15, 35, 107
Clothing, 100
   see also Fashion
Clubs, 84, 85
Coffee houses, 115
   see also Clubs
Colonization, 209
   see also British Empire
Commander of the British
   Empire, 153
Commerce, see Businesses and
   business practices
Commons, House of, see House
   of Commons
Commuting, 145
Concorde (plane), 35
Conservative Party, 63, 180, 184,
   189
Contraception, 92
Cooking, see Food
Courts, 79, 116, 181, 187
   see also Crime; Laws; Legal
      system

Coventry, 208
Craft guilds, 119, 143
  see also Labor unions
Cricket, 18, 52, 79
Crime
  and blacks, 68
  and guns, 193
  in old London, 118
  in Scotland, 127
  sex and crime, 100
  street crime, 35
  in U.S., 201
  see also Courts; Legal
  system
Cromwell, Oliver, 176
Cuckold's Point, 112
Cuisine, *see* Food
Culloden Moor, 124, 130
Cypriots, 107

D

Daily Express, 40, 121, 164
Daily Mail, 121, 187
Daily Mirror, 187
Daily Telegraph, 187
Debutantes, 121
Declaration of Arbroath, 124
De L'Isle, Lord, 56
Demonstrations, 139
Diamond collections, 58
Dieppe, 18
Diplomacy, 62, 159
Discrimination, *see* Racial intol-
  erance; Racism
Disraeli, Benjamin, 63
Divorce, 76, 170
  see also Marriage
"D" notices, 187
Doctors, 195
Dogs, 48
Drivers (automobile), 20
Drunkenness, 127

E

Economy, national, 34, 51, 114,
  155, 213
  see also Business and business
  practices; Foreign trade; Industry; Labor unions; Pov-
  erty; Prices
Education, 43, 46, 74, 124, 143
  see also Schools
Edward II (king), 173
Edward VII (king), 161, 166, 177,
  178
Edward VIII (king), 91, 158
Edward (prince), 166
Elections, 74, 183
Elizabeth I (queen), 25, 133, 151,
  174
Elizabeth II (queen), 19, 23, 55,
  121, 149, 169, 165
Elizabeth (Queen Mother), 167
Elizabethan Age, 99
Emigration, 200, 210
Employment and unemployment,
  23, 65, 114
  of management, 48
  and racism, 67
  of women, 72, 73
England, 134
English (people), 11, 126
English disease, 32
Equal Opportunities Commission,
  70
Europe, 202
European Economic Community,
  202
Execution Dock, 112

F

Family planning, 92
Fashion, 16, 17, 100
  and corpulence, 50
  from France, 208

Fashion (cont.)
  of the queen, 152, 156
  during Restoration, 101
  and sex, 95
Fast food, 51
Feminist movement, *see* Women
Fishing, 112, 113, 204
Folk heros, 33
Food, 32, 48, 50, 51, 58, 83
  see also Agriculture; Beer;
    Pubs; Restaurants
Ford Motor Company, 64
Foreign trade, 202, 210
Fox hunting, 53, 79
France, 25, 205
Fraud squad, 116

G

Gaelic, 124, 130
Gardens, 27
General strike of 1926, 30
Gentry, *see* Upper class
Geography, 15, 16
George I (king), 177
George III (king), 161, 174
George VI (king), 158, 174
Germany, 208
Ghettos, 67
Glasgow, 127, 128
Glasgow Airport, 64
Gold prices, 115
Gold Sticks, 160
Golf, 52
Government, 62, 72, 186
  Parliament, 150, 176, 177, 179
  see also House of Commons;
    House of Lords; Monarchy
Great Fire of London, 120
Grigg, John, 152
Guardian, 187
Guns, 193

H

Hadrian's Wall, 129
Haggis, 124
Heart transplants, 195
Henley, 17
Henry I (king), 120
Henry V (king), 98
Henry VIII (king), 16, 91, 133, 176
Hereward the Wake, 18
Hertford, Marquess of, 62
High society, *see* Upper class
Home, Lord, 28
Honors, 153, 154
Hospitals, 24, 195
House of Commons, 38, 39, 62,
  179
  lobby of, 188
  and monarchy, 151
  and St. Stephen's Tavern, 79
House of Lords, 39, 62, 151, 182
Housing, 105, 140, 144
Human rights, 192
Humor, 91, 126
Hunting, 53
Hyde Park, 108

I

Illegitimate births, 92
Immigration, 66, 68, 198
India, 61, 210, 212
Indians, 107
Industrial Revolution, 24, 42, 64,
  136, 137
Industry
  in north, 138
  and pollution, 113
  and social classes, 47
  and strikes, 65
  in Wales, 132
  see also Business and business
    practices

Inns, 80
Insurance, 114, 185, 195
Irish, 107, 127
Irish Republic, 146
Irish Republican Army, 147

J

James I (king), 177
James II (king), 176
Jews, 107
John (king), 175
Journalism, 188
  see also Newspapers
Judges, 181, 191

K

Keeper of the Queen's Swans, 160
Keeper of the Royal Philatelic
  Collection, 160
Keeper of the Royal Racing
  Pigeons, 160
Kidd, Captain, 112
Knighthood, 97, 153
Knox, John, 128

L

Labor, 22, 33, 40, 184
  and clubs, 88
  and human rights, 192
  and Industrial Revolution, 138
  servants, 122
  and social classes, 41, 47
  and social mobility, 41
  and women, 73
  see also Employment and un-
    employment; Labor unions
Labor Party, 43, 64, 133, 180, 184,
  189
Labor unions, 20, 22, 43, 64, 65,
  216

  in shipbuilding industry, 141
  and women, 72
  see also Strikes
Ladies-in-Waiting, 160
Landscape, see Geography
Language, 24, 54, 101, 102, 142
Laws, 182, 183
  British world influence, 24
  on brothels, 98
  and sex, 100
  and women's rights, 70, 72
  see also Courts; Legal system
Lawyers, 190
Legal system, 124, 181, 190
  see also Courts; Judges
Libel, 187
Liberal Party, 180
Lichfield, Earl of, 62
Life peers, 63
Literature
  etiquette books, 102
  folk heros, 34
  and love, 91, 96
  pornography, 92, 102
  Welsh poetry, 131
  women in, 97
Liverpool, 20, 67, 138, 140, 142,
  195
Lloyd's of London, 114
Loch Lomond, 36
London, 104
  brothels in, 96, 98
  climate of, 36
  clubs in, 85, 86
  commerce in, 39
  department stores in, 16
  land ownership in, 57
  racial unrest in, 67
  royal wedding in, 168
  Wax Museum, 35
  during World War II, 208
  see also City of London

London Museum, 119
Lord Chamberlain, 159
Lords, House of, *see* House of
    Lords

M

MacDonald clan, 16
Magistrate Courts, 191
Magna Carta, 175
Management, 47
Manners, 59, 102, 135, 152
Margaret (princess), 169
Marlborough, Duke of, 57
Marriage, 73
    affection in, 93
    between classes, 57
    and divorce, 76
    men's choices in, 94
    and sex, 94, 95
    upper class and, 121
Mary (queen), 174, 176
Master of Her Household, 160
Master of the Queen's Horse, 160
Master of the Queen's Music, 160
Mayfair, 120
Metal Exchange, 115
Middle class, 41–59
Military, *see* Armed forces
Mistress of the Robes, 160
Monarchy, 149, 157
    in London high society, 121
    queen, 150
    royal spouse, 71
    and social changes, 66
    sports liked by the, 53
Moscow Narodny Bank, 113
Moss Side, 67
Mountbatten, Lord, 61
Movies, 91, 93, 121, 201
Murdoch, Rupert, 19, 95
Museums, 21, 106, 119
Music, 80, 97, 141

N

National economy, *see* Economy,
    national
National Front, 67
National Health Service, 186, 194
Nationalist movements, 124, 132
Newport, Viscount, 62
Newspapers, 19, 91, 96, 136, 187
    see also names of individual
        newspapers
Nobility, *see* Upper class
Norman conquest, 18, 134
Normandy, Duke of, *see* William
    the Conqueror
North Atlantic Treaty Organiza-
    tion, 207
North Sea, 124, 128
Northern Ireland, 146

O

Oates, Lawrence, 30
Observer (London), 44, 187
Offa (Saxon chieftain), 134
Official Secrets Act, 187
Order of the Garter, 153, 154

P

Pakistanis, 107
Palace of the Holyroodhouse, 155
Palaces, 155
Pall Mall, 120
Parliament, 150, 176, 177, 179
Patrician class, *see* Upper class
Peasants' Revolt, 78, 176
Peerage, *see* Upper class
Pembroke, Earl of, 57, 62
Petroleum deposits, 124
Philip (prince), 155, 162, 163
Phillips, Mark, 172
Plaid Cymru, 133
Poet Laureate, 160

Poetry, 91, 131
Poles (people), 107
Police, 29, 68, 110, 116, 192, 193
Political parties, 189
  see also Conservative Party;
  Labor Party
Population, 11, 67, 104, 107, 123,
  132
Pornography, 91, 102
Poverty, 30, 40, 125, 140
Prejudice, see Racism; Religious
  intolerance
Press, the, see Journalism; News-
  papers
Prices, 23, 190, 191, 194, 204
Prime minister, 62, 150, 158, 182
Prince consort, 163
  see also Philip
Prince of Wales, 134
  see also Charles
Prostitutes, 91, 102, 120
  see also Brothels
Protestantism, 127, 145
Public schools, 28, 44, 45, 47
Public transportation, 109, 137,
  143
Pubs, 77, 81, 83, 111
Puritan Commonwealth, 100
Puritans, 31–33, 52, 99, 176

Q
Queues, 23

R
Racism, 66, 193, 198
Rainy weather, 35, 36
Refugees, 198
Religion, 33, 124, 127, 175
Religious intolerance, 127, 145,
  177
Restaurants, 49, 137

  see also Inns; Pubs
Restoration, 100
Richard II (king), 173, 176
Richard III (king), 173
Richmond Park, 53
Riots, see Violence
Ripon, Marquess of, 53
Roads, 120, 144
Robert the Bruce (king), 124
Roman Empire, 18, 36, 117, 135,
  174
Rothschild's Bank, 115
Rowing, 17
Royal Bargemaster, 160
Royalty, see Monarchy
Rugby, 52, 131

S
Salaries, see Wages
Sandringham, 155
Saxons, 50, 134, 174
Scholarships, 47
Schools, 25, 45–47, 52
Scientists, 126
Scotland, 29, 49, 123
  and France, 207
  golf in, 52
  landownership in, 57
  weather in, 35, 36
Scots, 123
Scouse, 141
Scrofula, 176
Seafood, 49, 51
Servants, 58, 59, 122, 160
Sewage system, 112
Sex, 32, 91, 95, 101, 102
Sex manuals, 93
Sexual equality, 70
Shakespeare, William, 16, 25,
  102, 173
Shelley, Mary, 16, 74
Shipbuilding, 141

Shipping, 22, 114, 140
Shooting, 53
Slavery, 211
Slums, 40, 140
Smithfield meat market, 107
Snow, 36
Snowden, Lord, 52
Snowdonia National Park, 132
Soccer, 24, 33, 52, 127
Social classes, 28, 31, 38
   and class status, 25
   and pubs, 81
   and labor unions, 65
   middle class, 41–59
   working class, 41–59, 64, 84
   see also Upper class
Social Democratic Party, 180
Socialist parties, 43
Social mobility, 41, 42, 60, 87,
   122
Solicitors, 190
South Bank complex, 111
Speakers Corner, 108
Speech from the Throne, 151
Spencer, Lady Diana (Princess of
   Wales), 166
Spies, 40, 86
Sports
   and class differences, 42
   cricket, 18
   golf, 52
   in London, 106
   and pubs, 79
   rowing, 17
   rugby, 131
   soccer, 24, 33, 52, 127
   tennis, 17
   in villages, 144
Standard, 187
Stansgate, Lord, 44
Steel industry, 23, 184
Stevedores, 140
Stock exchange, 116

   see also Business and business
      practices
Strand, The, 120
Strikes, 22, 64, 65
   by civil servants, 185
   General Strike of 1926, 30
   in Liverpool, 20
   in north, 138
Suburbs, 88, 105
Suffragettes, 74
Sun, The, 95
Sunday Times, 187
Surgery, 195

                    T

Takeover and Mergers Panel, 116
Taxes, 62, 150
Television, 24, 35, 56, 89, 201
   advertising on, 94
   humor on, 91
   royal wedding on, 168
   Welsh-language programs, 133
Temperance movement, 127
Tennis, 17, 53
Terrorism, 35, 147
Thames, 36, 110
Thatcher, Margaret, 19, 40, 64,
   182, 183
Theater, 35, 94
   censorship in the, 159
   in Elizabethan Age, 99
   critics of, 20
   during Restoration, 100
   stereotypes in, 139
Times (London), 19, 24, 40, 53,
   168, 187, 201
Titles, 56, 153, 154
Tolpuddle Martyrs, 65
Tory Party, see Conservative
   Party
Tourism, 15–17, 21, 144
Tower of London, 118

Townsend, Peter, 169
Toxteth, 67
Trade unions, *see* Labor unions
Traffic, automobile, 109
Train stations, 105
Tudors, 133
Tuition, 45
Turnbull & Asser, 16

U

Ukrainians, 107
Ulster, 146
Ulster Defense Association, 147
Unemployment, *see* Employment
  and unemployment
United States, 28, 198, 205
  American Revolution, 211
  British attitudes toward, 198
  colonies in, 209
  in London, 114
  language differences, 24, 55
  women's movement in, 74
Upper class, 42, 61
  accents of, 55
  clubs of, 85, 88
  and dogs, 48
  language of, 54
  in London, 121
  and politics, 62
  social life of, 88
  and sports, 53
  in Wales, 133
Urban renewal, 105

V

Vacations, 37, 40, 41, 43, 201
Vandalism, 33
Victoria (queen), 101, 150, 161,
  166, 177
Victoria Memorial, 161
Victorian Era, 101

Vikings, 117, 175
Village life, 83, 143
Violence, 30, 33, 67
  in Belfast, 145
  and guns, 193
  in House of Commons, 180
  in Liverpool, 140
  in old London, 118
  and racial problems, 67
  and soccer, 24, 127
  in U.S., 201
  in Wales, 133
  see also Crime
Voting, 74

W

Wages, 22, 40, 71, 72, 138
Wales, 29, 130
Wales, Prince of, 134, *see also*
  Charles
Walpole, Sir Robert, 119
War Museum, 106
Warrants, royal, 160
Water pollution, 112
Wax Museum, 35
Weather, 35, 107
Welfare, social, 24
Welsh (people), 130
Welsh Language Society, 132
Welsh National Party, 133
Wessex (ancient kingdom), 175
Westminster, 44
Westminster, Duke of, 57
Weymouth, Viscount, 56
Wife beating, 66
William II (king), 173
William of Orange, 177
William the Conqueror, 25, 117,
  175, 205
Wilton House, 57
Windsor, Duchess of, 91
Windsor, Duke of, 158

Windsor Castle, 155
Women
  club membership of, 90
  and honors, 154
  in literature, 97
  during Middle Ages, 97
  and sex, 100
  during Victorian Era, 101, 102
Working class, 41–59, 64, 84
World War I, 75, 200
World War II, 18, 24, 75, 200, 207

Wyatt's rebellion, 176

Y

Yorkshire, 52, 123, 138, 142
Yorkshire Ripper, 35

Z

Zimbabwe, 213